from the Heart's Closet

A young girl's WW II story

Anneliese "Lee" Krauter

FROM THE HEART'S CLOSET

THE SCHATZI PRESS
P.O. BOX 116
McCORDSVILLE, INDIANA 46055

HAWTHORNE PUBLISHING
DESIGNERS & PUBLISHERS
OF FINE BOOKS ABOUT INDIANA
AND ITS PEOPLE FOR 20 YEARS
15601 OAK ROAD
CARMEL, INDIANA 46033

ISBN 0-9772922-0-7 (Hardcover)
ISBN 0-9772922-1-5 (Trade Paperback)

Cover graphic is an original painting by Nhat Tran.
Interior book design by April Altman-Reynolds / Page by Page Design, Inc.

Permission to use photographs from the book: Attenkirchen—Bilder Erzaehlen Geschichte—
(trans: "Pictures Relate History") was given to the author by the 2. Buergermeister *(Deputy Mayor)
of Attenkirchen, Hans Kern. The Municipality of Attenkirchen published the book.*
*Authorization to re-print several pages of internees' camp newspapers was given
by Christina Hofmann, Rights & Permissions Department, K.G. Saur Verlag GmbH,
Ortlerstrasse 8, 81373, Munich, Germany. From the book* German-Americans in the World Wars.
Dr. Don Heinrich Tolzman. Vol. IV: The World War Two Experience. The Internment of
German-Americans. *Documents. Edited by Arthur D. Jacobs and Joseph E. Fallon. Section III:
German-American Camp Newspapers. Munich et al.: Saur, 1995/1996.*

Printed and bound in the United States of America

This book is dedicated to you, Joe. If I had just one day to live over—it would surely be March 8, 1952. There is no denying that the feelings you and I had for each other from that very first moment were not just instant attraction or mere infatuation. It was love at first sight and the feelings were real.

Thank you for not letting a day go by in all these years that you haven't made me feel so loved and cared for. You have made all things possible for me.

And to our four beautiful sons, Christian, Erick, Kurt, and Karl. I thank the Lord each day for each of you. You are the joy of our lives.

INTRODUCTION

For the better part of my adult life, the desire to tell the story of my family has been burning inside of me. Fanning these flames were the remarks friends and family would make after hearing bits and pieces of our history. Invariably, the responses would be the same: "Lee, you should write a book!"

My parents were German immigrants, but my brother Freddy and I always thought of ourselves as Americans. Our parents just happened to speak English with an accent. There was nothing unusual about that. Because we lived in New York, most everyone spoke with an accent of some kind.

Then the war broke out and we were swept into anti-Nazi hysteria. By mere association with German/American organizations, my parents were labeled "dangerous enemy aliens." Arrests by the FBI, separations, internment and finally repatriation to Germany during the war followed.

The choices my father made along the way, for whatever reasons, set us on a course more adventurous than I could have ever imagined, had I not lived it.

World events always seemed to dictate our family's destiny, and after the unprecedented tumbling down of the Berlin Wall, I was haunted by how much history was happening in our lifetimes and how quickly the years were passing. I was suddenly overwhelmed with a sense of urgency to tell our story, only to be stopped in my tracks by my mother, who wished not to have anything published while she was still alive. I guess she felt the FBI was still going to come after us. And so I continued gathering pictures, documents, letters, and interviews until several years after my mother had passed away. After getting through a period of mourning, I was finally able to concentrate on writing.

And so it happened on a beautiful late summer day in August of 2002, that our paths crossed. Nancy Niblack Baxter and I met at a writer's seminar and the rest is history. All the pieces fit and Nancy became my mentor, my editor and my publisher. I could have never written this book without you, Nancy. Thank you from the bottom of my heart for your knowledge, your experience, your expertise and above all you patience!

Final line editing and excellent suggestions were offered by Denis Glover, former Lifestyle Editor of the *Christian Science Monitor*. And, no better book designer could have been found than April Reynolds who "fell in love" with "her" book.

I also wish to express my gratitude to Dr. Don Heinrich Tolzman, Department of German Studies, Blegen Library, University of Cincinnati, Dr. Stephen Fox, author of *America's Invisible Gulag* and Arthur D. Jacobs, author, editor, and collector of almost 15,000 pages of internment documents housed in the United States Air Force Academy, Colorado Springs. I am grateful for their advice in how to go about acquiring my father's FBI file from the Department of Justice archives through the Freedom of Information Act.

Special thanks also to my Tante Karla in Hamburg and cousin Erwin Dreissigacker in Bettenhausen for all the family information they shared with me.

Last, but not least, I wish to express my admiration and gratitude to my friend, Nhat Tran, the cover artist, for wrapping my story in such exquisite beauty.

I'm a woman of two worlds, and this fact has colored all the events of my life.

I'm first of all an American, born in New York, but I'm also strongly influenced by my German heritage. Part of this may be in the blood. My heart stirs to German music, poetry, and the sound of the language, which I speak fluently, just as I do English without the trace of an accent.

But it's also a matter of place. I spent key years of my young life in several German towns and villages, among them the little town of Bettenhausen, which shaped me in ways I still don't realize. That, and World War II, which was the shadow over my childhood.

We came to Bettenhausen, in the heart of Germany in the Province of Thuringia, more than once during my childhood. We lived there when we were sent from America as hostages to a conflict of which we became victims as surely as those wounded by bombs. It was my father's *Heimat* (native home) where he was born and where he grew up. It is the place I often return to in my dreams.

Bettenhausen was typical of many villages across Germany. It had operated for centuries with a self-sustaining economy, with hard-working farmers caring for their fields, adding to their holdings, and producing all they required on their own land. My grandparents, Oma and Opa, and their children would rise at dawn and do all the things farmers had done for centuries.

Soap was boiled, sows (not boars—they were too strong-tasting) butchered, lard rendered, meats smoked, and many heads of cabbage shredded and pickled into sauerkraut stored in huge barrels. Apples, pears, and cherries were picked from trees, currants and gooseberries gathered from bushes, and all of these fruits were eaten fresh or canned and preserved for the winter. Garden vegetables were grown in huge plots not far from the house and served as they came into season, feeding the family from spring through fall. Vegetables, such as string beans and red beets, were also canned. Opa raised potatoes, wheat, oats, and rye, as well as field turnips and hay for the livestock.

My father was an expert butcher, trained and certified as a young man, and he could use every part of an animal for food or other purposes. The sow, for instance, would be clubbed on the head, throat cut, and hung up. As blood poured from the jugular vein, Oma would catch it in a bucket, stirring continuously so it would not coagulate. Then my grandparents would prepare the delicacy of the day: a dark concoction called *Blutsuppe* (Blood soup). What wouldn't be consumed at the main meal would later be used in the making of *Blutwurst*, another delight offered in every German butcher shop.

On baking day Oma and Opa formed a team with some of their children. Bettenhausen's two communal ovens, one in the upper village, one in the lower, were in a town cut in half by a stream called Herpf. The ovens were kept heated at all times, and each family was assigned a regular day every two weeks when they could bake bread. Depending on the size of the family, a sufficient number of loaves had to be readied for baking on schedule.

That presented problems: It wasn't easy to prepare that much bread. Fleischmann's yeast wasn't part of the process. Instead, the family making the bread for the day used another neighbor's yeast starter, a blob of leftover dough allowed to ferment in a jar to turn sour.

My job was to go to a neighbor's house and carry the *Sauerteig* (sourdough starter) back to my grandparents' home. A huge bread trough was set up in the center of the kitchen. As they mixed and kneaded it with their arms in the dough up to their elbows, I recall seeing flour dust all over.

Fires in the ovens were banked by the users of the day at sundown. Our bread was put to rise on breadboards the evening before. About three in the morning, Opa would get up to stoke the fire. At six o'clock he and the women arose and took the oven-ready dough to be baked. Fragrant loaves of dark rye bread came out and were carted home for the family's meals to last until the next trip to the oven some fourteen days later. To this day, whenever I smell freshly baked bread, it takes me back to those times when the aroma would permeate the air as I walked through the village.

All children were needed; they began seriously contributing to the farm and village economy by the age of seven or so. Women, young and old, tended the gardens. An herb bed for parsley and chives, dill and the like was planted near the back door, and a large plot of garden vegetables grew in a terraced garden on the side of a hill.

In German villages of the time, including Bettenhausen, farms were groupings of land, separated into individual fields surrounding the villages. The large, spread-out farms of America—with farmhouse, barns, outbuildings, and fields in one contiguous section of land—were not known.

My grandfather's acreage abutted the village, but some fields were half to 2 or 3 kilometers away. The barn adjoined the main house, cow stalls and pigpens under the same roof. The arrangement helped keep the animals, as well as humans, warm during the severe winter months—but it also made for an odorous environment.

When spring began, Opa would prepare his fields with a single bladed plow and his strongest ox. The women and some of the older girls would follow, planting potatoes and field turnips in the furrows.

Fall meant harvest. I recall the excitement when the threshers arrived. They would set up the threshing machine at one end of the village in whoever's barnyard was the biggest, and communal threshing would begin. Four or five farmers would help each other with their harvests. As soon as one group was done, the machine would move deeper into the village and repeat the process, setting up in another large barnyard, until the grain harvest of all of the farmers in Bettenhausen was in and stored in gunny sacks. It was also a busy time for the women; they cooked from dawn to dusk to keep the threshers and helpers fed. It was a happy time.

Root vegetables were brought in from the fields and kept in a root cellar close to the house. Potatoes were stored in the same place. When the potato harvest was underway in Bettenhausen, when I was visiting or living there later, I saw carts full of potatoes roll through the main road. There were potatoes all over the place.

This is the life my father led growing up, one I came to experience myself when we lived in Germany, repatriated by the American government when they suspected him of helping the Germans during the second world war.

My father was Otto Karl Wiegand, born in Bettenhausen, January 29, 1903. His father, my Opa, was Friedrich Karl Wiegand. Opa was a twin, one of two boys, born on April 30, 1882. Family history has it that his twin brother, Ernst, immigrated to South America as a young man, so somewhere down there is a branch of our family. I knew my grandfather as well as he allowed me to. A farmer with a large family and a skilled butcher and sausage maker, he was proud, strong-minded, and dedicated to the Fatherland. He had the respect of the Bettenhausen villagers and his family. His word was the last word. I don't recall hearing him laugh, but there was not much to be amused about during those war years when tragedy touched every family on a daily basis. He had been as distant a parent as he was a grandparent, so my father, whom I called Pappi (pronounced "Poppy"), said.

Opa and Oma had thirteen children, with ten still living by World War II. The oldest was a daughter, Lydia. Then came Otto, my father, the second child and oldest son, followed by Bertha, Hilda, Elsie, Erich, Erwin, Karl, Helene, and finally the lastborn, Willi. As the baby, Willi could do no wrong in the eyes of Opa. He was a mischievous, high-spirited boy who loved to play practical jokes and generally got his own way. My father was already an adult and had left home when Willi was still a baby, and so he didn't know his youngest brother during his growing years. Later, when we returned to live in Germany, he adored him just as his father did.

My grandmother, Emilie Laesser, born February 13, 1881, was a gentle, responsive woman, loved by all. My father revered her as only a German son loves and honors his mother. Having children and running a farm household took all of her time, and she experienced the usual sadness of the times. Twins she bore were either stillborn or died in infancy, and another little boy named Kurt died as a toddler.

When my father reached seven or eight, he became a helper to the village shepherd. Both were responsible for collecting and pasturing sheep from the village farmers. In springtime, the shepherd would walk through the village and collect the small flocks kept by each farmhouse. Twelve to fourteen sheep would be driven out, usually guided by the shepherd boy, my father, and the flock would grow while herded through the village, until at the head of the village the shepherd could look back and see nothing but a sea of sheep following. And there were wonderful, high-spirited herding dogs nipping stragglers in the heels to keep them from falling behind.

Bettenhausen was nestled at the foot of the Geba, a mountain at the upper end of the village. The sheep were pastured on the highlands of Geba to graze and fatten over the summer. Many lambs were born during this period, and it was my father's special chore to keep an eye on them, loving them and spending sleepless hours tending to their needs.

Pappi stayed in the same hut that had stood in these highlands for the keeper of the sheep for many years. At regular intervals, various villagers would bring food, drink, and additional supplies. Family members visited. There were hours of solitude, however, with only sheep as companions. My father grew to love the animals he protected, and his love of animals became a lifelong passion. Many years later, whenever he would see lambs with their mothers, he would show tenderness and love. Although spirited, adventurous, and fun, my father was the gentlest person I have ever known.

Not only sheep, but also other village animals, such as geese and ducks were herded communally. They all had a keen sense of where their homes were. When my father brought sheep down from the highlands, each flock would turn into its respective barnyard, baby lambs sticking close to their mothers. Even after weeks in the highland pastures, they knew instinctively if they stuck close to their mothers, they would be all right.

Bettenhausen was part of a larger region. The Province of Thueringen is one of the most beautiful areas in Central Germany, famous for its forests, namely the beloved Thueringer Wald. Bettenhausen lies within this region, as does Meiningen, one of its larger towns, the county seat of many surrounding villages, Bettenhausen included. Meiningen was a cosmopolitan town ahead of its time, which drew my father as a boy, offering many cultural activities, including a beautiful and famous opera house that presented operas, operettas, ballets, concerts and plays. Educational opportunities abounded if you were fortunate enough to be able to avail yourself of them. Meiningen also had mineral baths and became a well-known spa, which to this day attracts people from all over in search of waters that cure. Lovely hotels, rehabilitation centers, and private boarding houses were built to accommodate tourists, music and art lovers, health and back-to-nature seekers in their quest for natural healing, mind stimulation, and healthy bodies. All of this made Meiningen a prosperous town.

Beyond the Province of Thueringen was Germany, which when I was a little girl visiting in the late 30's, was already well on its way to National Socialism.

Opa was proud of the growing power of Germany. He was not in the military, but served in a home guard. Although the village had not been involved in world events earlier, during the time my grandparents were bringing up young children and Germany was under the rule of Kaiser Wilhelm, the nation was beginning to assert itself as a world power. After having emerged as a nation-state to be reckoned with following the Franco-Prussian War, a unified Germany was claiming colonies and developing what it hoped would be the best naval force in Europe.

As my father entered young manhood in the early twentieth century, the German nation tested itself by forming alliances and getting itself into World War I. Opa did not fight on the front, although there is a photograph that shows him proudly wearing the uniform of the German *Wehrmacht* (military). His occupation beyond farming, that of a butcher and sausage-maker, was considered an essential industry. Then, too, he was raising sons for the Vaterland, even though they were too young for that war.

Bettenhausen was not unaware of politics. Germans are by nature contentious and love to argue policy and debate ways of governing. They bang tables and argue strenuously when families and friends get together, and it was so in my grandparents' house. Inevitably, the men would end up telling war stories.

My father attended the *Dorfschule* (village elementary school) first through eighth grade, combining it with his shepherding duties as he grew older. The school calendar was regulated so children got time off during planting season and harvest time so they could take their place in the field.

My father was almost 14 when disease decimated the sheep in central Germany. He decided he should go to Meiningen into *Lehre* (apprenticeship) and become a butcher and sausage maker. A master butcher in Meiningen, a friend of the family, took him in for three years (1917-1920). He worked through the standard guild program: apprenticeship, journeyman, and master. He acquired his certificate as journeyman, passing examinations upon completing his apprenticeship with the goal of seeking employment on his own. But going on to become a master butcher was not his plan at this time. Instead, he had an irrepressible desire to travel—the wanderlust.

Contributing to his restlessness may have been the unrest in Germany. World War I had ended. Germany had experienced the humiliating loss of the war, some of the most awful inflation in modern times, and discontent over the Treaty of Versailles.

About this time, 1920, while in Meiningen, my father probably first became aware of the wider world of German political thought. "The Jews sold us out after the war," people grumbled. "Things are awful for us here in the Reich. Times have got to get better, or we'll have no future." My father was bright, intellectually curious, and eager to get ahead. I can't tell where his wanderlust came from since his family were fairly stodgy people rooted in their own land. But times were changing, and he was ready to go out and meet that change head-on. An opportunity for employment presented itself in Hamburg.

There he met the girl who became my mother. Alma Wiedrich grew up in Husum, a fishing hamlet on the North Sea in Schleswig-Holstein. Alma was an out-of-wedlock child whose mother was a girl named Pauline Wiedrich. Not much is known about her, other than that she was a housegirl who was in service to a family by the name of Harkson. Rumors in town had it that Mr. Harkson, a well-to-do businessman and owner of a concrete products company, got Pauline pregnant. In an age when unmarried pregnancy was a terrible shame, families cast out their own children, who had often been forced in one way or another to submit to powerful men in the homes they served. It followed that Pauline was sent far away to Kiel, close to the Danish border, to give birth in anonymity and surrender the baby for adoption. Possibly, Harksen discreetly funded expenses. But Pauline did not give up her baby. Instead this courageous young mother gave it her name. Records show baby Alma Wiedrich was born in Kiel, May 10, 1903.

Pauline returned to Husum with her newborn, and I can only speculate that the pressures of single motherhood at that time were overwhelming. My mother was presented as a baby in a basket at the front door of a kindly couple known to take in foster children. There she grew up in the nurturing home of Johann and Anne Christine Hansen. How often my mother told me later how fortunate she was, for "they were always so good to me." She called them "Mama und Papa."

Alma was one of four girls the couple took in. Clara was the oldest; then came my mother. When she was around seven, another baby, Karla, was taken in, and finally, a young girl, Friedl, was the last of four fortunate children to be raised by the Hansens. Karla was my mother's favorite sister. She is my godmother.

Growing up with the Hansens was a strengthening experience for the girls in their care. This couple seemed to have taken the children for philanthropic reasons. They loved children and were well suited to caring for them, treating them as birth children.

My mother went to elementary school until she was fourteen. Then she, too, was placed in service, first to a farm family, then to a business household. During her service, my mother was approached for the typical seduction and was probably afraid she would follow in the path of her mother. She was a strong-minded and independent young woman, however, even in her teens, unlike many others of her time.

It was practically unheard of for a young woman to break the arrangements, because society believed young women were to be protected in family situations until such time as they would marry. Ironically, the so-called protectors in their service situations were, more often than not, also their seducers. My courageous and goal-oriented mother, flaunting the conventions of society, took the risk of going to the big city to make a living.

That is not to say that other venturesome women were not trying to go it alone, particularly in the cities. After World War I, women across America and in Western Europe were finding their way into businesses.

They had always taught school and some became nurses. Now they would also become shop girls and train to be secretaries, making an income that would sustain them—barely.

My mother went to Hamburg in the early 1920s to work for the owners of a butcher shop and a small sausage factory. Room and board were offered as part of her compensation. She was by this time a knockout of a woman: chestnut-haired, full-figured, spirited, and independent. As fate would have it, it was there that she met the bright, handsome obstreperous young man who was to become her husband. Both of them were not only ahead of their times in attitude, but also part of the generation that fearlessly forged ahead with plans for life.

My father was not like the men she had known in Husum. He had been on his own for a few years. He knew how to work and where he was going in the world, and he was handsome, and full of fun and mischief. All of these qualities any woman would find appealing; none of these had she experienced before. She left her boyfriend behind in Husum, tall, handsome, and correct Gustav Gertens, who was probably more serious about the relationship than she. He would come to Hamburg occasionally to visit.

My mother learned to prepare platters of assorted cheeses and cuts of meat and sausages, as well as side platters of salads and vegetables for the butcher shop. Because of her talent she was put to work in the meat kitchen one-hundred-percent of the time. My father worked nearby in the slaughterhouse and meat-cutting area. He noticed her and made eyes at her, but she brushed him off.

The working area of the business was in the lower level, with the butcher shop at street level and a narrow staircase connecting one to the other. One day my mother, bearing a huge platter of tastefully presented wurst and salad, headed up the stairs. Coming down was the young man she'd come to know as Otto Wiegand. With a twinkle in his eye, he announced he was not going to let her pass unless she gave him a kiss. Fuming, probably wishing she could upend the platter in his face—knowing full and well if she did, her employment would end at that very moment—all she could do was demand that he let her pass. But she was trapped. He leaned over and took his toll: a few well-placed kisses. Soon they were seeing each other, and Gustav Gertens faded out of the picture.

My father, seeing an intelligent and spirited young woman, believed this girl of his dreams should have a career of her own. He encouraged her to apply for an apprenticeship at one of the finest houses in Hamburg, the well-known Ratsweinkeller in downtown Hamburg. She was accepted and began training to become a certified *Kalte Mamsell*, a defined profession in

Europe—salad chef.

Hamburg was a wonderful, complex city. Full of international atmosphere and culture, it was also beset with unrest. Germans took to the streets, demonstrating over a disintegrating economy, inflation, and the weak central government. The Kaiser had abdicated after World War I, and prejudice against the Jews was flourishing, though the happy young people in the boarding house of Irma Blaufuss must not have felt it as strongly as they felt the pull of making plans for the future.

My mother was on her way to a new career. My father's dream was to go to sea. There was a window of time to accomplish both objectives. But before he could go, he had one more loose end to tie up: he had to make Alma his fiancée. They became engaged, and she said she'd wait for him as he traveled the world.

Father: Friedrich Karl Wiegand—born 1882
Mother: Emilie Augusta Wiegand
(nee: Laesser)—born 1881

Lydia Augusta—born 1901
Otto Karl—born 1903 (my father)
Bertha Kellner—born 1905
Hilda—born 1906
Elsie—born 1908
Erich Wilhelm—born 1910
Erwin Karl—born 1911
Karl Otto—born 1913
Helene Lydia—born 1919
Willi—born 1921

There were three more children: a set of twins who died at birth, and a little boy named Kurt, who died as a toddler. There were thirteen children in all.

My father and his siblings: (back) Pappi (10), Bertha, Lydia, Hilda, Elsie (front) Erwin, Baby Karl on Oma's lap and Erich.

Pappi's "*Elternhaus*," the Wiegand Homestead built in the mid-17th century.

My Oma and Opa (Pappi's parents) Friedrich and Emilie Wiegand

Bettenhausen, Province of Thueringen. The Geba mountain is to the right.

Horses and wagons as well as oxen were standard on German farms in the 1930s. Here Opa with the handlebar mustache, son Erwin on the bicycle and Oma to the rear, wearing a headscarf.

HUSUM

As in de ganze Welt bekannt,
ligt Husum an de Nordseekant,
Dor swemmt de Austern fri herum,
doch jonich för dat Publikum.
Un wat för Ossen kamt to Stadt,
de sünd förwar nich för de Katt,
So draff un fett un kugelrund,
wie seht se blos un wischt de Mund,
Dat Husumer Gymnasium
deent keds uns als Palladium,
Datt wie nich geistig ganz versurt
un mang de Ossen ganz verburt,

De Haben, de de Fiskus hört,
is för de Stadt von grotem Wert
De harr all längstens Weltverkehr,
wenn he en beten natter weer.
Un dann de Stadtpark! O wat fin:
Son schönen hett nich mal Berlin.
Kost he ok dörtig dusend Mark,
is dat för Husum blos en Quark.
Dat Rathus het geheme Kraft,
sien Standesamt dar Wunder schafft,
Geiht en herin as ohle Brut,
kommt se as junge Fru herut.

Is Husum ok all old un grau,
pulseert ehr Blot doch warm un gau
Is för en Futjen jonich bang,
un lett de Fliep so licht nich hangn.
Singt geern en lustig Schelmenleed,
deit jede „Prost" ok geern Bescheed,
Un hölt dat weibliche Geschlecht
in vullen Ehrn, na Fug un Recht.
Drum, Jungens, wüllt jem Hütten buun,
blivt hier, gaht nich na Kamerun,
Sünd unse Döchter ok nich swart,
sünd se doch gräsig good von Hart.

Em. Gurlitt.

Husum, the fishing hamlet on the North Sea where Mommi was raised.

My Mother's Parents

Foster parents raised my mother. Their names were Johann and Anne Christine Hansen. She called them Mama and Papa.

She was one of four girls this couple took in. Clara, the oldest, was seven years older than my mother. Then came my mother, Alma, taken in as an infant. Later another baby named Karla was taken in when my mother was around seven. Then, eventually, Friedl came. Karla was my mother's lifelong favorite sister. Karla is also my godmother—still alive—and adored by me no less than I adored my own mother.

Interestingly, the Hansens never formally adopted my mother and that was always a source of sadness and disappointment for her. She never really understood why, but was too beholden to them to ask. The Hansens did have a biological daughter named Magda. When Magda got married, it turned out that she and her husband, Karl Ritscher, could not have children. The Hansens eventually agreed to an arrangement where Magda and Karl Ritscher would adopt Karla and raise her as their own.

Clara did not live very long. She died of pneumonia as a young woman in her twenties.

Friedl left the fold after a few years. She was still very young—under the age of ten. Her birth mother just had to get her life together. After she got married and in a position to provide a stable home life for her daughter, the Hansens, who had taken Friedl in as an infant, returned her to her biological mother. They once again demonstrated their devotion to their foster children and did what was best for them. During their entire lifetimes, they encouraged the sisters to remain close to each other.

Mommi's foster parents' home.

The Hansen family. Mommi, approximately 10, standing next to her foster mother. Karla, 3, is far right.

Baby Friedl is on a caregiver's lap. Standing, Mommi, 14, sitting, Tante Karla, 7. Baby is nine months.

$\mathcal{O}$*tto, my father,* had hired on with a shipping company out of Hamburg, Hapag-Lloyd, which transported goods all over the world. The food staff supplied meals for the working crew, with the butchers first cutting huge sides of pork, beef, and lamb, then preparing servable cuts of steaks, chops, roasts, and ground beef for the cooks. The butchery, with walk-in meat freezer and refrigerator, was near the galley. My father's motivation for taking the job was for the excitement of seeing the distant places he had dreamed about, far from rural Bettenhausen.

From 1923 through early 1926 his voyages took him to Asia, the Middle East, all over the Caribbean, as well as North and South America. His trips would last up to six or seven months at a time before the freighter returned to homeport. Adorning one of our walls when I was a child was a framed "baptismal" certificate he received upon passing across the equator. He was given the honorary mariner name "Stockfisch" as he was cleansed of all impurities of the Northern Hemisphere with the holy waters of Neptune, God of the sea. He was on board the SS *Cap Polonia* at the time. The certificate is dated the 4th day of the 9th month, in the Year of our Lord 1924.

Otto became a world-class sightseer. In Hawaii he mingled with tourists and hula girls whose dancing was probably more authentic than it is today. In Bombay he and other friends from the crew visited Bombay Temple and took pictures of schoolboys in white coats and knickers being educated in British ways to stand tall in straight lines. In Japan they rode in rickshaws around Tokyo. He dined at a restaurant in the shadow of the giant Buddha at Kamakura. In San Francisco, my father took a photograph of his best friend and seafaring buddy, Willi Dreissigacker, jaunty and confident in front of a bar in the most ridiculous pair of cowboy chaps the souvenir shop could supply.

Sandakan/Borneo, an oilrig near Sumatra, Singapore, Ceylon (now Sri Lanka), Port Said, the Suez Canal, the Panama Canal—all were ports of call.

His first experience coming into New York was in December, 1925, aboard the SS *Cleveland.* He and several buddies went on shore leave and explored the city, primarily the German section, called "Yorkville," on the upper eastside of Manhattan. It left an indelible impression on him, and he seemed to sense this was where he and Alma were destined to be.

Meanwhile back in Hamburg, my mother was busy completing her apprenticeship. After receiving her certificate through the Ratsweinkeller, she found seasonal employment in some of the finest resort hotels in the area. I have in my possession a stack of *Zeugnisse* (recommendations) from the places she worked testifying to her skill and character. She was so proud of them; they have become family treasures documenting her life as a young woman.

Even though my mother was engaged and living in bachelorette quarters, she was still being courted by Gustav Gertens. Gustav was tall, slender, quiet, and elegant. My father was short, muscular, and somewhat stocky, swarthy and handsome as they come. He was the one she loved, and she was willing to wait for the short times they shared when his ship was home.

※ ※ ※

By 1926 my father hadn't seen his fiancé for months, and his absence from her was beginning to wear on him. He signed on for one more voyage to the Americas, and they made the joint decision that this would probably be his last. Whether premeditated or not, when his freighter docked in New York, he made the decision to "jump ship." Jumping ship was not that unusual at that time; merchant seamen frequently left the companies for which they worked when they found their own Shangri Las. Some of his friends were already living in the German community in New York and were prospering. It was a time of burgeoning expansion then. Skyscrapers were going up; industry, shipping, and tourism were thriving; and there were jobs in construction, the grocery business, hotels and restaurants, and all the connected service industries. Whoever wanted to work found a job.

Although it was a melting pot, people lived in their own ethnic groups: Chinatown, the Irish and Italian neighborhoods, and a predominantly Jewish section. The diverse neighborhoods were all colored according to their homeland cultures and traditions. So it was that Yorkville was renowned for its cafes, German restaurants, meat markets, bakeries, and assorted specialty shops stocked with all possible imported goods. When strolling 86th Street from 1st Avenue all the way up to Lexington, one could overhear the pedestrians conversing in German. German music would drift from the cafes, and the abundant flower stands would at times crowd a visitor off the sidewalks.

Otto had some bachelor friends who had an apartment on East 83rd Street. He kept their address in his pocket, along with an open invitation to join them at any time. Through his acquaintances, his reputation as butcher and sausage maker had preceded him, and just two days after his arrival he was employed by the George Kerns Packing House on West 38th Street and 10th Avenue.

My father lived a rather carefree lifestyle for a while in the company of his friends, but this was not what he had come to America for. His plans were to build a future with Alma, have a family, and make it in this land of opportunity. And so he sent her a telegram, telling her to book passage as soon as possible, as he began preparing for her arrival.

My mother worked until two weeks before her voyage to America. She quickly got her affairs in order. The day of her departure, Gustav came to take her to the pier where her ship was docked. If things didn't work out with Otto, he'd be waiting. She smiled, thanked him, and bade him goodbye. She was on her way to her future.

My mother arrived in New York on May 30, 1927. My father had planned on taking her downtown to the Justice of the Peace to get married before they even went to the furnished apartment he had leased on East 86th Street, but it was Memorial Day and all government offices were closed. The next morning, they went to the County Municipal Building, 3675 Broadway, and tied the knot. How they must have felt! My father the consummate romantic, my mother, completely in love, now with her devoted life's partner.

Years later, when my brother Freddy and I were adults, we would ask Mommi whether she and Pappi spent that first night together, not being legally married. My mother, squeaky clean until the day she died, would never really fess up. "Surely you didn't make Pappi sleep on the couch that night!" All she did was smile with a twinkle in her eye.

In the late 1920s my parents lived the life of happy young newlyweds. They were very industrious and frugal. But they never denied themselves the pleasure of widening their friendship circle, going out, entertaining, and taking short trips. Pappi worked as a butcher, waiting on customers and going to night school to learn English so he could serve them better and get ahead. My mother found employment as a cook and housekeeper, mostly with wealthy Jewish families on the Upper West Side. She felt secure in these positions, inasmuch as her language skills were still lacking. Most Jewish families spoke German anyway.

It was now the time of the Great Depression although I don't recall my parents talking much about it. They certainly had no grand investments to lose, and those in food service were usually able to weather economic downturns anyway.

Freddy was born on May 11, 1931. I was born February 3, 1935. My parents continued working, with older German friends watching us. I vaguely remember a "Tante Ella," big and fat with ugly brown teeth and Jube-Jubes (little gummy candies) in her pocket.

Eventually my parents moved out to Queens, deciding to mingle in a more mixed and suburban neighborhood, where Pappi could find work in a butcher shop. He took employment with a grocery chain by the name of Bohacks as manager of the meat counter in one of their stores. They rented an upstairs apartment on Cotillia Road, a pretty, tree-lined street with postage-stamp back yards. Soon after, Pappi transferred to another Bohacks store in Ridgewood, Brooklyn. It was on the corner of Sixtieth Lane and Foxhall Street. We moved to another apartment, catty-cornered from Bohacks: 68-58 Sixtieth Lane, an old three-story brownstone where we rented the top-floor apartment.

Apartments in those days were different from those of today. We climbed the first flight of stairs, then walked a long hallway that led to the bottom of the second flight. Climbing that, we would arrive on our floor. Our apartment by design was called a "railroad" apartment. It stretched from one end of the top floor to the other, all rooms in a row—like boxcars. The apartment had two entrances. The one we used in the front led directly into the kitchen and living room area, my parents' bedroom, then the bedroom Freddy and I shared. The second entrance opened onto a hallway in the rear of the apartment, from which we could access two more connecting bedrooms. My mother always earned extra income by having "rooms to let," rooming only, no meals, and these two connecting bedrooms with their convenient separate entrance were never without renters. The only bathroom in the apartment was located in the hallway and had to be shared by all occupants.

Not in a million years would my parents dream that these two rented rooms would be a major contributing factor to the turmoil our family experienced after World War II broke out and the FBI showed up at our front door.

We spent our days happily in the neighborhood. My father, the butcher at Bohacks, obviously of German decent, was like our Irish, Italian, Russian and Armenian neighbors. Everybody spoke with an accent of some kind. English was just about everyone's second language, but that didn't mean that every one of these people wasn't proud to become an American citizen and have American-born children.

※ ※ ※

Freddy and I were raised by traditional-minded parents in a loving, though disciplined, atmosphere. Mommi took the greatest pleasure in our using good manners. Eating with knife and fork, saying *bitte* and *danke* (please and thank you), shaking hands with a curtsy or a bow when greeting her friends—all these things were the order of the day. Pappi, on the other hand reveled in our personalities, keenly aware of our inherent qualities. I recall he loved my fastidiousness. He would go through the apartment, purposely leaving doors ajar, opening drawers half way, mussing up clothes and shoes. Then he would send me to a back bedroom to get a book or something and watch as I, unaware of his peeking, put everything back in order on my way. When I returned, he was standing in front of the couch where I had put my doll. Pretending to almost sit down on top of her, he picked her up by one leg, held her up in the air, and asked me what he should do with her. Outraged, I told him to lay her down immediately. Didn't he know her blood would be rushing to her head? I was five years old.

We spoke German in our household, but English came easy once we played with the neighborhood children. My parents worked hard at learning English and got by. In the butcher shop, even though many of his customers spoke German, he wanted to be able to respond in English, rather than have to point and guess at which of the various cuts of meat on display the customer wanted.

My parents loved their life in America. They had come for a future rich in opportunity, eagerly embracing its culture, as well as adding to it. They attended neighborhood and city events conducted in English, but just as important, they supported German cultural activities. We belonged to the New York *Turnverein* (a gymnastics club), where we would meet with other German families for weekend dinners and traditional feasts.

There was always lots of music and German folk dancing. I made Pappi dance with me until he would finally find a reason to leave the room. There were gymnastic activities, a *Maennerchor*, a *Liederkranz* (choral groups) and a German *Volkstheater* (civic theater), where Pappi involved himself in amateur acting.

My father also belonged to the "German American Vocational League," and we attended many of their picnics and events as a family. In German it was known as the *Deutsche-Amerikanische Berufsgemeinschaft* - DAB for short. This group had a summer camp in New Jersey, which Freddy and I and Mommi attended for several summers. The organization encouraged professional contacts, assisted new German immigrants to get on their feet, and perpetuated German traditions and holidays. Membership was open to Americans as well as Germans. Pappi's membership was destined to become our nemesis, dramatically altering the course of our lives.

On weekends we would go to Forest Hills, a lovely public park in Queens. Here Freddy and I whirled about riding the horses on the carousel, Freddy leaning out precariously, reaching for the brass ring and snatching it most of the time. That would earn him another ride. Or, we might take the subway to visit Tante Elsie in New York, this aunt who had given in to her own sense of wanderlust. She was one of my father's younger sisters: the only other sibling who immigrated to America. She came in 1928 and settled in with my parents for a brief period in Yorkville. Mommi wrote long letters to her foster parents. Loyal to her foster family, she never sought out her birth mother as people do today, probably believing it would cause her parents pain. She also stayed in close contact with her sister Karla, inviting her to come for a visit, perhaps stay. Karla came, but she didn't stay.

The words "upwardly mobile" hadn't been invented yet, but that's what we were. One day when I was about five, Mommi sent Freddy and me to the butcher shop to get some lamb chops. She gave us a list, and I couldn't understand why we were taking a shopping list; Pappi always brought meat home from Bohacks. "Don't go to Bohacks," she said. "Go to that little butcher shop across the street. You might see something interesting."

We took the list in hand and followed her instructions. We had never gone to this little store before. When we opened the door, the bell rang to alert whoever was there to wait on us, but no one was behind the counter. We walked across the sawdust-covered floor, past the shiny new cases where steaks, chops, and roasts were beautifully presented. Everything looked perfect; we just didn't see the butcher. What was going on here?

All of a sudden Pappi popped up from behind the counter where he'd been crouching to surprise us. He was dressed in a white butcher apron covering his white shirt and tie, black trousers, wearing a white chef's cap and a great big smile. He came around the counter and caught both of us in one big bear hug and said, "Yes, here I am—this is our shop now." Then he took us to the back room, a kitchen and preparation area, where he already had frankfurters simmering for us.

Every Saturday Freddy and I went to the movies: the Glenwood on Myrtle Avenue. He hated to have me tag along because it cramped his style with the young girls he was already trying to interest. Mommi insisted. "You take your sister—or no movies!" He referred to me as "that little fart," although he did watch out for me and let me hang on to him when the scary serials came on, like *The Iron Claw*. The movies cost eleven cents, and Mommi gave us each a quarter. Freddy always used up his money. I usually had money leftover, with which I treated myself to a "Creole Sundae" at the ice cream parlor on Fresh Pond Road the next day. This was a parfait-like concoction consisting of three scoops of ice cream in flavors of my choosing, separated by various fruit sauces and topped off with whipped cream, chocolate sprinkles, and a cherry!

Pappi's sister, Tante Elsie, was now happily settled in America. She lived in New York and had married another immigrant, Werner Knoch. Onkel Werner, well off, came from Werdau, a small city in Saxony. His parents owned a hotel and restaurant called Hotel zum Goldenen Anker. Werner trained in some of the finest hotels in Germany, Switzerland, Austria, and the south of France. He was to eventually come back to Werdau, and as the only son, take over the family business. By the time Werner arrived in America, he had built an impressive resume and found immediate employment with Luchow's, a famous German restaurant in New York. He was also a first-class "Bon Vivant," and it didn't take long before he was having an affair with the owner's daughter.

As a young woman, Tante Elsie was a Madonna look-alike. Blond, sexy, very outgoing with a rich accent, she loved the good life! My mother never approved of her lifestyle, especially in the beginning when she lived with Mommi and Pappi. Then Elsie met Werner. They partied until the wee hours of the morning, and Elsie got pregnant. That ended Werner's affair with the boss's daughter and sent him looking for a new job. My cousin Marianne was on the way. She was born in November, 1934. The following February, Werner married Elsie.

During this same time, the mid-to-late 1930s, letters from relatives in Germany encouraged my father to come for a visit. "Perhaps you will want to return to Germany for good," some wrote. "Things are on the move. This new man, Adolf Hitler, is restoring our good name as a nation. He is building super highways [the famous Autobahn], encouraging economy and industry, rebuilding the German [Aryan] stock and restoring pride. Hitler is promising a Volkswagen in every garage and opportunities for families to have dream vacations. Children will be educated and given the most memorable camping experiences. Everyone will have a job. People will prosper as never before."

My father thought about it. A visit would provide the opportunity to experience the new Vaterland first hand, and his family, whom he hadn't seen in over a decade, would be able to meet his wife and children for the first time. Not incidentally, he would be able to rectify his alien resident status in the United States by re-entering the country legally.

And so on July 1, 1937, we sailed on board the SS *Hamburg* from New York to Hamburg, via Southhampton and Cherbourg. It was a wildly exciting trip with welcome-aboard parties and many activities: movies, concerts, children's theme parties, dining, and dancing.

When we arrived in Bettenhausen and experienced the things I described earlier, it seemed the quality of life did appear to be better and getting better all the time. The family Pappi had left behind was, indeed, growing prosperous. Only two siblings were still at home: my father's sister Helene (I called her Tante Lene) eighteen and very mature and sophisticated, and his youngest brother Willi, a sixteen-year-old wild man. He irritated my mother to no end with his smart-alecky ways. "He's going through his *Flegeljahre* (adolescent years)," Pappi told her. "Don't let it bother you." Friends in the village were welcoming. Pappi played soccer with his former schoolmates on weekends, and during the week when the farm work didn't stop, my parents willingly helped out in the fields. Freddy and I especially enjoyed riding home on the hay wagons.

At the end of the day, after the evening meal, relatives and neighbors would gather at the local Biergarten and tell stories. Children were never excluded and played with other children nearby. Freddy was six years old and I two and a half, but neither one of us had a language barrier. Although born in America, we both spoke German. This fact made an enormous impression on my grandparents, Opa taking personal credit for the talent his grandchildren demonstrated. It was a special treat for the villagers to visit with their old school chum Otto, now living in America.

Many of the younger men were already in the *Wehrmacht* (German Armed Forces). Teenage boys were in the mandatory *Hitler Jugend* (Hitler Youth). The young girls were in the *BDM* (*Bund Deutscher Maedchen*), the female complement to the Hitler Youth. Some of Pappi's brothers and brothers-in-law were also in the military. The Third Reich was here, firmly entrenched and mighty in its power to build a nation of loyal followers. We heard the German anthem played at every public event, followed by soul-stirring marching music and singing.

Upon entering a government office or even a private shop, instead of the usual *"Guten Tag"* (good day) people were getting into the habit of greeting with *"Heil Hitler!"*

Everyone was caught up in this atmosphere of unity, pride, and nationalism. My father was indifferent; my mother opposed. She loved America. Pappi had a gut feeling about the whole scene, especially the aggressive political views: *"Heute Deutschland, morgen die ganze Welt!"* (Today Germany, tomorrow the whole world!") And he didn't like the build-up of military might. Weren't these the political extremes they left behind when they went to America in the 1920's?

There was never a question in my mother's mind on which side of the Atlantic she was going to make her home. She had initiated proceedings to become a naturalized American citizen shortly after Freddy was born while my father procrastinated.

In 1937 he came to Germany with an open mind. He had met the family and experienced first hand what life was like under Hitler, and didn't like the uneasy feeling it gave him. His experience served to strengthen his resolve to go to the American Consulate in Berlin and arrange legal immigration into the United States. He had after all lived in the States illegally for more than ten years. Pappi was not only somewhat of a procrastinator, beyond that, he was very concerned with the fact that his being *schwarz im Lande* (German expression for residing in a country illegally) could possibly put him at risk for deportation. So, this trip to Berlin was uppermost on his "to-do list." He took the train to Berlin while we stayed in Bettenhausen.

During my father's absence, an unpleasant incident occurred between my mother and Opa. My grandfather hurt her feelings to such a degree that she never really forgave him. I don't know exactly what led up to it, but he said, "There's not a woman alive, worthy of any of my sons." It was the wrong thing to say to the woman in my father's life. Opa was an overly serious, dominant German man from the previous generation, and his wife tolerated his ways; my mother was a "new woman." Mommi felt much compassion for Oma, referring to her as "angelic." For my own part, I loved my Oma and enjoyed going into the barn to get chicken feed and scattering it all over the ground. This is the earliest memory I have.

When Pappi returned from Berlin and our visit was almost over, Mommi, Freddy, and I looked forward to returning home. We sailed from Hamburg on September 16, 1937, on board the SS *Deutschland*, the flagship of the Hamburg-America Line.

And so we took up life again in America, in Brooklyn. When I was about five, my parents sent us to a private German school. Freddy was already in public school. He had to do both. We were totally bi-lingual at this point, but they insisted we learn to read and write in German, including old German script. For me, this was in lieu of Kindergarten. Pappi was always very keen on education and often remarked, "What you have in your head, no one can take from you." There was no greater gift we could give him than to bring home good grades. When I did so, he'd point to my high forehead and say, *"Da ist etwas drinne!"* (There's something in there!).

We lived in a wonderful, all-American neighborhood, where we girls marked up the sidewalks for hopscotch. Boys and girls roller-skated from one end of our block to the other, chalking up the street. Hide and seek, stick ball and tag—those were our street games. I think we were quite popular among our friends because we could offer something nobody else had—a Dad who had a butcher shop on the corner and prepared hot dogs for us on the stove in the back room of his store. Sometimes when we entered the shop too often with our playmates, I'd see him waving his arms and good-naturedly gesturing us away.

Our neighborhood had many Germans, but there were other nationalities as well. Herr Roelke, my piano teacher, had a wife from Romania with a strong guttural Slavic accent and an apartment that always smelled like spicy soup. Mr. Draschbill was an old Russian and a gifted artist. My mother purchased a miniature oil painting from him. There were Italians around us, too. And the McMahon family stood out as a boisterous, loud, and hard-drinking Irish family. My mother warned us to stay away from their kids: "They could be trouble," she said, but I did not find that to be so.

Patsy McMahon, a few years older than I, went to the same dance studio. We both took acrobatics, but Mommi chose ballet for me, while Patsy took tap. I was in awe of her. She could tap-dance like one of the Rockettes. Our studio was rehearsing for a recital, "Junior Frolics of 1940," to be presented at the Manhattan Center. "Boisterous" probably described Patsy's performance best. When the music began, she hurled herself onto the stage tapping up a storm to the tune of "Stars and Stripes Forever." Her Uncle Sam top hat must have been glued to her head, and her feet flew across the stage, as beneath her royal blue vest and her short, red-and-white-striped satin skirt, she showed her pretty legs. I, too, had a number in the recital. Listed in the program as "Cupid in the Enchanted Garden," a solo by "Baby Anneliese," I danced on pointe to "Valse Lente" from "Ballet Sylvia" by Delibes. My mother was on cloud nine. Tante Elsie, always included in our lives, was there too. I'm sure these times were bittersweet for her, inasmuch as her daughter, my cousin Marianne, had been living in Germany with her paternal grandparents since 1938.

Marianne was just four years old when Werner took his wife and daughter home to introduce them to his family. Werner's mother disliked Elsie immediately. She was the daughter of a farmer—*ein Bauernmaedchen* (a peasant girl)—with barely an eighth-grade education and no certified profession. She was, in fact, a maid to a rich family in New York. Werner's parents thought of themselves as upper crust, and his mother simply could not envision Elsie as the lady of the house, once Werner inherited the family's Hotel Goldener Anker (Golden Anchor Hotel) and the social status in the town of Werdau that came with it. But they were enchanted with their only grandchild, who favored her father's side in looks and temperament. Marianne also spoke fluent German.

When their visit came to an end, the grandparents urged Elsie and Werner to leave Marianne with them and return to New York to gain more experience in Werner's hotel/restaurant management profession without the need to care for a toddler. Marianne would be raised in a privileged environment. It would only be for a few years, just until Elsie and Werner returned to take over the family business and live in Germany for good. All agreed to the plan. No one could foresee the outbreak of World War II that would leave Marianne stranded in Germany.

Freddy and I became Tante Elsie and Onkel Werner's surrogate youngsters. They lived in Manhattan and would often come to Brooklyn to pick us up on weekends while our parents worked, taking us to the Bronx Zoo, Central Park, the circus at Madison Square Garden, Coney Island, so many places our parents neither had the time nor the money to do. I'm sure we filled a void in their lives. Conversely, they made a lifetime of memories for us. Especially Elsie. She was my lifelong "Auntie Mame."

All of this worked well until about 1940 or so. The nationalism and military buildup we had observed on our visit to Germany was bringing bitter results in Europe. Germany had conquered Czechoslovakia and Poland in the spring and summer of 1939. Following those conquests, Britain and France declared war. This was Hitler's Third Reich in action, the new Nazi Germany everyone in our neighborhood was talking about. Most felt conflicted as anti-German hysteria grew to a fever pitch around us. The newspapers, the radio, the city at large, even our neighbors, began to look at Germans with a wary eye

The neighborhood churches began to reflect the conflict. Our family was Lutheran by denomination, and Mommi sent us to the Evangelical

Lutheran church across the street from our brownstone to attend Sunday school. She rarely attended services herself because the pastor's style of preaching made her uncomfortable. He was openly anti-German and laced his sermons with hate mongering of his own. My father, not a regular church-goer anyway, lost all respect for this man of the cloth. Pappi was a human-ist, an honest man who was dedicated to making his own way, treating people fairly, giving back to his community, and taking care of his family.

When we started being referred to as "Heinis," we stopped going. My father's business fell off, and Freddy and I began to feel a cooling in the neighborhood children's attitudes towards us. These were our playmates, kids we went to school with. It was a new reality. Germans were just not welcome anymore.

The butcher shop in Meiningen where Otto Wiegand served his three-year apprenticeship under master butcher Karl Seifert.

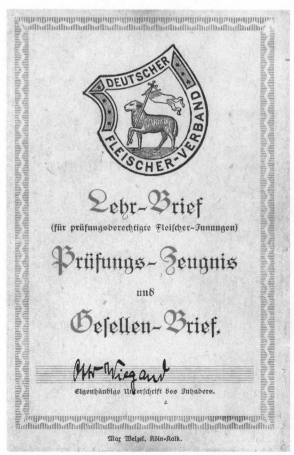

DEUTSCHER FLEISCHER-VERBAND

Lehr-Brief
(für prüfungsberechtigte Fleischer-Innungen)

Prüfungs-Zeugnis

und

Gesellen-Brief.

Eigenhändige Unterschrift des Inhabers.

Max Welzel, Köln-Kalk.

Pappi's certificatation of board exams passed, following three years of apprenticeship. He was a journeyman butcher.

Pappi aboard the *Monte Sacremento*.

My father Otto Wiegand in the 1920s.

My mother Alma in the 1920s.

Pappi's ship *Resolute* near an oil station in Sumatra.

World traveler Pappi (far left) at a Hindu school in Columbo, Ceylon, today Sri Lanka.

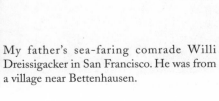

Another ship, another town: Tokyo.

My father's sea-faring comrade Willi Dreissigacker in San Francisco. He was from a village near Bettenhausen.

My mother Alma serving her apprenticeship at the famous Ratsweinkeller in Hamburg while her sweetheart was at sea. She is second from the right, dark hair.

Pappi (second row, second from left) in evening school in New York — learning English.

My Aunt Elsie and Uncle Werner met (top left), had a baby (top right) and got married, then left to take young Marianne (bottom left) to Germany to live with her grandparents (bottom right) in the lovely Hotel Goldner Anker.

1928. Aunt Elsie had lived with Pappi and Mommi in their New York apartment before she went out on her own.

My parents and big brother with little me on a Sunday afternoon family outing.

My parents partying in the '30s before children. Everybody was always dressed up.

Our first family studio picture. I am about six months,
Freddy, 4 years.

Anneliese, the author, at about sixteen months.

We sailed from New York to Hamburg via Cherbourg and South Hampton July 1, 1937 for a visit to Germany.

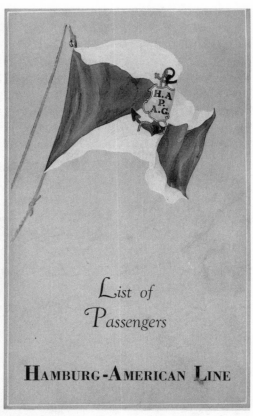

Our passport picture.

Our family vacation. Anneliese, Freddy, Mommi and Pappi onboard ship.

The two Wiegands with two other children pose with the lifesaver on the boat. Freddy is standing, wearing lederhosen.

We played with cousins when we visited Bettenhausen.

Here I am with Oma's chickens in the barn yard. It is my earliest memory.

On that 1937 vacation my Uncle Erwin showed us his glider. I thought the swastika was so interesting.

Pappi (front, 2nd from right) was invited to play soccer on the "old men's team" in Bettenhausen. Victory and swastika signs are on the tank tops.

The war had come. News of Germany's conquests came thundering in: radio accounts, the bombings on "Movietone News," magazine covers showing horror scenes from Europe in living color. Bold newspaper headlines told of an England increasingly under siege from the *Luftwaffe.* By late June of 1940, both Holland and France were occupied by German forces, and by Christmas season, 1941, after Pearl Harbor, the United States Congress declared war on Japan and Germany. It was all so ominous, and German families around us began the splitting of ideals and allegiances which would last the entire war.

As early as June of 1940, Congress had passed the Alien Registration Act. Aliens of all nationalities, especially Germans, had to comply. They were fingerprinted, asked questions about their history from birth on and geographical locations, occupations, and organizational memberships. My father had already registered and received his Alien Registration number at the time he re-entered the country legally following our German visit in 1937. In August 1938, he had filed his Declaration of Intention to become a naturalized American citizen.

However, the Alien Registration Act also gave the FBI, the INS, and the AECU (Alien Enemy Control Unit) sweeping authority to compile lists and issue warrants for the arrest and/or "presentation" of suspicious individuals for questioning. All of these orders were published over the signatures of the then Attorney General Francis Biddle or the Director of the Federal Bureau of Investigation, J. Edgar Hoover.

Threats to the East Coast were on the minds of those responsible for security in the United States. Because of perceived dangers to the West Coast (invasion by the Japanese), American citizens of Japanese descent came under the closest scrutiny and were being put into internment camps. But Germans knew the hostility, too. We as children felt the impact of the propaganda machine, which whispered all around us.

The name-calling by kids in the neighborhood, "Heini," "Nazi," the finger-pointing, the suspicious looks—all of that was on the increase. Even the adults picked up on this. It scared me and made me very unhappy. I don't think Freddy suffered as much as I. Perhaps I was just more sensitive. But I do recall kids skipping along beside or behind us on the way to school, calling us names and pointing—sometimes even pulling my long blonde braids. But Freddy was a born tough guy, the proverbial big brother, always ready to protect and defend. He made me feel safe.

Miss Chatfield, my second grade teacher, was the ultimate picture of a spinster school marm: New Englandish, tall, skinny, and hawk-faced. And a hypocrite. When my mother came to "conference" with Chatfield, she would praise me as an A-B student, take my cheek and pinch it, supposedly in affection (it hurt like anything), and call me a "lovely child." In the class-room, it was different. I was obviously a German child, connected with the enemy. My hand was always held high with answers; she would ignore me to make me feel overlooked and rejected.

One day I needed desperately to go to the rest room. I sat there, wav-ing my hand, trying to get her attention; she continued to look over my head and ignore me. In those days a child didn't speak out; you had to wait until you were called on. When she finally acknowledged me, she said, "You'll have to wait until this lesson is over." Once released, I was so bad off that I left a trail of droplets behind me as I ran to the rest room. When I returned, she further humiliated me by pointing to the trail. Naturally my classmates snickered. Chatfield was making a point, and I had experienced my first encounter with discrimination.

Air raid practices were a part of daily life. In front of our brownstone apartment building was a huge red sand box with a slanted top, on which we slid. A shovel was provided so that in case of bombings, the air-raid warden could put out fires. The kids started playing different games. In-stead of "Cowboys and Indians," they played "War." Which sides were Freddy and I supposed to be on? I remember volunteering to be a nurse.

We lived through this no-man's land during the early war years. Our family continued to be involved in the New York German community. We were especially active in the *Deutsche/AmerikanischeBerufsgemeinschaft*, DAB. (German/American Vocational League). It provided a social base for German families integrating into American society, while at the same time encouraging Germans to keep their heritage alive and to teach their children the best of German culture, music, and holiday traditions. Our social life to my recollection revolved almost completely around this organization and gatherings with other families.

Freddy and I especially loved going to the DAB camp Bergwald in Riverdale, New Jersey. The DAB developed this large property as a summer retreat for all member families. Cabins, built by volunteers, were connected by a path that led through the woods and ended in a clearing on top of the hill where the *Gemeinschaftshaus* (Community Building) stood. My parents were very committed volunteers, for it gave them the opportunity to offer Freddy and me wonderful summer vacations. During our school vacation my mother was one of the main cooks. My father would come from the city on weekends and work with the men. For the most part, however, I remember them always cooking in outdoor cauldrons over open fires. We children had to gather wood and keep the woodpile well supplied.

There were songfests, dances and concerts, German movies, and lectures. Weekends were usually packed with special events. German celebrities were often invited, and once there was even a reception for the German Consul, children with our group singing German folksongs for him. But what Freddy and I loved and lived for the most was swimming in the natural lake and participating in the athletic activities.

It had always been my perception that the DAB was strictly apolitical; at least my parents never spoke of the organization in any other context. The organization did do some philanthropic work. They either provided sponsorships or financial help and advice for Germans who wanted to immigrate and had neither family nor a financial base in the States. DAB assistance really became necessary after hostilities broke out in Europe in 1939 and German travelers became stranded over here. These German nationals had to find living accommodations until they could arrange passage back. The leadership of the league called on member-families known to have rooms for rent, short term, for the visiting Germans. We always had a room for rent; it was my mother's way of earning extra pin money.

In September, 1939, a boarder came to take our extra room. Herr Gruda appeared one day and brought his few possessions up the stairs in a suitcase. He seemed very mysterious. He was over six feet, had dark hair, wore a tan-gold trench coat, and took off his fedora hat when he greeted us with "*Guten Tag*" as he arrived on the landing. You could tell he was well educated and polite in a polished sort of way, but he wasn't friendly. He came, he went, very private and discrete, on what business we never knew. My father once said he thought he had ongoing official business with the German consulate. He always carried a dark leather briefcase and, as I think of it today, he fit the picture of a spy. Gruda lived with us until the latter part of February, 1940, at which time he left as suddenly as he had arrived.

As 1940-41 evolved, we began to feel the pressures of the national alien screening process more and more. We heard of members of German families being "picked up" by the FBI and taken in for questioning. Some were friends of ours, others mere acquaintances or friends of friends, but they all had some connection to the DAB or similar German/American groups. There were rumors that the Bund (the American arm of the German Nazi Party) had infiltrated many German/American organizations in the United States and that Nazi spies were active under the cover of these outwardly legitimate and harmless groups.

And so it turned out. The FBI had been tracking Herr Gruda, suspecting him of spying for the Nazi Party and infiltrating German/American organizations. They had a tight case against him: he was alleged to have been active in espionage in Canada, escaping from there in September, 1939, and subsequently making his way to New York. Noteworthy is the fact that the FBI was closing in on Fritz Kuhn, chief of the German American Bund, at the same time, arresting him on September 29. Could it be that Gruda was ordered to come to New York as an assistant to party chief Fritz Kuhn, at a time when the Bund was experiencing such intense pressure from the Feds? Piecing it all together, it seems more like fact than fiction. Once in New York, Gruda contacted the DAB and slid underground to a safe house, namely, a room for rent in the Brooklyn apartment of an unsuspecting member, paying his first month's rent in advance. Coincidentally, it was also in September, 1939.

On July 10, 1942, around 10:30 AM, two conservatively dressed men, courteous but non-smiling, rang the doorbell to our apartment. Mommi answered the door; they flashed their Federal Bureau of Investigation ID and asked to come in. Pappi was with them. He was already in their custody, having been arrested at his place of business, Wiegand's Quality Meats, one half hour earlier on a Presidential Warrant for Otto Wiegand, as it was called. The warrant ordered the Attorney General Francis Biddle to authorize the execution of this warrant by agents of the New York Field Office of the Federal Bureau of Investigation. It read in part: "I hereby authorize and

W A R R A N T

TO THE DIRECTOR OF THE FEDERAL BUREAU OF INVESTIGATION:

In pursuance of authority delegated to the Attorney
General of the United States by Proclamation of the President
of the United States dated December 8, 1941, I hereby authorize
and direct you and your duly authorized agents to arrest or
to cause the arrest of Otto Wiegand, 68-58 - 60th Lane, Ridgewood,
Long Island, New York,

an alien enemy whom I deem dangerous to the public peace and
safety of the United States.

The said alien enemy is to be detained and confined until
further order.

By order of the President:

FRANCIS BIDDLE

Attorney General

~~xDecemberx8pd2hx~~

July 1, 1942

direct you and your duly authorized agents to arrest or to cause the arrest of Otto Wiegand, 68-58—60th Lane, Ridgewood, Long Island, New York, an alien enemy whom I deem dangerous to the public peace and safety of the United States. The said alien enemy is to be detained and confined until further order. By order of the President." It was dated as early as December 8, 1941, subsequently updated to July 1, 1942 and finally executed on July 10, 1942.

The agents came into our apartment, asked to search the premises as they had asked to search the backroom of the butcher shop, and confiscated my father's passport, a bunch of personal papers, and a photo album containing snapshots of our family and others in the process of building Camp Bergwald in New Jersey.

By this time, my father had changed clothes and at the suggestion of the agents packed some toilet articles, then turned to us to say good-bye. He assured my mother, "Everything will be fine." He had nothing to fear; he had done nothing wrong. She was very strong, but could not hold back the tears.

I was very scared, crying and hanging on to him. "Why are you taking *mein* Pappi away? Where are you taking him?"

He comforted me, saying: "*Weine nicht, kleine Mutzi. Ich bin bald wieder da.*" ("Don't cry little Mutzi," [his pet name for me, pronounced "mootsie"] "I'll be back soon.") And with that, he walked out of the apartment, accompanied by the two FBI agents.

Pappi was taken to the Federal Bureau of Investigation, New York Field Division, with offices in Manhattan for questioning. It was evident they had other concerns than merely checking out the disposition of his citizenship papers. He would have become a naturalized American citizen that fall of 1942, final papers and all, but it was now just July 10.

The complete FBI file of my father's case was finally released to me in 2003 after I had requested it a year earlier under the Freedom of Information Act. In it his initial interrogation was revealed in detail, and the "Herr Gruda Spy-Suspect Story" was of uppermost interest to the authorities. How had he come to rent a room to this Gruda? What was the connection? Was there a connection? When my father offered to help "stranded Germans" by providing temporary housing and communicated this to the then German Consulate Fritz Zeglin via the DAB, did he know this Herr Gruda was a Nazi agent and most likely active in the Bund? How much overlap was there with the DAB and the Bund? They wanted to know if the DAB had been infiltrated and if my father had any internal knowledge of it,

```
                                      ....

                                   July 15, 1942
JRW:mcf
Special Agent in Charge
New York, New York

                              Re:   INTERNAL SECURITY - G
                                    ALIEN ENEMY CONTROL


      Dear Sir:

               Enclosed are copies of Presidential Warrants for the following
      subjects:
```

Otto Wiegand

```
               These individuals are a portion of the eighty-three members
      of the German-American Vocational League and the Reichdeutsche Vereinigung,
      for whom Presidential Warrants were requested by the Honorable Harold
      M. Kennedy, United States Attorney for the Eastern District of New York,
      by a letter which was received by the Department on June 30, 1942.

               Mr. Edward J. Ennis, Director, Alien Enemy Control Unit, has
      advised that the execution of these warrants should be held in abeyance
      until instructions to execute them are received from Mr. Kennedy. Two
      copies of each warrant are being forwarded to you. When these warrants
      is executed, one copy of each is to be forwarded to the appropriate
      office of the Immigration and Naturalisation Service, and the other copy
      is to be placed in the case file for the particular subject. At the
      time these subjects are taken into custody, their apprehensions as
      dangerous alien enemies are to be reported in accordance with existing
      Bureau instructions.
```

Mr. Tolson
Mr. E. A. Tamm
Mr. Clegg
Mr. Glavin
Mr. Ladd
Mr. Nichols
Mr. Rosen
Mr. Tracy
Mr. Carson
Mr. Coffey
Mr. Hendon
Mr. Kramer
Mr. McGuire
Mr. Quinn Tamm
Mr. Nease
Miss Gandy

Enclosure

```
                                       Very truly yours

                                                           100-123329-X

                                       John Edgar Hoover
                                            Director
```

JUL 23 1942

when Gruda left and where he went. Did he flee to Germany surreptitiously?

Pappi answered all of these questions as directly as he could. He steadfastly maintained that both he and my mother were unaware of Gruda's status; he was just a boarder, albeit a very private person. When all of this came to light, my father was convinced he had been used and set up by the DAB. He asserted he was never a member of the Nazi Party and had never joined any political organization while still a young person in Germany, nor had he ever joined the Bund in the States. It wasn't enough. He was photographed and fingerprinted following his initial "interview" and delivered to the Immigration and Naturalization Service authorities at Ellis Island pending a hearing before the Alien Enemy Hearing Board.

A day or so later, two FBI agents returned to inform my mother of Pappi's detention and the procedure for us to visit him on Ellis Island. They requested another search of the apartment, but were non-specific about just exactly what they were looking for. They came in and poked around, hardly raising an eyebrow at what they saw. Lots of German books, quite natural for families like ours. Many were on history and geography, probably some on politics. My father was an avid reader, always seeking to broaden his horizons. Did he have Hitler's *Mein Kampf*? It was probably there. The agents noted a little German flag we had stuck in a bookcase. But there was something that caught their attention even more. We had on the wall among our other pictures the famous print of Hitler bending down to receive a bouquet of flowers from a lovely little blonde Aryan girl. I guess it was one of the bad choices my parents made, surely through innocence, to have that in the house. This was 1942. To us it was just a nice picture of the man leading our nation of origin, the Vaterland. But he was not a nice man, and we should have realized that and not hung his picture.

I have my own suspicions about what they were looking for. As I read through my father's FBI papers, I discovered an order given to the DAB membership by Fritz Schroeder, president at that time, to destroy all membership books and dues cards for this and any other German organization the members might have belonged to, having been told that if they kept the books there might be trouble.

My father had also been a member of the *Reichsdeutsche Vereinigung* (Association of German Nationals), as well as participating in a program called *Rueckwanderer Marks* (Re-emigration marks). The latter was a program that afforded Germans living in the United States the opportunity to transfer US Dollars to savings accounts in Germany and draw 4% interest.

The exchange rate at the time was 4.10 Marks to the dollar, and as my father explained at his interrogation, he considered it a good investment. He already had over $1000 (4,100 Marks) saved. Purchasers of these Marks were automatically held suspect; for in order to qualify; one had to voice his intent to return to Germany permanently in the future. My father told the FBI that was not his intention. Still, he liked having this money in reserve over there for his family to take trips back home or for his children to study in Germany later on. Perhaps they would want to stay.

Had our countries not been at war and had there been no suspicions that Germans were funding Hitler's war effort from over here, this all would have been a non-issue, for American banks were profiting as well in the collection of transfer fees. But under the circumstances, all of these activities only added fuel to the fire of my father's case and landed his name on too many suspicious aliens lists.

My mother did not waste any time arranging a visit to Ellis Island. She didn't have to take us out of school, since it was July. Our store had a sign on the front door: "TEMPORARILY CLOSED." This was the first of many trips we made to Ellis Island. We took the subway into midtown Manhattan, transferred and continued all the way down to Battery Park in lower Manhattan, where all the ferries trafficked to Staten Island, Governor's Island, Liberty Island, and Ellis Island. I was too young to realize the emotion an immigrant would feel, passing through this magnificent harbor. My mother loved America and especially New York with all her heart, and I often wonder how conflicted she must have felt at that moment.

There were quite a few other passengers on the ferry, probably all on the same mission, since most were Germans, as I overheard conversations in German. After we arrived on Ellis Island, we were led to a large building where everyone's name was checked off and then went through security. It was not nearly as thorough as we know it today, no metal detectors that I recall, but we couldn't take anything inside the visitor's hall. My mother had to leave her purse with a guard and anything we might have brought along as a gift for Pappi. Homemade cookies, personal care items, pictures Freddy and I drew for him—these things were all taken away from us with the assurance they would be given to him after they were inspected.

The hall we entered was huge: stark white, high ceilings, windows all around, but high up, so there would not be a good view of the outside world. Many long, dark-brown tables ran parallel down the center. We could pick any place we wanted to sit, as long as it was on the side marked "Visitors." As soon as all visitors were seated, guards came out and took up their stations at the ends of each table. Then a door opened, and the men entered the room single file, and we all looked in anticipation to spot that one familiar face. There was much emotion in the room. Many men and women wept audibly, and that contrasted with the squeals of delight when the children saw their fathers.

There was no falling into each other's arms. We were pathetically separated by thick wooden partitions that ran down the center of each table. All my parents could see were each other's faces. If they as much as reached for a hand, the guard would admonish them immediately. Freddy sat on top of the table. I went even higher and sat on top of the board so I could comb my father's hair and tickle his mustache. The guard looked the other way. After a while, Freddy went out into the hallway and played marbles with some of the other boys. My mother and I carried on conversations with Pappi. There were so many questions. From simple ones, such as, "Are you being treated well?" "Are the accommodations adequate?" "Is the food okay," to the most prying: Did they connect him with Herr Gruda? And what had he told them?

On one of our weekly visits, anger shone in my father's eyes as he told of an interrogation incident. When the agents had searched the apartment, they confiscated his passport. It showed, of course, a trip to Germany in 1937 with all of us. That in itself might have been suspicious, although thousands of new German immigrants had returned to the Vaterland to see relatives and show off their new prosperity in the years just before the war. In the interrogation room on Ellis Island, several FBI agents surrounded him and shoved the passport in his face. They rifled through until they came to the page showing the trip to Germany. "How do you explain this?" one of the agents demanded harshly, pointing to a stamp on the page. My father looked at it and realized it was the stamp of the Nazi Party, indicating his membership in the Bund, the American arm of the Nazi Party.

He told us he had stared down at the red stamp in total disbelief and then looked up at his accusers. I remember his exact words: "Gentlemen," he shouted, "this is a fraud!" He even pounded the table with his fist as he told us about the stamping, which made our guard turn around and look at him. He had been framed! Some person within the purview of the investigating authorities had placed that stamp in there after the passport was confiscated. Today we call it "Dirty Tricks." And this was the beginning of my father's disillusionment with the new country he had come to love, disappointed that he should be picked up, separated from his family, lose his business, interrogated like a criminal, and accused of being a traitor, even the insinuation he enabled a known German spy to ply his trade. All he had ever wanted to do was to make a living for his family in the land of opportunity.

Today I have no delusions about my father's love for the Vaterland. Pappi cherished German tradition and made every effort to keep it alive in our family. He loved the natural beauty and culture of his homeland and was a student of German history. Although not passionate about politics himself, he did enjoy joining in on lively discussion. He could lay out the rationale of a political situation based on his knowledge of world history. But that's about as far as it went. The political mess Germany found itself in after World War I was the reason he left and went to sea, ultimately landing in America. Now, after all that had happened to him, with no end in sight, his feelings towards the two countries were becoming increasingly complex.

Pappi had not yet become a citizen when the troubles started, and his "German-ness" was deep in his heart. Still, he was at the beginning intensely loyal to America; then a series of incidents undermined his love for it. Suspected of consorting with spies and of being a spy himself, having records falsified to incriminate him, being incarcerated—how could this be the land of the free? He did nothing in retaliation for the injustices he experienced; he just became very introspective. I'm sure he went through many inner struggles, trying to sort it all out.

By nature my father was a very focused man, solidly anchored in his life with goals and long-range plans for himself and his family. Now he found himself totally out of control of his destiny, adrift in a sea of turmoil. My mother, on the other hand, saw America in all positives. All the joys of her young womanhood were tied up with the new land. Here she followed her love when he called for her, here she married him, here her children were born, and here she began making a home for her family. She was a citizen of the United States of America and never turned back, even when enormously taxed.

My mother made a valiant effort to keep our store open. She hired a butcher to fill the display cases with fresh cuts of meat, while she became his number one helper. Freddy and I kept on playing in our neighborhood, we just didn't go home to the apartment. Instead, we'd go to the store, where we kept busy in the back room until Mommi closed for the day and we all went home together. But it didn't work. Rumors were rampant in the neighborhood: "Did you hear that Herr Wiegand got arrested?" "The FBI picked him up!" "He's allegedly an enemy alien!" Our customers from the first day my father opened the store in August 1940, stopped coming. Hostilities soon went beyond scuttlebutt and became real when one morning the word "Heini" was scrawled all over the store windows along with swastikas. The window washer came and cleaned everything off. Several mornings later, the store windows were smashed in. My mother closed Wiegand's Quality Meats, and we went on welfare.

Pappi was still being held on Ellis Island, waiting for his case to be heard before the Alien Enemy Hearing Board. In spite of everything, my parents still held out hope that things would resolve themselves and he would be released.

Life for us on the outside became increasingly difficult. Nazi hatred and propaganda were running at fever pitch. With the business closed, my mother had no income for daily necessities. The walk to and from school PS 88, a block away on Fresh Pond Road was scary. Kids would make hurtful remarks and try to pull my long blond braids. I recall my mother going to school and complaining to the principal, telling her what was happening. She said she'd take care of the problem. Nothing happened; it didn't get any better. The neighborhood kids would play war games, and, if they let us play at all, we were the bad guys who got captured or shot. Nothing was fun anymore.

My mother had a lady friend named Mrs. Deininger about a block away in a half-in-the-ground basement apartment in one of the brownstones. Always interested in the supernatural, my mother attended séances in Deininger's living room along with several other people. I sat off to the side and watched as they lay their hands on a small three legged table and concentrated. Pretty soon the table started rocking and Deininger (whom I later found out was the medium) started asking which spirit from the other side was in the room. One time I had to leave because the visiting spirit would not communicate with a child in the room. It was all very spooky. Nevertheless, Mrs. Deininger turned out to be a friend to my mother. She not only gave her moral support, she also came through with some very specific help.

My mother needed assistance in filling out welfare applications. Deininger introduced her to Attorney Rosenzweig, an elderly, kind Jewish man, who lived in our neighborhood. He did all our work *pro bono*. Soon the welfare checks started coming in. Mommi cried when she opened the first one. Accepting public support was a source of shame in her generation; it symbolized having hit bottom. But I think it was also a matter of German pride.

Finally, on one of our Ellis Island visits, my father told us that his hearing before the Alien Enemy Hearing Board had been scheduled. This was the definitive event, the opportunity to explain everything and speak in his own defense. Again, it wasn't good enough. He was ordered to be interned.

A document in my father's FBI file reads as follows:

> *In the matter of OTTO WIEGAND — Alien Enemy — OR-*
> *DER —*
> *WHEREAS, Otto Wiegand, of Ridgewood, Long Island, New*
> *York, a citizen of Germany, over the age of fourteen years, is within*
> *the United States and not a naturalized citizen thereof and has here-*
> *tofore been apprehended as being potentially dangerous to the public*
> *peace and safety of the United States; and, WHEREAS, the Alien*
> *Enemy Hearing Board has recommended that said enemy alien be*
> *interned; NOW, THEREFORE, upon consideration of the evidence*
> *before me, IT IS ORDERED that said alien enemy be interned.*
> *Signed Francis Biddle, Attorney General. September 10, 1942.*

On September 30, 1942, J. Edgar Hoover, Director of the FBI, sent out three letters over his signature. One to Rear Admiral H.C. Train, Director, Office of Naval Intelligence, Navy Department; another to Brigadier General Hayes A. Kroner, Chief, Military Intelligence Service, War Department; and another to the Special Agent in Charge, New York Field Office of the FBI, Internal Security, Alien Enemy Control. Two days later, on October 2, 1942, my father was formally interned and delivered to Fort Meade, Maryland, for confinement.

⁂

The stark reality of our situation set in after Pappi was gone and no longer in a place where we could visit him. To make matters worse, he was only held at Fort Meade, Maryland, for one month. Records show that on November 3, 1942, he was transferred to the Alien Enemy Internment Camp at Camp Forrest, Tennessee.

For Freddy and me, it meant we would not have Pappi home for Christmas. *Der Heilige Abend* (Christmas Eve) was the most festive and wondrous occasion of the year for German families, celebrated with much reverence and tradition. We always started our evening with Mommi lighting candles, as we sang *O Tannenbaum* (O Christmas Tree). Then we sang *Stille Nacht, Heilige Nacht* (Silent Night, Holy Night), followed by the traditional *Gaensebraten* (Roast Goose) dinner. For dessert there were colorful tin boxes filled with *Lebkuchen*, marzipan, and sparkling foil-wrapped candies. My parents drank wine as we gave each other gifts.

It was not going to happen this year, a least not in the traditional manner. Instead, my mother got us all dressed up in our finest Sunday clothes, and off we went to a photography studio on Myrtle Avenue for a sitting. I can only imagine the tug on my father's heartstrings when he opened his Christmas mail and saw these beautiful portraits and read our letters. I never loved nor missed him more in my entire life. Sadly, we could not even look forward to Christmas with Tante Elsie and Onkel Werner in New York.

Onkel Werner took a totally different route than my father. He became a citizen early on and was ultimately drafted. He served in the United States Army as a chef in the officers' mess hall on some base in California. He was never assigned to overseas duty. Tante Elsie sublet her apartment in New York, packed up and left for California for the holidays and part of the winter. Werner had rented a hole-in-the-wall apartment near the base. I recall Elsie's telling me later in life that in the autumn of 1942 both of the men in her life were taken away. Her brother went to a camp surrounded by barbed wire, her husband to a camp surrounded by cactus plants.

If my mother felt inner turmoil, she didn't show it. She was never despondent or frightened. Through the German cultural network we were a part of, she found out that family camps existed for Germans detained on the East coast. She went resolutely forward in her battle to get us reunited. Even if it meant being interned in a family camp behind barbed wire, at least we would be together. But she needed help in the process.

Attorney Rosenzweig to the rescue! He drafted a letter for my mother addressed to the Department of Justice, Eastern District of New York, Harold M. Kennedy, United States Attorney, in which she requested internment in a family camp with her husband and two children. The only result that action got was a review of her link to my father's case. Additionally, it surfaced that there had also been a warrant issued for her arrest as early as October 12, 1942. She, too, was "an enemy alien deemed dangerous to the public peace and safety of the United States." My correct and law-abiding mother! The warrant just hadn't been executed yet. Only on orders from Kennedy could it be set in motion.

Having had no movement in her case, Rosenzweig followed that action with another letter he drafted for her, this one addressed to the Immigration and Naturalization Service asking for a hearing. Shortly after the hearing was granted, I recall our taking the subway to Grand Central Station and boarding a train to Philadelphia.

The result of the hearing was just another of our many disappointments, only this one was major. My mother was told there was simply no way she, a naturalized American citizen, and her two American-born children could be interned in an alien enemy camp. The law would not allow it. I remember the interviewer, a lady, pointing at Freddy and me and asking my mother how she could even consider internment for herself and her two "beautiful American children" as Freddy and I sat there looking like Hansel and Gretel. It was at this point that my mother either made the statement or wrote a letter to the authorities, perhaps both, that she would relinquish her American citizenship if that were the only obstacle keeping her from being interned with her husband and children. It was not what she wanted to do, but if that's what it took, she would do it.

In one last-ditch effort, she took it on herself to seek an audience with the Swiss Consul. Perhaps a representative of a neutral nation could work as a liaison and plead in her behalf. All he could do was verify and agree with the law.

My mother's good friend, Mrs. Deininger, remained steadfast in her support. She invited us shortly after Pappi was arrested to attend church services with her and meet her pastor. Not having a church, he held his services in a banquet room in the Hotel McAlpin in Manhattan. Pastor Greber was a soft-spoken, elderly man, who struck one as being very kind and compassionate and taking all the time necessary to listen. He was Protestant although I'm not sure of which denomination, and a published author. My mother had several of his books, all written in German. He seemed to have important friends in high places with considerable influence. His ministry was to help people with problems beyond the ordinary.

It was now going on nine months since Pappi had gone away, and soon it would be springtime. The New Year had been acknowledged only with thoughts of "What will 1943 have in store?"

My father's FBI papers reveal several more interrogations, both in Camp Meade as well as Camp Forest. The passport business was a nail in the coffin. His name kept coming up on various lists, in addition to the red stamp that had mysteriously appeared in his passport. To his dying day, my father maintained he was not a member of the Nazi Party or the Bund, and the testimony sounds convincing. The transcript shows him responding, "You are confusing my membership in German cultural organizations with this other thing." About the dollars he transferred to a bank in Germany, he reiterated that one time he sent $400 to help his father with a mortgage payment, and this was documented. On the other occasion, he purchased $1,000 worth of *Rueckwanderer* Marks not only as an investment, but as a reserve for his personal use, should the need arise during some future visit back home.

On one occasion he was asked if he would be willing to defend America. The authorities were suggesting that by volunteering for active duty, he would automatically become a citizen. He told them he had already registered with the Local Board #283 in Ridgewood, Brooklyn, in February 1942, several months before he was arrested. He went on to answer the question with a qualified "yes," as long as he could be assured not to have to fight on the Western Front. He had too many brothers, brothers-in-law, and nephews in the German *Wehrmacht* and could not possibly lift a gun against his own family, but he would fight in the Pacific. The interrogators responded they were not in a position to strike such a deal.

Then they asked him which side he was for? Which side did he want to win? He responded, "Gentlemen, I just want this war to be over." I know my father was controlling his outrage at this point. He felt he was being baited and badgered. One of the most poignant responses he gave during all of his interrogations was when he was asked to describe his feelings for America versus his feelings for his homeland. He said, "I look upon Germany as my mother and feel about the United States of America as I do my wife." This logical and direct statement says so much about the kind of man my father was.

The most shocking discovery in my father's FBI files revealed a "Confidential Informant" who was passing on all sorts of personal information to the authorities. He must have been more than a friend. My father employed him several times to help out in the butcher shop. On one occasion he testified he was working for "the subject" (my father) and that subject's son was attending some kind of "Bund Youth Camp." Freddy never even heard of a Bund Youth Camp, much less belonged to one. If this was the spring of 1942, Freddy was only ten years old! Ironically, Freddy was able to recall and identify this fellow as the teenage son of the Dry Cleaning Establishment in our neighborhood, who delivered meat orders to our customers when Freddy was not able to do so.

The informant also told authorities he saw "electrical equipment, wires and dials" in the back room of the butcher shop. That was my father's short wave radio. Most likely the wires were extra antennae he had jerry-rigged for better reception. Practically every German family we knew had a short wave radio at that time and listened to overseas broadcasts. It was perfectly legal to have one. But I recall my mother asking Pappi to take the radio out of the apartment because all of the squawking and static noise got on her nerves. He liked to listen to the BBC and the *Deutscher Rundfunk* (German broadcasting station) to compare broadcasts from over there with what was being reported over here. The so-called "electrical equipment" was nonsense. But by this time my father had been unfairly accused of so much that anything that would further incriminate him and add to his case became gospel. Earlier this confidential informant even told the authorities that he overheard a conversation my mother had with a trusted friend that she wanted to be interned with her husband and children, repatriated, and, if it meant relinquishing her American citizenship to accomplish that, she would do it. The authorities therefore knew of her intentions before she ever advised the INS or made an application to be repatriated.

In early April 1943, when my father was still interned at Camp Forrest, Tennessee, the Memphis Field Office was ordered to deliver him to the Immigration and Naturalization Service in New York for a re-hearing by the Alien Enemy Control Board. A United States Marshal escorted him to Ellis Island, where he was held to await a re-hearing. Neither of my parents made a specific request for this re-hearing. It appears from some statements gathered out of Pappi's file that it came as a result of an appeal by Pastor Greber to Attorney General Francis Biddle.

Both were ordered to appear before the Enemy Alien Hearing Board #2 on April 15, 1943. They were questioned separately. [Transcripts of the interrogations and testimony given by my parents as taken from my father's FBI file appear in the appendix.]

Although my father's return trip to Ellis Island for a re-hearing presented a wonderful opportunity for us to see him—it had been almost a year—the recommendation by the board read as follows: (as taken from his FBI file) "After re-presentation of all the facts in this case and after permitting OTTO KARL WIEGAND an opportunity to be re-heard on his own behalf, the Board recommended for a second time that he be interned for the duration."

This was a major blow to my parents, both of whom held out such hope that we would finally be interned in a family camp. Instead, my father was sent to Fort Lincoln in Bismarck, North Dakota, to be re-interned with German and Japanese internees and German prisoners of war. When my mother found out, I recall our going home to our apartment in Brooklyn in a dejected frame of mind and getting out the atlas to see how far away they had sent Pappi.

Throughout this entire period, my mother had been the pillar of strength, but I think she was deeply distressed by this latest turn of events. She called on Rosenzweig for help one more time. He phoned a physician he knew and asked that he certify that my mother was ill and on the brink of a nervous breakdown and had to be reunited with her husband or face serious health consequences. Documents were prepared and submitted to the powers that be.

The health gambit worked. We could go together as a family. My mother was advised to pack our overseas trunks, have them ready for pick-up by a certain date, and report to Ellis Island with her children. We were heading out for Crystal City, Texas, to be interned in a family camp.

At this point, there is a large gap in my father's FBI papers. All of the last pages in his file bear the stamp, "COPIES DESTROYED 1/8/59." However, according to notes I made after questioning my mother, we were quartered on Ellis Island for approximately one week, awaiting the arrival of my father who was being transferred back from Fort Lincoln, North Dakota. Upon his arrival and final processing, we boarded a train in the company of other families like ours and headed out for Texas. We were guarded by plain-clothes agents of the Immigration and Naturalization Service. We ate in dining cars, slept in Pullman cars, and Freddy and I and the other children on board generally had one good time staring out the windows, playing cards, and sharing in the excitement of a new adventure. As for my parents, I have never seen them happier. We were together. That was all that mattered. Their love for each other had grown to greater, more meaningful, heights by having been separated, and it encircled Freddy and me as well. It was a poignant family bonding.

The countryside of the southern states, then the West, flew by the windows. The dry-gulch area south west of San Antonio with only cactus, mesquite, and scrub pine looked desolate. When we finally arrived in Crystal City, Texas, the town with its wooden buildings and wooden planked walk-ways looked like something out of a Western. The camp itself was a short distance outside of town. We were loaded onto old, olive drab busses and transported to the front gate, which stood wide open, almost welcoming. The time of year was August; the average temperature 110 degrees in the shade—and no shade! It was so dry just walking kicked up dust. Dust covered everything.

We proceeded into a compound surrounded by a barbed wire fence about ten-feet high, interspersed with strategically placed watchtowers to overview the camp and the nearby area. Guards, wearing cowboy boots and ten-gallon hats and riding horseback, patrolled the fence, gun belts slung low on their hips. They were very friendly, especially towards the children, and later we spoke with them a lot. Inside the entrance to the camp were communal buildings: camp administration, a hospital, a gathering center, a building with schoolrooms, and a café, called Café Vaterland, with an area for sitting outside to enjoy coffee and cake in the company of fellow internees. There were also some other service facilities, such as a sewing room and a beauty salon.

The German population lived in barracks at the front end of the camp, Japanese families at the far end. We were divided by nationality, but did not feel as though we were being segregated. On the contrary, we exchanged many traditional events, demonstrating the cultural diversity of our backgrounds. Some barracks were duplexes, some triplexes, and some quadroplexes. We were lucky to be assigned an end unit in one of the triplexes, situated on the main road that ran through the center of the camp. Our quarters consisted of one large room: kitchen space with running water, a kerosene stove, an ice box, and a cozy sitting area arranged by my mother with the furniture provided. To the other side of the room my parents hung blankets from the rafters to privatize their sleeping area. Freddy and I shared an adjacent bedroom. We had a toilet, but I do not recall having a bath. To clean up we went to shower houses, built between the rows of barracks and serving many families.

All the buildings were on stilts. Varmints and crawly things abounded. I had never even heard of termites or giant red ants. The only bugs we previously had to deal with were occasional cockroaches in our New York apartment. Snake alerts were frequent, and toads would surprise us often. They blended in so perfectly with the environment, we didn't always recognize them right away. Scorpions crawled up the walls and onto beams overhead inside our quarters. Every night when we went to bed, Freddy and I would shine our flashlights around to make sure the coast was clear. The ugly scorpions scared me. Black widow spiders were another story. They crept around in the damp shadows of the showers. We children would take jars and spot them. Whenever the younger children saw a black widow, we called the older ones like my brother Freddy, who bravely tapped the spider into the jar and took it to the dispensary in the hospital. There a laboratory attendant would relieve him of his scary burden and pay a quarter or so for the venom they'd be able to collect. To this day I have a real affinity for spiders.

My parents spoke German most of the time. We children spoke English with our playmates outside. When we came in and continued conversing in English, we were commanded by our parents to "*Sprech' Deutsch!*" ("Speak German!"). They wished us to remain totally fluent in the mother tongue.

To my recollection camp life was very structured. Adults worked at various occupations to feed, clothe, entertain, and provide services for fellow internees. My father worked as a butcher in the canteen, a well-stocked grocery store where we would turn in the food coupons we received. We could also spend the camp money of pressed cardboard coins our parents earned on other merchandise. US currency was not allowed. The school system inside the camp was as well organized as any on the outside.

My mother decided to make an appointment at the camp beauty shop one day to have her hair styled by Herr Dietrich. Prior to being interned himself, he reputedly had a salon on Park Avenue, where his clientelle consisted of upper crust New York society. He now found himself no longer cutting and curling in his crystal palace on Park Avenue, but in Crystal City, Texas, with combs, bobby pins and curlers, beautifying interned women from all walks of life, who sat on simple stools inside wooden barracks. Nonetheless, when my mother came home after having her hair done, she felt like a 5th Avenue society queen.

One of my most pleasant memories was going to the Café Vaterland on Sunday afternoons for *Kaffeetrinken* (a favorite German tradition: coffee-drinking) and eating a *Berliner*. A *Berliner* is a well-known German pastry, similar to an American jelly donut, but filled with delicious vanilla custard. Café Vaterland offered an astounding variety of pastries, confections, cookies and beautifully decorated layer cakes called *Torte*. One could choose from all flavors and varieties of Torte, many of them regional specialties in Germany. Everything was prepared and served by internees.

Most of the German, non-naturalized intelligentsia from the whole Eastern seaboard and larger cities in the Mid-West were there, all in a state of limbo. Keeping a stiff upper lip and staying busy made life not only bearable, but actually quite pleasant. Women did lots of sewing, arts and crafts; men cared for and improved the barracks; men and women planted flower gardens at the entrances to their quarters. Cultural activities abounded. Musicians organized concerts, singing groups performed "under the stars" in the old German style, and those with acting ability, my father included, performed their skits, comedies, and tragedies on stage in the community house. We saw movies several times a week. Both American and German films were projected on the outside of one of the larger buildings. Many times we paid more attention to the shooting stars in the beautiful Texas skies above than to the film being shown.

To my knowledge, most internment camps had a newspaper. Crystal City's weekly was called *Das Lager* (The Camp) written in German, compiled, edited, and published by internees. I found a book during the course of my research that held a collection of many of these newspapers. Among the numerous copies of Crystal City's *Das Lager* I discovered my father's name listed on a *Fussball* (soccer) roster under *Alte Herren* (elderly gentlemen or what we would call a "seniors" team in America). One of his best friends "BREITENBERGER" was listed just below. It was Issue #15 of *Das Lager,* Crystal City, Texas, December 24, 1943. My father was all of 40 years old.

The philosophy of the Crystal City Internment Camp seems to have been non-punitive, at least it seemed so to our family. It was to keep those whose loyalty was being questioned and those deemed dangerous to the public peace and safety of the United States out of further trouble and with their families. Many Japanese incarcerated on the West Coast have complained, justifiably, of demoralization in the camps there: scornful and indifferent treatment and rigid, military-like rules. To my knowledge, this was not the case with the Japanese families in our camp. During our family's internment, we never had to fall in, were never subjected to inspections or made to feel like criminals. I do not recall ever having to stand up and be counted.

I speak for my brother as well as myself when I say we children had a great time. It was even better than Camp Bergwald in New Jersey, the camp the (DAB) German/American Vocational League owned. Our internee families were together, and the interesting environment offered much exploration and discovery within the confines of the camp. The educational, cultural, and social life in general kept us busy and for the most part content. We often heard comments, passed on to us by those internees who had direct contact with camp staff and workers from the Texas community, that our life in camp appeared to be much more interesting and pleasurable than their lives on the outside.

Christmas, 1943, at the camp was an attempt at warmth and tradition. Pine trees were trucked in and distributed among all the families who wanted to gather their loved ones around the "Tannenbaum," the Christmas tree, probably the most symbolic centerpiece of this festive holiday for German families. Freddy and I cut out and painted cardboard stars and made festoons of curly paper to decorate the tree. My mother baked almond crescent cookies to hook onto the branches. The canteen had special holiday candy, and we were able to purchase candy canes with our camp money to hook onto the tree.

A group of adults, all of them talented internees, put together a Christmas program, to which everyone was invited, with special invitation going to the camp administration. It was a beautiful, festive evening, filled with German Christmas music and lots of singing, though ending on a very emotional note when the children gathered for the finale and sang "Ihr Kinderlein Kommet" ("Let All the Children Come"). There wasn't a dry eye in the room, and for a moment I think I felt what the adults were feeling: that even though we were in a safe place for now, we were all somehow either marooned on an island or awash in a sea of uncertainty. Were we lost? I felt uneasy. Perhaps I was growing up. But these feelings all went away after we returned to our barracks quarters, and the beautiful tree we had decorated was all aglow. We exchanged homemade gifts and drank wine with Mommi's cookies.

Our parents allowed a sip of wine on special occasions, a common custom among European families. Pappi had homemade wine going all the time. I recall lying in bed, the house dark and quiet, but I could still hear the blip, blip, blip of gas created by fermenting mash escaping through the water seal. There was no objection in camp to the men making wine, and Pappi was very good at it. Others would come over and consult with him or ask for recipes. He used raisins, apples, and very ripe bananas with lots of boiled raw sugar water and cakes of yeast. He called his brew "Chi-Cha."

We made friends. One family in particular, that of Kaspar and Rosa Wohlpart, seemed so like us. When we first met, their children were near in age to us. Inge was a beautiful, curly-headed blonde girl of eleven; Freddy, who had an eye for girls, pursued her. Alfred, her brother, two or three years younger than I, was the ultimate nerd as far as I was concerned. Still, we all played together.

After Christmas, we were directed to put the pine trees we had decorated between two shower houses to be picked up. When they were not, we dug holes in the sandy soil deep enough to upright the trees and create a forest. Then we all played "Jungle." Freddy was Tarzan, Inge was Jane, and the rest of us had to be the chimps and other wild animals. Our job was to get chased, as we dashed about making wild animal sounds and hiding between and underneath the boughs. Inevitably we got captured, brought back to Tarzan and Jane's treetop home, and held in pretend cages. One of us would then escape and return to free the others. Sometimes compassionate, animal-loving Jane would set us free, and the hunt would begin all over again.

We did not play war as other children in America did; it was too painfully close. We were all American-born children; the parents we loved were the Germans. The bad guys.

Stickball and roller-skating until our knees were criss-crossed with band-aids kept us occupied. The older boys played at soccer, but the serious soccer players were our fathers. I never saw an American football there.

The Texas sun in August and September took getting used to. The desert-like landscape, no shade, and temperatures reaching 100 degrees and above made us wilt. No air-conditioning, though I do recall our having a fan. There was a swampy area in one of the far corners of the compound, filled with water and snakes. Some of our camp leaders got together and proposed building a swimming pool on the site. It was a project we enthusiastically supported.

Camp officials agreed and promised construction materials if we, all able-bodied men, that is, could build it ourselves. It was very exciting, watching the project take place. During the land clearing, the men caught so many snakes they couldn't kill them fast enough. So, they threw them into a barrel, and I recall looking at more writhing snakes than I could count. After the snakes were killed and gutted, the harvested snakeskins were handed out to anyone who wanted them. Freddy came home with one, of course. Unfortunately, we never got to swim in the pool. There were construction delays, and we had to leave before its completion.

The only time we felt looked down upon during our internment experience was one day in San Antonio. Internees were sometimes bussed into town to shop for necessities not found in the camp or for medical or dental services beyond the skills of our dispensary. We were held to small groups and easily identified as "those Germans from the Crystal City Internment Camp," easy to spot because of uniformed and armed escorts. Our guards were very nice to us and tried to make it look as though we were not being herded. Nonetheless, there was much staring and finger-pointing by the populace as they mumbled, "There they go, the Germans." Nobody spat on us or yelled hateful things, and for that we were grateful. I held onto Mommi's hand and stuck close to her the whole time.

It was clear that we would not be released until the conclusion of the war. We were undesirables, always suspect, and would remain so in this situation. The camp was not unpleasant, and eventually after the war, the internees would have their cases reviewed. Many would be repatriated, a few deported, others would return to pick up the pieces of the lives they left behind in their American neighborhoods—if they were proven loyal after all.

But we would not wait for that. My father requested repatriation, an option offered at some point during our internment. My mother agreed. The decision was not a surprising one if one considers what had led up to it. His allegiance to the Vaterland had always been strong, but that was not the determining factor. He had been disillusioned with the new land of his choice. Subterfuge, wrongful accusations, repeated and grueling interrogations, and finally incarceration had been the results of the faith he had placed in it. Everything they had worked for and accomplished in America was lost, the butcher store, Wiegand's Quality Meats, closed. Accumulated personal and household goods, except for what my mother could pack into two overseas trunks, gone. Sixteen years of work and savings, making the American Dream come true for his family, over and done.

When my mother, Freddy, and I closed the door of our Brooklyn apartment for the last time and headed for Ellis Island to be reunited with Pappi in internment, we simply walked away from everything. Now my father was ready to leave. Many in Crystal City shared his views.

I don't know how my parents felt in their hearts and minds, nor how they shared their most intimate thoughts about our situation. All I know is they never demonstrated any hatred for the United States government. Disillusionment, resentment, disappointment, yes, but hatred, no. Nor did they blame the United States justice system. They certainly never verbalized or instilled anti-American feelings or bitterness in Freddy and me towards the country of our birth. We were all victims of the war that had separated our two peoples. My parents were not waffling people. What happened, happened. They made their choices, and whatever the future held, we would face it. And we would be together.

It is difficult to know how much talk there was among the adults, our relatives, about the war. In the Germany we were going to, it was common knowledge that one had to be careful about whom one talked to. It was not wise to voice anti-Hitler opinions. It was now early 1944. German fortunes were fading, but not desperate. Fighting on the Russian Front continued to be fiercely intense with huge numbers of casualties on both sides. The cold and unrelenting Russian winters killed as many soldiers as did the battles, and the winter of 1941 had been particularly devastating for the Germans. A counter offensive referred to by the Russians as "The Great Patriotic War," in response to a major attack on Moscow, caused the German *Wehrmacht* to lose over 145,000 ground soldiers in that battle alone.

The Germans were unequipped to wage war in the unbelievably low temperatures, and the harsh winter contributed to the high number of casualties. Equipment froze up, and men froze to death on the battlefield. The siege of Leningrad, lasting 900 days from September 1941, to January 1944, left 700,000 dead from cold, hunger, and bombings. Another half-million military from this city alone were sent to the front, most of them never to return. On the Western Front, the Germans had taken France and the northern countries and intended to do their best to keep them under control, in spite of active underground movements and sabotage.

❊ ❊ ❊

We were among the first group of internees to be repatriated from Crystal City. Men, women and children were told to get ready. Out came our two overseas trunks; my mother started packing again. There was much scurrying about and finding out who else was on the list. Freddy and I were happy to hear our best friends, the Wohlparts, were also going.

There were many disappointments. Families who were not included in this first Crystal City exchange had to say many emotional good-byes. *"Auf Wiedersehen* (till we meet again)" was the by-word in camp. Shortly before the middle of February, our belongings were loaded onto baggage cars, we boarded Pullman cars, and we were on our way to New York. We were all "pinned" with white lapel tags that bore our names and identifying numbers. The "SWPD" (Special War Problems Division / State Department) planned and orchestrated these inland transfers, as well as the exchanges with Germany. I recall guards at each end of our car, unsmiling, unlike the friendly guards we had come to know in camp. No one was allowed off the train, nor was anyone allowed to walk through to the next Pullman car. Our lapel tags indicated exactly to which numbered car we were assigned. On February 14, 1944, we were delivered to a pier in Jersey City, where the SS *Gripsholm* was awaiting her varied groups of "Persons being repatriated to Lisbon." We gazed at the ship, impressed with her majesty and promise, to take us safely across the Atlantic, supposedly homeward bound.

Breathing the salt air excited all of us, especially that unique, slightly putrid odor of the harbor waters. At nine years of age I could already wonder what my father must be thinking. Was he reliving memories of his adventurous youth at sea, the day he jumped ship in New York harbor, his wonderful hope for his family in a young and vibrant new land? Or was he now just facing the reality of this moment? My mother was strong; my father a very sentimental man. Often I remember her saying to him as he was lost in reverie: *"Was symbolierst Du denn jetzt schon wieder?"* (What are you pondering now?) We were waiting to board the *Gripsholm* on a life-altering voyage, and Mommi was ready to move on.

The *Gripsholm-I* was built by Armstrong, Whitworth & Company, Ltd, in Newcastle-upon-Tyne, England. She was launched on November 26, 1924. Upon her delivery to the Swedish American Lines a year later, she was hailed for her exquisite exteriors and the planning of the interior passenger areas. For the first time, modern Swedish design was plying the oceans. A "floating palace" is how enthusiastic passengers referred to her.

The *Gripsholm* would become particularly famous because of one novelty. Fitted with two six-cylinder, double-acting four-stroke engines, she would be diesel powered and thereby become the first trans-Atlantic diesel motor vessel in history. Geared with twin screws, her service speed was 17 knots.

The US State Department chartered the *Gripsholm* during World War II from 1942 to 1946 as an exchange and repatriation ship, sailing under the protection of the International Committee of the Red Cross. Thus she went from her earlier reputation as a "floating palace" to now being dubbed "The Mercy Ship." In 12 round-trips to various parts of the world, she carried over 27,000 passengers—POW's, diplomats, nurses, missionaries, oil people, and internees—safely to their pre-designated ports and on their way back home. The crew was Swedish. I recall our Captain's name was Gunnar Nordensson.

On February 15, 1944, we departed New York, destination Lisbon, Portugal, sailing the south Atlantic route. Flooding lights, beacons spilling onto the sea, warned adversaries in the war, if they happened to be in more southerly latitudes, that we were a Red Cross ship. We were easily identifiable by day with huge red crosses painted on the decks and the smokestacks. During the night, when we were all lit up, our ship must have been a magical sight on the dark waters of the wartime Atlantic.

The *Gripsholm* could transport over 1500 passengers during peacetime. Our exchange group was comprised of several contingents of internees from various camps, as well as a large number of German POW's. We seemed to be filled to capacity. In addition to all the exchange passengers and support personnel, there was the crew, food, and support material to supply all on board for the crossing, estimated to take two weeks. Most of the POW's were submarine and other naval crews who had been captured by the US. We were not being deported. We were being repatriated and exchanged for an equal number of Americans who were trapped in Germany due to the war. On the other side, ready to return to the US were stranded tourists, diplomats, and many American POW's. A United States repatriation/exchange plan with Germany, designed immediately after Pearl Harbor and approved in the spring of 1942, proposed exact lists of subjects be filed with both governments and followed through with a one-on-one exchange, after approval of the lists submitted by appropriate diplomats.

As usual, we children frolicked our way through trouble. We had free run of the ship (there was no formal security), and we only had to heed the admonitions of our parents. Freddy and I were in heaven when we found a small swimming pool on one of the lower decks and received permission to dive in. It sure made up for the pool fun we missed out on in Crystal City.

The *Gripsholm* was a most luxurious ocean liner for her time. We ate good food in the dining room, walked the decks, and breathed the ocean air. We were treated as decent, civilized human beings and were fortunate to have such a pleasant crossing. The adults were free to talk to the German POW's. These men also on occasion enjoyed talking to us children. Many were fathers with children of their own they hadn't seen for years. We played card games, read books, and talked of the future. One day there was an air of excitement all over the ship when there was a sighting of a German U-Boat. It allegedly traveled underwater alongside the *Gripsholm* for an entire day. Some passengers claim to have seen it; I didn't.

Officials from the US-SWPD (United States Special War Problems Division) and the representatives of the International Red Cross who accompanied us called us all to assemble in the large dining room. We were briefed on what to expect upon arrival in Lisbon. Disembarkation procedures were explained, gathering areas designated, and information given for the formal hand-off from the accompanying American officials to the sole responsibility of the International Red Cross.

The crossing offered a brief respite from our lives, which had been so long in upheaval. We enjoyed the moment; now it was time to stop wondering about the future and live it. Necessity and disillusionment had my father making choices that drove him to pragmatism: be where you can live some sort of natural life. Live where people would once again accord you respect, where you could unite in soul with a place with deep roots. All of us wayward souls on that ship, my father possibly most of all, were ready and eager to return to Germany and seek a real life again. Forget what lay behind, difficult as that was; there was nothing there for us anymore. After all, they had rejected us; we had not rejected them.

And so we landed in Lisbon, full of wonder and expectation. Bathed in sunshine and nestled by the sea, it was a pastel city of Mediterranean-style buildings. We left the *Gripsholm* in groups and were introduced to our Red Cross escorts. All Crystal City families were asked to assemble and board the busses standing ready to take us to hotels in the coastal town of Estoril. As always, I found myself with my nose pressed against the window, eagerly observing and absorbing the landscape and the people.

Estoril came into its own from the curious needs of two World Wars. Once a small spa area, conveniently located between Lisbon to the south and Cascais to the north, it became a prime location for European royal exiles to take up residence. Along with its fabled new residents and inevitable glitzy development, it soon became the "Portugese Riviera." But to us it was just a sunny haven.

Our busses stopped in front of a string of somnolent hotels across the boulevard from wide and sandy beaches. It was shirtsleeve weather with glaring sun and crashing, bright-blue Atlantic waves in the background. Freddy and I had to contain ourselves not to dash down to the water's edge, remove our shoes and socks, and wade right in. But we were so programmed for obedience, having been under guard for so long, that we did not break from the group.

How many were we? A Crystal City camp newspaper published in February 1944, put the number of German inhabitants at 1297. Of these, 634 made up the first group of families that left the camp and were repatriated. We remained a large group when transported on trains and ships, but were broken down into more manageable groups when it came to interim housing in Europe. There were at least twenty families in our hotel, more down "hotel row."

We received room assignments quickly and were told to rest a while, freshen up, then come down to the dining room for dinner. It was a lovely old hotel, quite grand compared to our previous barracks-apartment. At the required dinner we were informed we would be resettled in areas of our roots. The Red Cross was charged with investigating whether or not each individual family still had an *Elternhaus* (house of parents, i.e., homestead) to go to. There might not be a home left because the war in Germany had so intensified that some families had lost everything through bombings and had to be evacuated, or they had been overrun by the enemy and became refugees, or they had lost their lives. So the Red Cross had to find out if all of us waif families had a place to go. Those who didn't would still be transported back to Germany, but routed into a *Sammellager,* a safe collection or holding facility (camp) from which they would eventually be mainstreamed.

My father's parents were alive and well in Bettenhausen, but our good friends, the Wohlparts, had to go to a *Sammellager* in Prien am Chiemsee. The other family we were close to, the Breitenbergers (Herr Breitenberger was my father's soccer buddy), also went home to their family village, Herrsching am Ammersee. Both of these towns were in Bavaria.

The plan was to keep us all together and move us out in the direction of the German frontier in one transport. We had to wait until the Red Cross researched each family and confirmed their destinations, a process that took three to four weeks. During this period we enjoyed wonderful conditions in our hotel, good meals, and time for relaxation. Our parents were again ladies and gentlemen, waiting in a jarringly pleasant situation. Who was funding this? Probably a consortium of international sources: the

International Red Cross for sure, designated funds from the United States and Germany as well.

We had never been deprived of world news reports during internment or while waiting in Estoril for processing. The war and how it was going was all the men talked about. The Vaterland was fighting hard in the face of determined opposition by the Russian Army, as Hungary ultimately fell to Germany, but not without significant loss of life on both sides. American troops staged an assault against the Germans in Anzio and were beaten back repeatedly. Not until the battle of Cassino did the Allies attain victory in Italy. Some months later, I found out my oldest cousin Winfried Kirchner, serving as a paratrooper in the German armed forces, jumped in the battle of Cassino. Fortunately he lived to tell about his experience.

The Allies were bombing aircraft factories around Leipzig and Regensburg, and ball bearing factories in Schweinfurt. The worst news was always when major cities such as Berlin, Hamburg, Frankfurt am Main, and cities in the industrial Ruhr Valley were bombed so heavily that civilian casualties sometimes ran into the tens of thousands in just one air-raid. Apprehension over what lay ahead started creeping into everyone's conversation. Each head of family had turned his face from the country of his choice to the country of his birth. Had he traded his insecure life in a secure America for a life fraught with indescribable danger in a Germany at war? What would be left when he got there? What if Germany lost?

We children, on the other hand, could not be concerned about such worries. We had not experienced freedom of movement in a long time. We roamed the beaches across the street in search of unusual shells the waves tossed onto the sand and spent hours exploring the foreboding old ruin of a nearby fortress. When the tide came in, the waves crashed against the foundation, submerging its base. When the tide went out, we could hardly wait to hunt for the treasures of the sea that the waves deposited in the nooks and crannies of the old fortress. It was a daily adventure.

One day we were provided escorts and taken by bus to the sophisticated stores in Lisbon to shop. The powers that be, whoever they were, provided us with escudos, the currency of Portugal. My father, multilingual from his many years on merchant ships, spoke enough Portugese to function as a translator for all of us. I recall downtown Lisbon as a bustling metropolis. People moved about quickly and seemed happy, very friendly. The sales clerks were especially helpful and desired to please. So I have fond memories of Lisbon.

Still, when we took walks and strolled in the streets behind our hotel row in Estoril, we saw poverty none of us Germans from America had ever experienced. Shantytowns with open sewers,and crowded narrow alleys were a marked contrast to the glitz and glamour of the hotels and private beachfront villas.

We knew we had to be ready to move out on short notice. Finally, the word came. We would be leaving for Bairritz, France, where we would be received by the German military. The responsibilities of our international escorts would terminate at that point. But first, a group made up of one adult member from each family was taken to the docks in Lisbon to identify their respective trunks in the warehouses. The shipping authorities tagged them with addresses in Germany.

When we left Estoril, we boarded the day coaches of an outdated and uncomfortable train. It didn't take long to get through Portugal without stops. As we passed through Spain, and as the train slowed down for station towns and stopped, we pushed down the windows to get fresh air and take a look around. We saw faces of hundreds of peasant women with children, begging for food, money, anything—their hands pleadingly thrust out to us. I didn't like the way they shouted at us with words we couldn't understand. We couldn't tell whether they were angry at us or begging out loud. They looked very poor.

When we finally arrived in Biarritz, France, we were handed over to the German military. It was here that the war became a reality instead of a far-off story told by newspapers and radio broadcasts by Walter Winchell. German officers in smart, belted uniforms welcomed us with a snappy, heel-clicking "Heil Hitler!" They gave us all hearty handshakes and even hugs of affirmation and respect. We were the lost sheep returning to the true fold, those who had strayed from the Vaterland, who through all kinds of adversity endured enemy blandishments and punishments and had determined to return to its embrace.

There was no culture shock. By this time all of us interned at Crystal City had experienced various sorts of rejection and were alienated from any feelings of loyalty to America. German was now spoken exclusively, and we all felt as though we had truly returned home.

The prodigal sons, daughters, and children were taken to a huge glamorous hotel, which also served as area headquarters for the German occupational forces. Two soldiers—stereotypical "movie Germans," tall, with blond hair and smooth polished manners—escorted us to our rooms. "Beautiful German children" they murmured, patting my brother and me on the shoulders. As we passed through the carpeted corridors of the elegant hotel, we couldn't help remembering life in Crystal City, where we walked from sparse wooden barracks to the shower houses amidst scorpions and snakes. Now our accommodations were impressive, high-ceilinged rooms, with luxurious furnishings and ornate bathroom fixtures. Fresh flowers and an inviting fruit basket sat on one of the tables of our room.

But we quickly realized we were, indeed, in a wartime situation. One obsequious, almost fawning soldier pointed to the blackout shades on the windows and gave us a quick briefing on how and why they were to be kept pulled down during the nighttime hours. Allied bomber pilots flying over could see even the smallest light in a town below. Light bulbs were painted black halfway down, so there would be no flash of light and it would flow only towards the floor. Smoking was only permitted indoors. We were told that the tiny red glow at the end of a cigarette could actually be seen at 20,000 feet and become a bombsight target.

"There is a formal reception and a splendid welcoming banquet awaiting you in the hotel grand salon," our escorting soldiers told us. We freshened up and went downstairs, where festive German music filled the room as we were being seated. At least a dozen huge, crystal chandeliers hung suspended from the high frescoed ceiling, and oversized German flags draped the walls from floor to ceiling. A stage at one end of the room with a lectern promised there would be speakers. The tables were set in grand style with linen tablecloths, ornate silverware, the finest china, and an assortment of crystal goblets for each place setting. Beautiful floral centerpieces, complete with flickering candles, decorated each table as well.

My mother was in her element. She loved this kind of table presentation. Never mind the blacked-out windows! It was time for a celebration, and we were welcomed with a lavish German feast: smoked eel and caviar, *Wienerschnitzel*, rouladen, roast-goose, and venison. Familiar side dishes, more than you could possibly consume, completed the sumptuous meal. French champagne and wines of all descriptions flowed like water. There is a saying in German when your life is particularly abundant: you describe it as living *"wie der Herrgott in Frankreich"* (as God would live in France) and this was it.

Brown shirts surrounded us at other tables, all wearing armbands with the swastika. Soon soft dinner music, Viennese waltzes, and familiar semiclassical pieces began to fade, and a military brass ensemble played German national airs. The tapping of a baton quieted the room, and the band struck up the familiar German national anthem *Deutschland, Deutschland Ueber Alles*. Standing, we sang its words with emotional fervor. There wasn't a dry eye among the returnees. If there is one thing Germans do really well, it is to rally the troops and move the nationalistic spirit within the heart.

As I now try to examine the feelings of this band of wayfarers caught between the nation they had admired and adopted, but which had rejected them, and the homeland they had left, to which they were now returning, I recall no real fervor for the Nazism of Hitler. After several years of realistic observation of the man and his policies, there was no blind acceptance of those negative policies, by this time evident even to many Germans. This was during the time when a band of Hitler's most trusted officers and cabinet members were hatching a plot to assassinate him. We had, after all, been living in the United States, where we were not constantly exposed to the Third Reich and Hitler's hypnotic philosophy and plan: *Heute beherrschen wir Deutschland—morgen die ganze Welt!* (Today we rule over Germany, tomorrow the entire world!) Instead, there was only the joy of returning to the Vaterland, this piece of earth, far older and larger than any one regime could ever hope to be, no matter what time in history.

Towards the end of our dinner, the program called for introductions, hearty welcomes, and fulsome speeches, delivered with animation and drama. Many toasts were delivered to us, heralding our German heritage and our courage in the face of discrimination in a foreign land. Clinking crystal goblets resounded at each table all around the room. We were told to be proud to be on the winning side, as these fair-haired, uniformed Aryan leaders described the cause at that moment. The glory of victory was certainly soon to come. Yes, bombings were happening, but they were as a result of the barbaric Allies. Yes, our cities were suffering destruction, our people were being evacuated, but do not worry, right will prevail. We are in control! *"Sieg Heil!"* (Hail Victory!)

Our souls were stirred as the soldiers sang *"Die Fahne Hoch,"* the famed "Horst Wessel" song that was the anthem of the Nazi Party, chosen to glorify Horst Wessel as a Nazi martyr. The stirring strains of the cornets, trombones, and the marching beat of the drums rang throughout the hall. I must say, I always loved the music associated with each and every gathering of Germans, no matter what the occasion, but my eyes and Freddy's, too, were straying from the little swastika-marked favors on our table for us children to the table loaded with luscious German pastries. *Schwarzwaelder Kirschtorte* (Black Forest cherry cake) here we come! And we thought of what lay outside the banquet room.

We were situated along the Biarritz coastline, in a dramatic setting with thunderous waves of the Atlantic Ocean crashing against the huge boulders in front of our hotel. Freddy and I were itching to go out and explore the beach, but we were not allowed to. It was too dangerous. It's not that we were being guarded as before; we were now being protected. Normandy was still a few months off, but the German high command had knowledge that there would be an Allied invasion somewhere along the French coast. Exactly when or where this would occur, no one knew. But it was going to happen, and it could be soon.

They needed to get us out of there fast. Beneath all the bombastic welcome and the patriotic bluster, there was an efficient organizational push at work, the reality of which none of us realized. The bureaucracy of the Third Reich had its tentacles and paper trails spread all over Germany. Family roots had been researched, specific destinations for each family established; and when these destinations received final confirmation, we were once again on our way.

Soon we boarded trains under the escort of German military and passed through France as quickly as possible. Though we did not fully realize it, it was extremely dangerous for a trainload of Germans to journey through the French countryside. The French Resistance was active, and, had they discovered us, we would have been sabotaged. As we crossed into Germany at Saarbruecken, our train stopped rolling. We were put off onto a siding to await re-routing.

We were now on German soil. The landscape didn't look that different. We didn't feel that different; not until the air raid sirens sounded! Nobody had told us children about bombs crashing down on us. We rushed off the train and were directed below into a sort of bunker, really the lower train platform of the station. We couldn't have been in a worse place. The Allies always targeted the railway systems, anything to disrupt transportation and cause chaos. The noise, the fear was horrible. I was afraid we were all going to die. We were American by birth, Freddy and I, but because Pappi was German, we were German by law. Now we were really Germans, sharing the fate of our countrymen. We had landed in the midst of a hot war. Welcome to World War II.

Following another long, steady blast of the siren, indicating the "all clear" (we soon learned the difference between the "take cover" siren and the "all clear"), we were taken into the city and put up for the night, while the tracks and equipment were somehow speedily repaired. The next morning we re-boarded our train, good-bye tears streaming down our cheeks, as we said our farewells to families with whom we had shared so much. We promised each other to stay in touch if at all possible and then were off to Meiningen.

My parents were somber but resolved. The population in general seemed grim to me. There were no smiling faces, no laughter. It was a totally gray society, not at all like the Germany I expected, filled with happiness, music, and dancing, the way we lived in America among our own kind.

The train tracks did not go all the way to Bettenhausen. When we finally arrived in Meiningen, we were put on a bus for the last leg of our journey to my father's village. Opa, my grandfather, and Tante Lene, my aunt, greeted us when we arrived along with a bunch of cousins I didn't know. All I remember is how muddy the main road through the village was and how everything smelled like cows. This was the same place we had spent that wonderful summer of 1937. It was now a distant memory. Everything had changed, but it would now be our home. Freddy and I just looked at each other.

A few days later, our two overseas trunks that had been following us around the world like a couple of German shepherd dogs, arrived.

Mommi's Christmas card to Pappi while he was interned.

Pappi sent this Christmas card in 1943 while he was interned at Camp Forest, Tennessee.

P.S. 88. I am row 2, 3rd from right. Miss Chatfield, the teacher who constantly sent messages of dislike and prejudice to me in every way she could think of, is in the back corner.

Pastor Greber was one of our angels, helping us appeal to people we couldn't otherwise reach.

Pappi had been a volunteer chef on weekends at the Bergwald, the camp owned by the German/American Vocational League.

My Uncle Werner took his chances and enlisted. Fortunately, he never had to serve overseas. Here he is with Aunt Elsie. He stayed in California his entire tour of duty. She visited him several times.

In 1984 I visited the Crystal City Internment Camp in Texas and had my photo taken in front of a barracks exactly the same as the one we lived in.

Crystal City newspaper.

Sport und Spiel.

Faustball:

Da Kam. Mährlein durch anderweitige Arbeit, hauptsächlich als Turnlehrer in der Schule, zu sehr in Anspruch genommen ist, hat Kam. E.Meister die Leitung des Faustballsportes übernommen.

In Anbetracht der Tatsache, dass Faustball nicht nur ein schöner, sondern auch ein sehr gesunder Sport ist, sollten sich viel mehr daran beteiligen. Knochenbrüche u. Schienbeinpolieren, was beim Fussballspiel etwa vorkommen kann, ist beim Faustballspiel so gut wie ausgeschlossen, auch verlangt es nicht so viel Puste.

Nach Weihnachten sollen die Spiele um die Lagermeisterschaft wieder aufgenommen werden. Da Sonntags die Fussballspiele stattfinden, ist geplant, die Faustballspiele an Wochentagen nach 4 Uhr auszutragen. Die Spielführer der bisherigen Mannschaften, sowie neue Spieler sollen sich möglichst bald bei Kam. Meister, C 40, melden.

Am Dienstag, den 28.Dezember, spielen folgende Mannschaften:

Wolff - Reising	4.30 Uhr
Benz - Moeller	4.30 Uhr
Meister - Peters	5 Uhr
Kornoffel - Reuter	5 Uhr

Die Spielführer haben darauf zu achten, dass ihre Mannschaften zur festgesetzten Zeit antreten.

Fussball:

Hochbetrieb herrscht zur Zeit beim Fussballsport. Die Sportanhänger werden zu den, jeden Sonntag stattfindenden 3 Spielen, die immer interessanter werden, eingeladen.

Vorgangenen Sonntag spielten 2 Jugend-Mannschaften um den Sieg, der dann auch der besser eingespielten Mannschaft mit 2:0 zufiel.

Viel Spass gab es bei dem Spiel der "Alten Herren." Auf beiden Seiten wurde tüchtig geknallt, was das Torverhältnis mit 7:6 beweist.

Beim Hauptspiel am Nachmittag, das von Kam. Reinbold fein geleitet wurde, siegten die "Braunen" 4:1.

Am Sonntag, den 25.Dezember spielen die Mannschaften in folgender Aufstellung:

Jugend 11.30 Uhr

Christ
J.Fuhr - Volker
E.Fuhr - Krauss - Siegel
Eckstein-Needing-Siegel-Vogel-Koch

Egner-Christ-Kupfer-Kuhn-E.Moeller
Drewes-Fuchs-Vogel
Geier - Rehner
Fleckenstein
Ersatz: E.Fuhr, Schmitt

Alte Herren, 2 Uhr

Niepken
Albers - Löffler
Winkler-Brödel-Petzold
Rehner-Häusler-Bauer-Plaschke-Meyer

Roller-Winkler-Berndt-Kolb-Dietrich
Wessel - Fiedler - Wiegand
Abele - Breitenberger
Rinner.

Hauptspiel 3.30 Uhr

Knieriemen
Eckstein-Beyer
Faatsch-Feller-Therre
Schuwark-Winter-Weiss-Henger-Steiger

Richter-Benz-Reinbold-Evert-Moeller
Betzler-Heins-Rechl
Keller - Reeser
Meister
Schiedsrichter: Kerherr.

Alle aufgestellten Spieler müssen pünktlich erscheinen.

L.Winter.

Kino-Nachrichten

werden in Zukunft an der Westseite der Toiletten für Shelters u.Triplexes,der Waschhäuser für Quadruplexe und am Nordeingang des Ladens angeschlagen.

Wir gratulieren Fam.G.Krichbaum zur Geburt ihres Sohnes Erich am 23.Dez

My father—Wiegand—listed under "Alte Herren" on the Fussball (soccer) roster.

The welcome in Bettenhausen was very hearty. When we entered the kitchen and greeted my grandmother, Oma, it was a moment packed with emotion, especially for my father. He was Oma's oldest son, the first to leave home. He'd been all around the world, settling in America, had a family of his own; and now, a quarter of a century later, he was back. The wanderers had come home. She arose from her bench near the cook stove and walked towards him, arms outstretched, crying, "*Mein Otto, mein Otto, mein lieber Sohn,*" and with that she fell into his arms, her sobs muffled by his embrace. Pappi was crying, too; I saw his shoulders heaving.

I remembered a little of the summer we'd spent in 1937, but now my eyes were wide with excitement to realize we had returned to the village where Pappi grew up. The entrance, which I didn't recall from before, was imposing. The house fronted on the street with a bench and espaliered trees. There were two side-by-side gates. One very large one was for teams of oxen, carts, and carriages to pass through; the other was a garden gate for people. The farmhouse was typical of German architecture: white stucco on the first floor, half-timbered with stucco on the second and third floors. The third floor was actually the attic where grain was kept. The house, reportedly constructed in the seventeenth century and today an historic landmark, had a steeply pitched, red-tiled roof. The eaves provided much shelter for roosting pigeons. But the birds became a nuisance when they found a way into the attic and looted the grain designated to feed chickens and geese for the winter. In the earthen-floored cellar amidst the root vegetables and jars and jars of home-canned fruits, one could see the sturdy foundation the huge house was built on. All interior walls were brick.

Inside were steep steps leading to the upper level. To the left was the kitchen, to the right the parlor, where on Sundays *Kaffee und Kuchen* were served to friends and relatives. Beyond the parlor was Oma and Opa's private bedroom. It was totally off limits. No one dared enter my grandfather's domain. I was never in it, but will admit to having taken an occasional peek. At the end of the narrow hallway, past the staircase, was one more small bedroom. It served as a guestroom and was referred to as *"die Kammer."* My parents spent their first night back home in the *Kammer.* Freddy and I were bedded upstairs with our aunts and several cousins.

There were four bedrooms upstairs, one in each corner of the house, and another *Kammer;* although this one was used as an all-purpose catchall room.

I stayed with Tante Lene, my grandparents' youngest daughter, who occupied two of the upstairs bedrooms. She had a two-year-old little girl named Gudrun. We took to each other right away, and she became my favorite aunt, much like the Tante Elsie I had left behind in New York. Her husband, my Uncle Willi (Buechner was his last name), was a first lieutenant in the German *Wehrmacht*, serving on the Russian Front. We met him when he came home on leave, as his outfit was being transferred from Stalingrad to a developing Russian offensive in Hungary. I had only seen photos of him up to this point and found him dashingly handsome. In person he was the epitome of a German officer. His visit lasted only a few days, during which all of us children had to camp out with Tante Lisbeth, who occupied the other two bedrooms upstairs.

Tante Lisbeth was the daughter-in-law in the house, married to my father's younger brother, Karl, who was also serving in the German *Wehrmacht* in Russia. They were the parents of two daughters, seven-year-old Marlene and Ulla, an infant born a year earlier. Marlene and I became good friends, but as playmates we were not the best match. I wanted to play sports or go out exploring, and she didn't always want to do what I wanted. Perhaps it was because she was two years younger than I.

When Onkel Karl was young he had left Bettenhausen to establish himself in Berlin as another Wiegand butcher. That's where he met and married Lisbeth, a typical *Berlinerin*: quick witted, cosmopolitan, somewhat of a playgirl and never at a loss for words. She was often a bit sharp-tongued, which was a source of irritation to Opa, but I loved her sense of humor and constant chatter. She always had something to say, mostly comical, sometimes sarcastic, about everyone and everything. Today we'd call her a "motor-mouth." Tante Lisbeth and her two girls had landed under the same roof of the *Elternhaus* because raids over Berlin had become so intense that any kind of a normal life was impossible, to say nothing of the danger to human life. Families who had a safe place to go left. Freddy had no problem bunking with Tante Lisbeth for the time being. He liked her as much as I did.

The evening of our arrival drew deep into the night. After a meal Oma and Tante Lene prepared for us, word had gotten around that Otto Wiegand had come back from America. Soon a continuous parade of neighbors, friends, former schoolmates, and more relatives stopped by to welcome him home and meet his family. Some even came from neighboring villages. It was amazing. But even more amazing was our impression on them. I don't know what everyone expected, but we appeared just as German as they were, fluent in the mother tongue, not at all like a bunch of *Amerikaner*. I think Freddy and I surprised them the most, not only with our accent-free German, but also with our confident way of addressing adults. As children we were never shy.

When this eventful evening finally ended and everyone turned in, I remember lying awake. I thought about the long train ride from Saarbruecken. The military had seemed to be running everything with their neat gray uniforms, spit-and-polish boots, and always "*Schnell, schnell, schnell.*" (Quick, quick, quick, or go, go, go). As we had headed for Thueringen, traveling on a train hurtling through the darkness, we had been hoping there would be no more air raids before we reached our destination. It was all so frightening. Still, despite the incessant bombings of the railway system by the Allies, the Germans had the tracks repaired and ready to go within a matter of hours. Fortunately, we had been spared another bombing on our way home.

There was a constant sense of urgency in the Germany of 1944. The German officers at the grand banquet in Biarritz had presented the Vaterland as triumphant over all. In daylight, Germany did not look all that triumphant to me with many of its cities lying in ruins. Now that we had arrived at the little hamlet, it did seem we had landed in a safer haven, certainly in a wonderful family environment and a farmhouse that exuded history and staying power.

So this was to be home. I had to get used to the smell that pervaded the farmhouse. A mixture of food cooking, homemade cheese stinking away on top of the cupboards in the overly warm kitchen, meat curing in the smokehouse, and cow manure—all under one roof. The smell of manure was overwhelming. No wonder, the *Misthaufen* (dung pile) was directly opposite the front door on the other side of the barnyard. This was going to take some getting used to.

Freddy and I made a stunning discovery before we went to bed. There were no toilets! What were we supposed to do if we had to go in the night? A *Nachttopf* (chamber pot) had been placed under the bed. And all of the bedrooms were ice cold. That's when we figured out why Oma sent us upstairs with a brick, which she wrapped in newspaper after taking it out of the warm oven chamber. This was the Bettenhausen-style hot water bottle we placed under the covers, while we quickly got undressed, jumped in, and disappeared under a mountainous feather tick. We soon became deliciously warm and fell asleep in the feathers.

The next morning, we found out where the toilet was. Out the front door, across the barnyard, was a shed that had cut wood stacked on one side and the *Misthaufen* on the other. It was called the *Abort*, the privy, complete with neatly cut squares of newspaper hanging from a nail. There was no such thing as toilet paper during the entire war. I did not like the *Abort*. On a warm and humid day, the stench would choke you. I was always so grateful when my mother let me use the chamber pot inside in the privacy of one of the upstairs bedrooms.

I was fascinated, perhaps dismayed, by the proximity of the cows and other livestock, pigs, and sheep. Their stalls occupied one whole side of the house, an extension to the rear of the main house and all under one roof, and the smell of farm animals was strong. Dung was piled room-high into a square concrete pit, and the rain leaching through the pile made for a very stinky liquid, which my Grandfather used to fertilize the fields. I recall Opa coming in from the fields that spring season reeking of the *Jauche* (dung water) that had splattered all over him. Oma made him take off his work clothes and clean up in the back hall before she let him in the kitchen. I had a really difficult time getting used to the stench that always hung in the air.

There was not as much bathing as there had been in America. Every Saturday night Oma would heat huge kettles of water on the stove, which were then dumped into a large galvanized tub, and we children would take turns bathing, one after the other, all in the same water. Adults bathed upstairs in privacy about once a week.

The house was filled to capacity. Tante Lisbeth had a newborn besides Marlene, and I suppose because of Uncle Karl's military service, a nice one-bedroom efficiency with cooking space and a verandah was soon found for her in the village. Living quarters were assigned by the local authorities and extremely hard to come by. It was generally known, "You had to have pull." I'm sure Opa also used his political connections inasmuch as he held a leadership position in the local representation of the NSDAP (the German Workers Party that was formed when Hitler came to power in 1933). Tante Lisbeth was happy to move out. She didn't get along that well with Opa anyway. But then Opa had his differences with my mother as well. Perhaps women of the new generation were simply too strong-minded for the old-fashioned gentleman. Nontheless, we took Tante Lisbeth's space upstairs and settled in

I liked my grandmother, and I think the feeling was mutual. She made me feel as though my helping her with chores around the house made a difference. On bread baking day, she would send me to the neighbor's to pick up the starter dough. When she baked cake for Sunday afternoon coffee, I would pit the plums she put on top of the *Zwetschgendatschie* (a delicious cheesecake concoction) for which she always seemed to have enough hoarded sugar. Food that wasn't raised on the farm was rationed, and families received food stamps, meted out according to the size of the family and sometimes, as in the case of milk, the ages of the children. Many Germans were suffering from shortages and deprivation by this time, especially those living in the larger populated areas. But we did not go without food on this farm, at least not until the front began to advance.

Outside in the chicken house I reached underneath the nesting hens and gathered eggs. I would fetch jars for supper from the cellar shelves: home-canned blueberries, pears, raspberries, and cherries. Also in the cellar were potatoes, turnips, and red beets, and I scooted down there to bring them up for our supper stews and soups. There were also apples spread out on shelves, so the air could circulate around them and they would keep all winter. They were called *Lederaepfel* (leather apples), and as the name implies, they had very tough skins, but were ever so crunchy and sweet inside. It was a treat when Oma let me have one.

There was also a pantry at the end of a hallway behind the kitchen. There the mainstay of every farmhouse was kept, a big barrel of homemade sauerkraut. From the pantry ceiling hung smoked meats, sausages, and slabs of bacon. Opa did all the butchering and smoked all the meat products in the smoke house behind the farmhouse.

Farm life was a grueling existence for Opa with no other men around to help. Karl, Willi, and son-in-law Willi Buechner were on the Russian front, son Erich on the Western Front, and tragically son Erwin had fallen shortly after the beginning of the war when Hitler invaded Russia in the summer of 1941.

Opa had no automated farm machinery; so all of his fields were plowed with a walking plow pulled by an ox. The spring planting, summer hay-raking, and fall harvesting were all done by hand. Oma helped as much as she could, but for the most part, she was busy taking care of the chickens, geese, and rabbits and supervising all food preparation. Tante Lene and my mother became Opa's main helpers. I had another aunt living in the village, Tante Bertha, and her three boys came often to help Opa. The oldest, Friedhold, was in his teens.

Freddy was put to work, too, lifting heavy bags of grain in the barn to feed the animals. Sometimes he had to load bags of wheat and rye onto a handcart and pull it to the gristmill in the center of the village where the water wheel mill would grind the grain into flour for bread. Much of the food produced on farms like Opa's was delivered to pick-up points in the village, where it was sold and managed by government agents and trucked to collection centers in the larger cities for distribution among the population as well as transported to the fronts to feed the troops.

Our parents enrolled us in the *Dorfschule* (village elementary school). It was a huge three-story building, housing the entire school system of Bettenhausen: Kindergarten through eighth grade, with multiple classes in large rooms on the second and third floors. Freddy and I had no problem adjusting to the German grade school. Besides public school, we both had gone to a private German school in New York; we could speak, read, and write by the time we left there and had continued our education in German as well as English in Crystal City. So German was now the tongue of daily life, especially now that we were among native speakers.

I liked school, and I especially liked my teacher, a young person very interested in how life in America compared to our lives now. I was in the third grade in the spring of 1944 and started in the fourth that fall with the same teacher for both grades, and teachers taught every subject except music and singing. Total organization and hands-on discipline were standard in German classrooms. My motivation was not only driven by myself, but to make Pappi proud of me when I came home with a report card full of *Einzer* (ones).

Freddy didn't fare as well. He was in the seventh and eighth grades that year and had a man named Lehrer Granner for his teacher. They disliked each other from the moment they met. Granner ruled by intimidation. He resented Freddy's free and easy attitudes towards his studies and life in general, misinterpreting his nonconformist attitude as being anti-establishment, anti-German, demonstrating everything he disliked about Americans. Granted, Freddy was by nature a bit of a rebel and full of himself, especially at this time in his life when he was at the advent of the *Flegeljahre* (the teenage years), but to me he was my brother, wise and street smart beyond his years.

Lehrer Granner was continually looking for reasons to discipline, punish, and openly embarrass Freddy. The day Granner blind-slapped him from the back across his face and ear, Freddy exercised all the self-control he could muster not to hit back. Granner also hated the fact that Freddy spoke English and would mutter things under his breath, which he couldn't understand, and ultimately forbade him to say. Needless to say, my brother had a difficult time acclimating, and I believe his teacher, Lehrer Granner, planted a seed in Freddy's heart, the longing to get back to America.

What little free time we had in Bettenhausen was mostly spent in the company of our four cousins, Friedhold, Edith, Erwin and Erich, and that time was usually in connection with Opa's assigned farm chores. Our cousins would often ask us to "Say that in English" and to teach them, too. Bad words and naughty phrases came first. They loved "kiss my ass" and "shut-up." Freddy warned them about letting their parents or Opa know, for we were basking in the praise of our relatives, who valued the cultural advantage of bilingualism.

Word got back to Opa about Lehrer Granner's difficulty in dealing with Freddy and the disruption it caused in the classroom. As a result he gave Freddy quite a dressing down, but he didn't dare dole out any physical punishment. He would have had to get past my mother first on that issue. She had the motto: "My children right or wrong. First I stick up for my children, then I will deal with the problem in private." It was just another thing that made us close all our lives.

Opa made short shrift of Freddy's rebelliousness and promptly signed him up for the *Jungfolk*, a branch of the *Hitler Jugend*. They did the same things as the Boy Scouts, but they marched more, singing marching songs, with words everyone had to learn by heart. Freddy loved the competitive sports: sprinting, handball, and swimming, where he particularly excelled. He finally got the attention of the other boys in the village, who heretofore had trouble accepting him, but now started to show him respect, even admiration when it came to swimming. He could do the Australian crawl, which left all others behind in his wake, as they were trying to catch up doing the breaststroke, more common in Europe. He was also an excellent diver and could perform a swan dive from the highest diving board, which made all the girls swoon. My brother was quite a show-off!

Slowly Freddy worked his way back into the good graces of my Opa; he just had to continually prove himself. The one remaining frustration Opa had with him was how he always managed to disappear when there was work to do. Hormones were beginning to kick in, and although the boys were slow to befriend him, he had no problem getting acquainted with the girls.

We had truly arrived in the heart of Germany. A good deal of German history and culture was centered in Thuringia. After World War I and the abdication of Kaiser Wilhelm II, its capital, Weimar, became a town with unusual political significance. The powers-that-be shunned Berlin, a city in political turmoil, and convened in the German National Theater in Weimar, giving birth to the Weimar Republic, the first democratic state on German soil. Johann Wolfgang von Goethe, the most beloved of German poets, lived in Weimar for fifty years until his death in 1832. Von Schiller, another poet, composer Franz Liszt, philosopher Friedrich Nietzsche, names we recognize from history and the arts, were once citizens of Weimar.

The school of design and applied arts known the world over as Bauhaus was rooted here. Not far away is the town of Eisenach, birthplace of Johann Sebastian Bach and the place where Martin Luther lived as a child. Although not born in Eisenach, Martin Luther, pursued for his religious views, received protection in the Wartburg Castle high above the city, where he translated the New Testament into German in 1522. Bettenhausen was located a mere twenty-five kilometers south of these historic cities, nestled among the hills of the beautiful Thuringian Forest.

It was obvious that we would move beyond Bettenhausen. Shortly after our arrival, my father was employed by the Organization of German Police Forces in World War II, namely the "ORPO" or *Ortspolizei* (regular local uniformed police). He was assigned to duty in the town of Meiningen, the county seat, 15 kilometers from Bettenhausen. His daily commute was on a bicycle. I'll never forget the evening he came home dressed in his newly issued uniform. It was not exactly military looking, and yet it did present him as a person of authority, mostly because of the black belt across his chest and around his waist, complete with holster and handgun. He also had a nightstick and handcuffs dangling from his belt. I was not sure I liked it. He looked so out-of-character. To me, the worst parts of his uniform were the *Wickelgamaschen* (puttees), pieces of fabric wrapped around his calves, resembling Ace bandages. They made him look like a World War I doughboy. Where were the spit-and-polish boots? Well, there were none. Then he donned his *Pickelhelm* (spiked helmet).

I thought my mother was going to split her sides. She was laughing so hard, she could hardly get it out when she told him he looked like a character out of a Laurel and Hardy movie or the Three Stooges. "Whatever you do," Pappi said to her, "don't let Opa see you having this much fun!" He was quite amused himself, but Opa's sense of humor would not stretch this far for matters touching on the traditional.

Pappi was assigned to an Allied prisoner-of-war camp, where he served as interpreter and liaison between the ranking officer of the prisoner population and the German camp command. The Brits and Yanks confined there were largely US Army, Air Corps, and RAF personnel shot down over Germany. The prisoners had all kinds of issues: Could they have better heat in the barracks? Could the food be improved? Could they perform a play? How about some updated books in the library, and so forth. There were no clashes between prisoners and their German captors during this period. That was yet to come.

Bettenhausen showed no visible signs of war damage, but not a single house went unscathed. Every family was affected, losing husbands, brothers, sons, and cousins. In a village of old Germany, generations of families had grown up and grew old together. Many former schoolmates, lovers, and lifelong friends and neighbors had died in the war or were captured. My father's youngest brother, my Uncle Willi, was with the *Panzers* or tank corps. He was captured during an offensive on the Russian front and held in a POW camp in Vladivostock, about as far to the east as one can go in the former Soviet Union.

We lived in Bettenhausen one entire planting season. I saw how much we were needed to help in the difficult world of farm life where there were few adult men left and many of them were disabled. Only the neediest farmers, those who had no extra hand, qualified to be assigned a *Fremdarbeiter* (foreign laborer). Hitler had put a program in place right after the onset of the war called *Arbeitseinsatz*, using "forced laborers" to maintain production, while his more valuable German workforce was utilized in all phases of the war effort. These forced laborers were mostly men; some were women, primarily from the conquered territories of Poland, the Soviet Union, and France, where they had been rounded up and sent into Germany.

The Poles were usually assigned to agricultural operations, of which there were several in Bettenhausen. They were quartered in primitive areas in the farmhouses they were assigned to, and although they were not guarded, they had absolutely no interaction with their countrymen in other farmhouses or with the general population. They could interact only with their host farm families and do as they were told, which was not always easy because of the different languages.

We worked our farm with every available family member, old and young alike. My mother joined the rest of the women working the fields, while Opa did the heavy work requiring his team of oxen. My father helped on weekends and long summer evenings if he could get home early enough. I learned how to plant potatoes and field turnips, and turn hay and rake it into long rows when it was dried out enough to be loaded onto a hay wagon, Opa throwing it in the air with a pitchfork. We children were allowed to ride home atop the pile of fresh hay. My favorite chore was herding geese in the meadows at the foot of Mount Geba, the same mountain on whose highlands my father had herded sheep as a boy. I was a *Gaense Liesl*, the traditional name given to a young girl whose job was to herd geese.

Our lives were relatively undisturbed by the war raging not far from us during this period. Bettenhausen was located in a pocket of quiet, having no large cities or munitions facilities in the area. The only reminders that we were in grave danger were the daily overflights of hundreds of B-29 bombers heading for their targeted areas, carpet-bombing entire German cities and unleashing terror, death, and destruction. Often we could hear the distant explosions, and we would hike up Mount Geba to look in the direction of the blood-red, pulsating horizon. Opa could always tell us which city was getting hit. Erfurt was a frequent target with its many wartime munitions factories. I remember the night Eisenach was bombed. It frightened me a lot, because it seemed the bombings were getting closer to home.

One afternoon Freddy became the village hero. Down at the millpond he was walking along the banks of the Herpf, the millstream that wound its way through Bettenhausen, when he looked up and saw a baby carriage rolling downhill towards the water. Running as fast as he could, he did not get there in time to stop the carriage, but he did get there in time to save the infant who was tossed out and was already underwater and being swept downstream. The hysterical mother came running towards Freddy, took her wet, screaming baby from his arms, and ran into her house. Freddy retrieved the carriage and placed it on her porch upside down, so it could dry out.

That evening a grateful father came to our house and gave my brother 100 Marks. The following day in school, Lehrer Granner, the teacher who couldn't stand Freddy, made the announcement of his heroic deed and praised him publicly for his quick action and courage. The accolades the villagers heaped on Freddy didn't match the pride I felt in my heart for my brother. I know Opa secretly took credit for his inherent grit and swift response, and it made a real difference in their relationship.

Before our term ended in late spring of 1944, we were given assignments and dates when the schoolchildren were to assemble over the summer. Our first assignment, which we could accomplish independently, was to pick chamomile blossoms when they were in full bloom, take them home to dehydrate, then bring bags full of dried-out flower heads to school in the fall. Oma taught me the drying process and helped me package the dry chamomile. We would always withhold some for ourselves. Everyone brewed it into tea. It would cure just about anything that ailed you. The product we children brought to school was taken to collection points, from which it was distributed by pharmaceutical houses.

When the potato fields were in full bloom and the top growth about 1/2 meter tall, we had to assemble in groups and walk through the furrows, picking off potato bugs and dropping them into jars. They were the ugliest things, black and yellow, crawling all over the plants, stubbornly adhering to stems and leaves. You had to peel them off, and I wore gloves. Adults had a fire going at the end of each field to burn these pests, which left unchecked could destroy an entire potato crop in several days. There was no such thing as spraying for bugs as we know it today.

In late summer, we would again assemble, and accompanied by our teachers, walk deep into the Thuringian forest to gather beech nuts. We found them all over the ground, baskets full of them. They were shiny brown, about an inch long and three-sided. When I asked my teacher why we were collecting them, she said they would go into huge presses to extract their oil. Although non-edible, the oil had many uses in the war effort, primarily as fine machine oil.

Our leisure time was mostly spent playing with our cousins when our parents visited each other on weekends. We would go on long walks together. A special time of the summer was when wild blueberries came in season, and Tante Lene would lead the family outing deep into the woods to pick buckets full. From years' experience, she knew exactly where to find them. The next day, we children had to pick them clean, and Oma would can them for the long winter.

I recall my cousin Marianne coming to visit from Werdau, a small city in Saxony. As toddlers we had lived in New York with our respective families. Her parents, my Tante Elsie and Uncle Werner, left her with Werner's parents after visiting in 1938 and never returned to Germany before the war broke out to bring her back to America. Now, doting grandparents and an aunt in an upper-class environment were raising her. She was the only child in an elegant, family-owned hotel, and to say she was spoiled was an understatement. She was the little princess in her grand hotel. Our life styles were worlds apart. We had acclimated to life on a farm in rural Thuringia; she arrived in a taffeta dress and patent leather shoes. During her visits everyone in the farmhouse all at once became very well mannered, even Opa. Marianne enjoyed the rare opportunity to play in the barn with a bunch of cousins and was not afraid to jump in the hay mound from high beams. She didn't even mind getting cow dung on her pretty shoes. I liked her.

Disruptions to our daily lives became routine. We got used to seeing hundreds of bombers flying overhead in an eastwardly direction and returning several hours later heading back west. We adapted to the constant drone of the engines. In these tense days prior to the Normandy invasion, when chores and work were over, conversation in our house centered on the war. In spite of recent reversals, Germany surely had a chance to win, or so the reasoning went. Besides, there were secret weapons being developed and rumored to be almost ready for launch. They would turn the tide. The Fuehrer had it all under control, most were certain. Reminders of the stake the Third Reich had in the war were everywhere. You walked into the local grocery store and did not say, "*Guten Tag.*" You said, "*Heil Hitler!*" Pictures of the Fuehrer and swastikas were on the walls in every public place.

June 6, 1944, changed everything. The Allies had landed in Normandy, and the news was ominous. The long rumored-invasion was now reality, and people were beginning to have doubts. Optimistic reports given out by the Third Reich sounded hollow. The attack on the Western Front was too strong and too well armed for the *Wehrmacht* to resist. My Uncle Erich came home heavily wounded. Though his legs were not amputated, he could not walk without the use of two canes for the rest of his life. People hoarded food, and civil unrest reared its ugly head.

My father heretofore had not feared street crime on his daily bicycle commute from Bettenhausen to Meiningen. Now, he frequently found himself in danger. Gangs of homeless people were roaming the cities and stealing from farmers. The POW's in the camp, the Yanks and the Brits, started having serious disagreements with each other, as well as the German command. My father's interpretive services were imperative to keeping lines of communication open, and sometimes he would not be able to come home. We often spent sleepless nights worrying about him.

There was a sense of urgency in our village that year about harvesting the crops and preparing for winter. We had a *Schreber Garten* close to Bettenhausen, as did everyone else, an allotted plot of ground, where village families could plant vegetables and berry bushes. The individual plots were not fenced off; instead they were marked by rows of cutting flowers that were jointly tended. I watched and helped my Tante Lene plant the garden in the spring. But mostly I had to keep an eye on my cousin, two-year old Gudrun, so she would not wander into the carefully stepped-off seedbeds. All summer we combined an evening walk with watering, weeding, and generally tending the garden.

When it came time to harvest the vegetables, carrots, onions and string beans, we discovered they had been stolen. And the currant and gooseberry bushes were picked clean. Worse yet, when Opa hitched up his team of oxen to the potato wagon and all of us rode out to our fields to help with the harvest, we discovered many rows of potatoes had already been dug up and the potatoes stolen. At one end of the field were our apple and pear trees. They, too, had been shaken, and the fruit gathered by unknown plunderers before we ever had a chance to pick our own apples. Opa was livid. This was unheard of. But so many strangers had come to our area—refugees, evacuees and homeless wanderers—that food was in short supply. One could hardly blame these people for stealing to keep themselves and their families fed. They were not farmers, could not raise their own food. What other choice did they have? The only recourse Opa had was to continue harvesting and bringing in the crops as quickly as possible. I recall Oma consoling him saying, "Don't worry Frieder, if we run out of potatoes, we'll survive on *Linsensuppe* (lentil soup)."

Storing wood for the winter also began earlier than usual in late summer 1944. The local Master Forest Ranger assigned to our area tagged trees to be cut in the Thueringer Forest surrounding our village, and logging began. Logs were dropped in front of each farmhouse, and we had to saw, split, and stack it. Those folks who were not in a position to cut wood themselves reported their need to the town hall, and chopped wood would be delivered to them. Coal was rationed and meted out according to the size of a family or facility, such as the schoolhouse. It was delivered by chute into a basement window. The call for children to come to the schoolhouse and help carry wood came earlier than usual that year. We had to assemble in the schoolyard, load each other's arms full of as much chopped wood as we could manage, then climb four flights of stairs, and stack it up in the attic. We were exhausted at the end of the day, and though this activity repeated itself year after year, usually laced with fun and laughter, this year it was carried out in a no-nonsense atmosphere. Who knew what was to come?

The *Volksschule* (elementary school) resumed in the fall, and I entered the fourth grade. Freddy had to go to the *Gymnasium* (secondary/middle school for boys) in Meiningen. On Monday mornings Freddy and Pappi would begin their commute to Meiningen earlier than usual because they had to share the bicycle. The system they worked out was clever. They would leave the house together, Pappi walking at a snappy pace, Freddy on the bike. Freddy would ride through the village and keep going for an additional 3 kilometers. He would then lean the bicycle against a tree and secure it with a combination lock and continue walking. Pappi would catch up to the bicycle, unlock it, mount up, and begin his rotation. As he biked past Freddy they would greet each other, and Pappi would continue for his 3-kilometer ride farther, stop next to a tree, lean and lock the bike, and continue walking. In this manner, they leap-frogged all the way to Meiningen, 15 kilometers away and had fun doing it.

Freddy had to stay in a *Schuelerheim*, a boy's dormitory that was part of the gymnasium system. He didn't like it. Too much heel-clicking "Heil Hitler" stuff. Also, much too rigidly organized for him. Freddy always had a problem with organization unless he was the chief organizer. On Friday evenings, Pappi would meet Freddy outside of his school. Pushing their lone bicycle, they would walk to the edge of the city and begin leap-frogging their way back home.

One day in October, a horrible day I'll never forget, the war came home in a striking and tragic way. We were sitting in the kitchen in the late afternoon, my mother upstairs, Opa not yet in from the fields. Oma was at her spinning wheel, my little cousin, Gudrun, on the floor beside her, reaching into a linen bag and handing her clumps of freshly shorn wool. I was at the kitchen table with a bowlful of threshed lentils, picking out the chaff, cup by cup. Tante Lene was knitting and had just gotten up to stoke the fire in preparation for warming the food for our evening meal.

There was a knock at the door, to which Oma responded, "*Herein!*" ("Come in!") The door opened, and two imposing German officers entered, one with a briefcase. They looked solemn. "Are we correctly here at Family Wiegand?" We nodded. "Is Frau Willi Buechner here?" That was my aunt's married name. Gathering her little girl to her, she listened as one of the officers delivered his tragic message: her husband "*Oberleutnant Willi Buechner*" had been killed in action in Hungary.

"*Mein Willi, mein Willi ist tot,*" my aunt cried. "*Mama, ich sehe meinen Willi nie wieder,*" she cried out again, as she collapsed into my grandmother's arms. ("My Willi, my Willi is dead"—"Mama, I'll never see my Willi again.") My little cousin, not understanding, believed her mother was hurt. "*Was ist los, Mama?*" she asked. ("What's the matter?") She, too, was crying, frightened and pulling at her mother's skirt.

I stood immobilized, horrified. The officers tried to continue talking to Oma, wanting to know where my grandfather was. As they spoke, my grandfather pulled up with his team, and seeing the official military vehicle on the street, hurried inside. He knew the importance of the parked car in front. Was one of his sons gone?

The news was again given, and he, too, dissolved in grief over the loss of his son-in-law. It brought back all the sorrow he had experienced, when

Erwin, his third oldest son, had fallen early in the war. Now Willi Buechner, a young man he loved as much as his own sons had given his life for the Vaterland. Career military, Willi was a patriot and a soldier through and through, everything my Opa admired and would have wanted for himself.

My mother had been upstairs and now arrived in the kitchen, disturbed by the loud crying. She was shattered when she heard the news and put her arms around her inconsolable sister-in-law. All stood around stunned, looking at the small package of Oberleutnant Willi Buechner's effects, the *Ritter Kreuz* on top. Germany's highest military award was the Order of the Iron Cross, which came in eight different classes, from the Knight's Cross to the Iron Cross. *Ritter Kreuz* was the sixth highest. Only about 7,500 were awarded.

The memorial service held the following week was one of a chain of these sad events in the village. Every house had been affected by this time. My aunt put on mourning black and wore a black veil on her hat, and we all observed a long mourning, joining others in the village whose sons, brothers, and fathers had fallen. Soon personal mourning evolved into grieving for an entire people, a futile cause, bitterly destroyed dreams, betrayal, privation, and anguish.

Only the names of all those who fell remain in the villages of Germany to attest to that terrible time, engraved on war memorials, along with the war in which they sacrificed their lives.

My aunt asked that Oberleutenant Willi Buechner be honored by having his name engraved on Bettenhausen's war memorial, even though it was not his birthplace. The request was granted, and his memory stayed alive for many years. As fate would have it, his own village of Schmerbach was razed when occupational zones were drawn after the war and the Russians created a 1/2 kilometer wide no-man's-land/death strip that became the border between East and West Germany. Anything that lay in its path was destroyed, including Schmerbach.

Many years later, after the Berlin Wall came down and East and West Germany were reunified, I returned to Bettenhausen. My cousins drove me to where Schmerbach used to be. There are now just open fields. All we could heard were birds, insects, and the breeze gently rustling the grasses that had grown up around the foundations where houses and barns used to be. Lives were lived here, children raised, animals and fields tended. The land and the families that once lived here were at rest and finally at peace.

The atmosphere in the house after Willi's death was one of overwhelming sadness. I overheard my mother tell Pappi she didn't think Tante Lene would ever get over her loss. Willi was her *Grosse Liebe* (the love of her life). It had been established that the farm would be passed on to them when the war was over, after he had returned to Bettenhausen. In exchange, Oma and Opa would be given the right to live out their lives there, which included care-giving responsibilities by the young couple, should my grandparents become ill or infirm before their passing. All of these plans had now been shaken.

Several weeks later, our family of four received authorization to move to Meiningen. The Housing Bureau assigned us a third-floor apartment in a typical German blockhouse apartment building on the edge of town in a section called am Weidig. It was a lovely, spacious apartment, featuring a large central foyer with WC, an eat-in kitchen, living room, three bedrooms, and a huge bath. The ceilings were high and the windows oversized, all of which made the apartment light and airy. It was also completely furnished.

My father was not exactly treated like a VIP, but when possible, we were given some special privileges because he chose to return to the Vaterland during the height of the war. The privileges included this beautiful apartment. Additionally, his language skills placed him in key positions, and he needed to live close to his duty stations.

Our apartment was located in a quiet suburban neighborhood on the banks of the Werra, the river that ran through the city. The building was on the edge of the flood plain and gave us lots of green space to play in. Freddy became popular with the neighborhood boys, teaching them how to play baseball. They in turn taught us how to walk on stilts, which was especially fun and challenging when the Werra overran its banks and we stilt-walked through one-half meter of water.

For a brief period, life became normal. My mother was happy; she was not a farm girl at heart; city life was her milieu. Freddy did not have to live in the boys' dormitory anymore and came home from school every afternoon. I transferred to the public school in Meiningen and started ballet again, as well as piano lessons. My father welcomed not having to commute thirty kilometers per day on a bicycle. He was home every night, although his hours were irregular, depending on whether or not there was unrest in the POW camp. It was Pappi's daily contact with the Allied prisoners as well as the constant overflights, air raid sirens, and mad dashes to the bunkers that were daily reminders we were in a war. The news that entire German cities were being blanket-bombed, flattened by fire-bomb attacks with civilian casualties running into the tens of thousands, devastated and broke down the resolve of the German people.

Still, catastrophe did not always seem near us. Our town was a cultural one with a renowned opera house, concert halls, and beautiful parks. During peacetime it was famous as a *Kurort*, a city that offered many health spas with healing waters, first-class hotel accommodations, and restaurants. Here is where people came to get rejuvenated in body, mind, and spirit. There were also sanatoriums for the chronically ill.

It was for all of these reasons that Meiningen was easily converted to a *Lazarettstadt* during the war; a "hospital, rest and recovery" city, for German war wounded, as well as for enemy soldiers. POW camps were in the same location. These were all facts known to the Allies. Meiningen was designated a safe city and although we were blacked out at night, there were huge red crosses painted on the roofs of the hospitals, sanatoriums, and other large buildings, indicating we were not to be bombed.

The enemy was moving across the land that winter of '44. The Western Front was especially threatening with all its firepower. The battles were fierce, and the Allies were closing in from all sides. We had not been bombed yet, but felt we would ultimately not escape the threat. We were all aware that before we could be liberated we'd have to be either conquered or overrun. No one knew how much or what kind of resistance Meiningen would put up. I always clung to the hope that the people would get out the white sheets and flutter them from their windows the day the Yanks showed up at our doorstep in their tanks. It was also our fervent hope that the Americans or the British would reach us before the Russian Army. The Russian soldiers were notoriously vicious fighters and had many scores to settle with the Germans. They did terrible things to women and children.

At eleven o'clock in the morning practically every day towards Christmas of '44 one lone airplane circled over Meiningen. You could almost set your clock by its regularity. The air raid sirens would go off, frightening everyone and making us run to the bomb shelters. We couldn't understand what was going on. Was this overflight to unnerve us, or was the aircraft on reconnaissance missions? Perhaps both. We got so accustomed to this daily flight that many citizens didn't bother to make a dash for the shelters anymore.

Then one day it happened. It was shortly after Christmas because I remember our tree was still up in the living room. The time was late morning, our usual nervous time. We heard a strange whistling followed by massive explosions. The earth trembled, and the whole house shook as we flew down three flights of steps to the cellar.

We huddled together with the rest of the residents. In spite of extra beams that shored up the cellar, dirt and debris were falling from the ceiling.

"How close are they? The bombs?" I cried. Some evacuees who were now residents in our building had already experienced bombings replied, "Close, very close. Let's be thankful this is not a blanket-bombing, or we could all be *verschuettet,* buried alive under a collapsed building." It was everyone's nightmare.

"Where is Pappi? Where is Freddy?" I asked my mother in an anguished voice. She shook her head. She did not know.

Finally, the all clear sounded, a long uninterrupted blast of the siren, and we emerged from our cellar like animals after hibernation. Not knowing what to expect, we looked around in the strange quiet and saw a haze hanging over the river near our house. As we approached, we discovered our floodplain pockmarked with craters on each side of the footbridge that crossed the river Werra in our neighborhood. Our eleven o'clock airplane visitor had dropped his load but missed his target, if in fact his intent was to blow up the bridge.

As the weeks went by, concerns for our safety became paramount. My parents huddled together and spoke in solemn tones. My father told us about a brewery at the edge of town near the main bridge, which handled all the traffic coming from the west and the north. The brewery had a tunnel dug deep into the side of a mountain meant to lager beer, but now it had been designated a bomb shelter. Fortunately for us, this was at our end of town; it was the safest bunker in Meiningen. The only problem was its limited capacity. Pappi made us promise to make a run for it whenever air raid sirens sounded.

The morning of February 23, 1945, began as most every other morning. It was Friday. Pappi went to work at the POW camp; Freddy went to school. I had dress rehearsals for the ballet that afternoon in readiness for opening night performances at the Meiningen Opera House and was excused from school. It was still early, not even mid-morning, when the sirens sounded. Down three flights of steps we sprang, and grabbing my hand, Mommi led me to the brewery.

Hundreds of people headed in the same direction, carrying the young and pulling the ailing and elderly along, trying not to stumble for fear of getting trampled in the rush for safety. The droning noise of approaching bombers grew ever nearer. They sounded ominous, not at all like the lone airplane we had heard often before. And then all hell broke loose. The bombs began to fall. Whistling preceded the hits, followed by the bombs exploding. We didn't have to wonder how close they were, we were in the midst of an air raid. The entrance of the tunnel was in view, but we were not quite there. When we finally made it, people screamed as they pushed their way through the doors. Some were already hurt; others were trampled and didn't have a chance.

I don't know how my mother made it. I only remember being dragged inside and pulled deep into the tunnel, crying for Pappi and Freddy. Men were forcing the doors shut, pushing, pulling, kicking people out of the way to close the doors on the inferno raging outside. Voices screaming, pleading: *"Aufmachen, bitte, bitte aufmachen!"* ("Open, please, please open!")

Then, silence. The earth, trembling under foot, muffled prayers and children's crying in semi-darkness. The one light bulb in the tunnel fluttered before it went out. There were only a few shafts of daylight coming through air vents.

It seemed like an eternity before the all-clear sounded. Cautiously some men opened the doors. Before we could emerge, they had to pull bodies aside. Casualties, people who didn't make it into the shelter in time. Bodies lay sprawled all around, and I remember hearing groaning in the unsettling quiet. The smell was overpowering—putrid, sulfuric. Incendiary bombs had exploded, delivering their earth-scorching aftermath.

An ugly yellow haze hung over everything; our world had been altered to look like a moonscape. At a nearby tree a German soldier had attempted to shield a woman; they were burnt into a grotesque statue, standing upright, fused to each other at the trunk of the tree. The image remains scorched in my memory. Like a severe burn injury, it has healed over, but the scar will be with me forever.

"Come," Mommi said, "don't look around," and she took me by the hand and hurried me along.

As we picked our way through the rubble and debris on our street I asked, "Do you think Freddy was sheltered at school? Do you suppose they bombed the POW camp where Pappi was?" We both wondered if our apartment building would still be standing.

It was, and eventually Freddy came home. But where was Pappi? We waited as the afternoon wore on into evening. Finally he came home, worn out and tense. There had been a riot inside the camp. The two sides of the Allied prisoners of war had accused each other of staging the air raid. Had their respective commanders ignored the fact that Meiningen was off limits? A declared safe zone, not to be bombed? With tensions running high over other issues anyway, the English and American prisoners had surged at each other. They had to be separated, and eventually the RAF officers were moved to another location.

Freddy had been at school and along with the other students had scarcely had time to make it to the bunkers on the school grounds. After the all-clear sounded, they were dismissed, and Freddy started to make his way home. As he tried to go his usual route, he saw scenes of death and carnage that shocked and sickened him. Many of the traffic bridges over the Werra had been bombed, including the one we used to get into the city from our end of town, the same bridge next to the brewery that sheltered us in the tunnel. Taking the footbridge by our apartment house, coming from the other side of the river, Freddy passed warehouses that had been partially destroyed. Hungry people rushed inside to grab sacks of flour, sugar, oats, and tubs of lard, then ran from the scene as fast as they could, giving no regard to a group of bodies, buried under rubble. He said he saw a young mother, dead, reaching out for her baby, also dead, who lay half buried in a pile of debris with its skull crushed. Terrified, he raced home.

We were hungry, too. Food deliveries had been disrupted ever since that first bombing. Freddy, resourceful as always, took it upon himself to run back to the warehouse and try to get some sacks of flour and sugar for us as well. He knew the lady in the apartment below had a handcart, and he asked to borrow it. She said yes, but the building superintendent had to get it out of the cellar where it was locked up. When he accomplished all of this, Freddy returned to the warehouse, pulling the cart, and loaded as many sacks and tubs as it would hold. When he got back, he divided his booty three ways. One third went to the lady with the handcart, one third to the superintendent, who bellied his way into the deal, one third to us.

Shortly, the housing authoritiy advised us that we had to take in a bombed-out family. Frau Ruth Segelke, widow of a high-ranking German officer, and her two teenaged children came to be with us. They had lived in a beautiful villa in an up-scale neighborhood in Meiningen. Having lost almost everything in the bombing, their house was uninhabitable, and most of their possessions either destroyed or plundered by street gangs.

A representative from the authorities brought the three in, assigning them one of our bedrooms and explained their kitchen and bathroom privileges to us. Fortunately, Frau Segelke was an educated, cultured woman with whom my mother could connect. The young people were polite and friendly, soon fascinated with Freddy's and my command of English, not a customary talent at that time in that part of Germany.

Friends and neighbors told horror stories of uncongenial evacuees, arbitrarily assigned to live with families, pushing them around their own kitchens and bathrooms, making all sorts of unreasonable demands or simply taking over. People who were already suffering some loss were being thrown in contact with those from other fronts who had been through many more tragic experiences. Often they berated their host families: "You haven't been through enough yet!" The homeowners' lives were forcefully disrupted by strangers who lived intimately in their midst.

Lots of arguing and hateful behavior became the norm; society was becoming dysfunctional. People change when faced with life-threatening situations, and their daily existence becomes a matter of survival. Thankfully, we were spared this. Our two families became friends.

Frau Segelke was a collector of fine arts and an artist herself. My mother's passion was original oil paintings. One day she gave my mother one of her oil paintings, a vase filled with yellow and white daffodils, so lifelike you could almost reach out and touch them. It had to be one of her prized possessions, one of the few things she salvaged from her villa. My mother loved and appreciated this painting her entire life. It now hangs in my dining room and reminds me of those terrifying, yet unbelievably adventurous, days of my childhood in Meiningen.

The continual air raids became the only thing we could focus on, day after day, hour after hour. Freddy and I continued to go to school, but many times I begged Mommi to stay home, and she let me. What truant officer was going to come and get me, or admonish my parents? In spite of Hitler's rallying speeches, the entire system was breaking down anyway. Soon there was no more school.

The only enjoyable times we had were when friends or relatives came for an afternoon visit. My mother would brew some "moogge-fook." That's what we called our ersatz coffee in jest. It was brewed of ground, roasted barley, steeped in boiling water. Not too palatable, but it was the *Gastfreundschaft* and *Gemuetlichkeit* that mattered (hospitality and geniality). My uncle Erich came often, struggling up three flights of stairs with two canes. Though he had been heavily wounded in France, he was thankful to have his legs. A sweet and gentle man, one of my father's younger brothers, he always managed to bring me a treat, usually an apple or a jar of home canned plums from the tree in his garden. I liked him a lot.

Another frequent visitor was Willi Dreissigacker, my father's comrade from the carefree days of his youth when they cruised around the world together in search of adventure. He never settled in America as Pappi did, returning instead to his childhood sweetheart in Herpf, a village midway between Meiningen and Bettenhausen. They were first cousins, but got married anyway. Despite warnings from relatives not to have children, they went ahead and had three, a boy and two girls. Tragically, all of them were born with severe birth defects, suffering from dwarfism. I often caught him looking at Freddy and me and thought I saw sadness in his eyes.

Many evenings we could hear the muted roar of dull explosions to the south and to the west. We would go out on our roof and see the horizon.

People in our building who were familiar with geography would say, "Look, Schweinfurt is getting it again." Schweinfurt was a town well known for its ball bearing factories, built far underground. The Allies bombed it repeatedly, but were never successful in completely shutting down production.

At the same time, the streets of Meiningen began to be dangerous because bombs might fall at any time and *Auslaender* (outlanders/foreigners) formed into gangs and broke into businesses, robbing homes, mugging citizens, and generally causing civil unrest. The citizenry was advised not to resist if they were mugged—or risk losing their lives. The elderly were especially warned of the hazards. These gangs who were wreaking so much havoc were the forced laborers Hitler had captured during his conquests of Slavic countries and sent to Germany to work in agriculture and in factories.

With the Allies and the Russian fronts advancing and liberating them, the *Auslaender* roamed the countryside, towns, and villages, staying alive by plundering, pillaging, and stealing everything they could get their hands on. Their hearts were so filled with rage and revenge for the German people that it left them with little regard for human life. Often bodies were found among the ruins, thrown in the weeds along a fence or in a ditch alongside a roadway. Some had gunshot wounds; others had been bludgeoned or stabbed to death. No one knew who the victims were, where they came from, or who had committed the crime.

My father's job working for the authorities as interpreter in the POW camp involved civil defense policing of these gangs. He often confronted them by breaking up riots and interfering with their assaults. Gang members began to recognize and hate him. Death threats on his life were becoming commonplace and always stated the same: *"Wenn Russki kommt— Du Erster!"* (When Russians come, YOU - FIRST!) They would point their fingers at him when they shouted these words, then follow up with a throat-slitting hand motion.

When I overheard my father relating this to my mother the first time, I was petrified. I didn't want Pappi to leave the house again. I was so afraid he would get murdered I could hardly sleep alone. Many a night I asked my parents if I could come to bed with them, and they let me.

It was now March, 1945, and we were running out of food. One morning my mother and I and our neighbor, Frau Schott, and her young son started to walk the 15 kilometers to Bettenhausen to get food from my grandparents' farm. We needed bread, potatoes, eggs, and butter. The Western Front was within 200 kilometers of Meiningen, but we were pretty sure we could make it out and back before nightfall. We soon found otherwise.

We had hardly gotten out of town, with forest all around us, when low-flying enemy fighter planes began strafing the woods. The little Schott boy wore a bright red stocking cap, easily seen from above. We scuttled into the drainage ditch on one side of the road, with bullets zinging over our heads. The planes turned around and headed back in our direction. Frau Schott yanked the red stocking cap off her son's head, and we ran across the road and dove into the ditch on the opposite side. We did this about four times, criss-crossing and diving into ditches to avoid the strafings. I do not believe the planes were shooting at us though it seemed that way. We discovered the forests around town were full of retreating German units and the intense strafings were meant for them. We didn't have a chance to get through.

Returning to our apartment, my mother searched the kitchen and found the end of a loaf of bread. She discovered a couple of ration coupons for milk and took them to the store to get a liter of skim milk—all they had left. Frau Schott had a few pieces of smoked wurst and several apples. So we managed to put together a communal meal.

When Pappi came home after work, he realized this couldn't go on. "I know the back roads to Bettenhausen. Emil and I will go tonight under cover of darkness and get whatever food Oma and Opa can spare." Emil Schott was the other husband and father and was a childhood friend of Pappi's since Emil's parents were also farmers in Bettenhausen. As fate would have it, after so many years and a lifetime apart, we were now neighbors in Meiningen.

During this episode, Freddy had to stay home with a serious middle-ear infection. There was no doctor available, and we had no medication. My mother wrapped him in a warm, wet sheet like a mummy to break his fever. We spent a sleepless night, sponging Freddy's forehead hoping for Pappi's safe return. By daybreak, Freddy was soaking in sweat. His fever had broken, and he was beginning to chill. My mother gave him a sponge bath, quickly dressed him in dry pajamas, and put him back in a dry and warm bed. He fell into a deep, healing sleep.

Finally we heard Pappi coming up the steps. My prayers were answered; he was home. We had breakfast together, eating modest portions of the wonderful food Oma sent. After a short nap, Pappi went to work. Freddy slept most of the day. He woke up much improved and rejoined the dangerous world that made up our existence.

My father came home from work earlier than usual that evening. He looked beaten and defeated. "Did you have a bad day on the streets? Were the gangs of outlanders plundering and delivering death threats again?" my mother wanted to know.

"It was a day about as unruly as always," he said, "but there is something else on my mind, something so much worse. We'll talk about it later tonight."

We ate, and Freddy and I were sent to our room early. Night fell, and my mother and father sat down at the kitchen table with only candlelight flickering between them. Pappi spoke, "Remember last night when Emil Schott and I walked to Bettenhausen to get some food for all of us? It gave us the opportunity to talk for many hours, and he took me into his confidence. He told me things I could not have imagined in my most horrific dreams. *Ich bin seelisch ganz kaputt.* (I am emotionally shattered)."

Pappi and Emil could trust each other, a rarity in these days when conversations with those you thought you could trust would be reported to the German authorities, especially if you said anything negative about Hitler, the war, or the Third Reich. Talking to the wrong people, sometimes even including your friends or relatives, meant risking the Gestapo's showing up at your door in the middle of the night. You would be picked up and put away, never to be seen or heard from again.

Freddy and I were not in bed. Our little bedroom was off the kitchen, accessed from a narrow door we could barely slip through. During more peaceful times when families had household help, our bedroom with its immediate access to the kitchen was probably designed for live-in servants.

Pappi was speaking in hushed tones. At times we couldn't hear him, so we crept to the door and listened, lost in the darkness of the corner. He told of his friend Emil Schott and related to Mommi the conversation they had had, as they made their way to Brettenhausen. Emil had been a member of the *Wehrmacht*, who was taken off combat duty and assigned to duty at a concentration camp. He told my father all about what was really going on in the "KZ" (the concentration camps). He told of Hitler's Final Solution for the Jews.

No word had come to anyone in our family about this up to this time. Others in the city may have known; I cannot say. I only know this was the first time these unspeakable atrocities were even hinted at by anyone we knew. In subdued, anguished tones Schott spoke of the herding of lines of Jewish men, women, and children, of their being forcefully separated, the subterfuge of the showers, the gassings. "We can't keep up with the cremations," he said. "We have to throw them into mass graves." He had drawn a complete verbal picture of what the Allies were to find.

Pappi's voice broke as he told my mother about the concentration camps. He sobbed uncontrollably, his head on the table. I was crying, too, and wanted to run to him. Freddy held me back and muffled my sounds by putting his arms around me. I think it was at that moment my father's entire world came crashing down. He saw that a whole line of decisions he had made through the last five years—decisions he had thought were good ones, with loyalty to a Germany he had known and loved—had come to this. Everything he had brought his family back to, all we had gone through for the Vaterland collapsed into hideousness.

My father, a deep humanitarian and lover of all that had been good in German tradition, culture, and history was a broken man, but my mother showed incredible strength. Although sobbing with him, we heard her say, "Otto, here's where we have landed. We are here now, and we will survive."

Freddy and I crept back to our beds, feeling our way in the darkness of our blacked-out room. I had never seen my Pappi so hopeless, so lost. I was frozen in fear, such as I had never experienced before, and crawled in bed with my brother.

In spite of the sky falling on us, we kept functioning although classes no longer met at school. I kept going to ballet lessons, but soon gave that up, too. Our bridge into the city was still out, and the footbridge in our neighborhood took me so far out of the way, I was always afraid I wouldn't make it home safely. The footbridge detour took me through the industrial area where the gangs were hanging out. Pappi's death threats now included going after family members. Consequently, Freddy and I stuck close to home—by Pappi's orders.

Frantic runs to the air raid shelters were still common, even though the actual bombings had ceased. Still, wave after wave of B-29 bombers in perfect formation flew over, heading towards German cities to the East. The strafings by low-flying fighter planes were becoming more intense as German fighting units were retreating under cover of the thick growth of the forest. The front was coming closer. Often we could hear explosions and artillery fire.

Food became increasingly scarce. Everyone resorted to *Hamstern*, an expression we used meaning to go on food-hoarding missions. Mommi and I would walk to close farmhouses and trade stuff for food. My mother had an abundant supply of sheets and table linens, all new. A set of sheets would bring a large round of black bread. Add a tablecloth, and we'd get butter and a few eggs.

Refugees were adept at hoarding. Many were homeless, living in make-shift quarters dug out of ruins, owning nothing but the clothes on their backs, but for one thing: many had salvaged their jewelry. They traded family heirlooms for a measly gunny-sack of food. My brother had his own solution. Disregarding my father's order to stay close to home, he took off anyway, not to come home until after dark with vegetables stolen from other people's gardens and tiny new potatoes he had dug from farmers' fields. The thing that upset Opa so much when it happened to him, Freddy was doing to others. But we could no longer risk going to Bettenhausen for food. Retreating German soldiers appeared all around us, putting up pockets of resistance. We were hungry and a potato was gold. It meant we could eat for another day.

Some time around April 11, 1945, the Yanks were rumored to have arrived from the south and southwest and were surrounding us. Everyone was terribly apprehensive. Were we going to take much artillery fire? Would the gangs not only plunder, but also take advantage of their freedom under the Allies and turn on German civilians in one last act of revenge? We could only hope for a bloodless surrender of Meiningen.

Fortunately, the bombed bridge, which caused such disruption in accessing the city from our end, turned out to be our salvation when the tanks advanced. We were spared the firefight that ensued upon entering the city. It was brief, and although some buildings were destroyed, there was no significant loss of life. The town was not particularly hostile; large hospitals filled with German soldiers and the Allied POW camp, complete with its own hospital, were good reasons for the Germans to seek a peaceful surrender.

Soon white sheets began tumbling out of the windows and fluttered in the breeze. Cheering for the jeeps and troops walking down the streets, the citizenry came out of their houses and walked alongside them with outstretched arms and handshakes. Children squealed with delight as they caught Hershey bars and packs of Juicy Fruit gum the GI's tossed out. Gum-chewing American soldiers, so young they looked like kids themselves, were our conquerors. This was the enemy? The average German could not believe the friendliness of these crew-cut American boys riding on top of their huge tanks, laughing and smiling through their dirt-smudged faces. The dirt made their smiles seem much broader and much brighter.

But some stood and looked solemnly at the parade going by. They were women the war had turned into widows, or, perhaps had experienced the worst atrocities of a war while fleeing from the Russian front, possibly seeing members of their family tortured and killed, or their children lost as they themselves were raped and otherwise violated. Elderly men with hats off stood in silence with canes supporting them, in tribute to the victors. Old honorable warriors, perhaps having fought for the Kaiser, they could have been grandfathers to these young soldiers. I saw a GI jump down from his tank and shake an old veteran's hand, as he handed him several four-packs of cigarettes. I was only ten years old, but these moments shaped my values.

Our family didn't dare tell anyone what to expect from the Americans when they would finally arrive, or what they would be like. "Given a fight, they will be killers. Given a handshake, they will be your friends." We simply had to hold our tongues or risk having such statements taken out of context and ourselves winding up on the wrong side of a barbed wire fence in the nearest concentration camp. That is not what we returned to Germany for, but that is how paranoid and fanatic the system had become.

After we left Lisbon we landed to a grand welcoming and glowing German promises in Biarritz. I believe the hotel we stayed in is rising from the center of the photo.

This is the reality we experienced in the Germany we returned to.

The *Dorfschule* (Elementary School) in Bettenhausen.

My Tante Lisbeth and cousins Marlene and Ulla, who lived with us under Oma and Opa's roof.

Onkel Erwin, who was the first in my father's family to lose his life for the Vaterland. Onkel Erich, out of uniform and Onkel Karl, Tante Lisbeth's husband.

Onkel Erich, seriously wounded
on the Western Front.

Oberleutnant Willi Buechner, the
handsomest soldier I had ever seen.

Oberleutnant Willi Buechner with his wife and family. The saddest day in the lives of the Wiegand family was when he fell in the war.

Marianne came to visit us from Werdau during the war.

Entrance to the city of Meiningen.

Our apartment house in Meiningen.

The floodplain where we played with footbridge we used when the main bridge was bombed out.

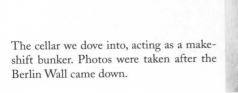

The cellar we dove into, acting as a make-shift bunker. Photos were taken after the Berlin Wall came down.

Frau Ruth Segelke, the lady assigned to live with us in the confused days as the German Reich was dying.

The painting Frau Segelka gave my mother as a thank-you. It became a life-long treasure.

My father did not leave the POW camp during the march-in of the American troops. He was keeping a lid on both the Allied prisoners and German staff, who were in the process of organizing a peaceful transfer of the soon-to-be released prisoners.

The first necessity for the Americans was to establish a command post. My father's position as translator and liaison in the camp put him in a key position to facilitate the orderly transition from the German city government to Allied military occupation, as well as the safe evacuation of prisoners. The American Military Commandant of Meiningen immediately retained my father's services. Pappi became his personal aide, civilian status, and was assigned a Jeep and a driver. This was a huge stroke of luck, inasmuch as it provided safe transportation around the city for my father, as well as to his duty station and home.

On the second or third day of occupation, my father overheard a conversation in Command Headquarters that the US Forces were encountering many pockets of resistance on their drive to the North and the East towards the river Elbe, where they were to rendezvous with the Russians. He heard "Bettenhausen" mentioned. Some retreating German soldiers were allegedly holed up in farmhouses in the village.

The Americans generally left villages and towns alone if they had no issues in surrendering, respecting the sheets hung from the windows. But if a town harbored dissidents and was sullen, resentful, or outright defiant, they could make it very hard on that town. Army tanks now sat in front of Bettenhausen, ready to lob artillery shells into suspected farm safe houses or blast their way through the entire village if they had to.

My father told the Military Command that Bettenhausen was his home village, that his parents and extended family were living there, and that he knew just about everyone else in the village. He asked permission to go to Bettenhausen to smooth the way. He was given the go-ahead and driven to the entrance of the village, accompanied by four American soldiers, two of them officers, two of them sergeants. Pappi got out of the vehicle and walked to the *Gemeinde* (the village town hall), located in the lower end, close to where Pappi had been dropped off.

The Buergermeister and several other officials immediately recognized him, and after a brief explanation of his mission, they asked to meet with the four accompanying military. The officials knew exactly which houses harbored the German troops and arranged for the farmers to bring them to the center of the village, the *Brunnenplatz*, for surrender. This was the town square that had the common fresh water well, from which the villagers would fetch water in the olden days. The German soldiers, most of them wounded, were then led away, their weapons and ammunition confiscated.

It was at this point that one door after another slowly opened, and the villagers came walking, then running to the *Brunnenplatz* to thank my father and shake hands with the Americans. As my cousin Gudrun related the details of this to me over fifty years later, she added one more note. One of the officers was a black American. His presence fascinated everyone. He was especially kind and playful with the children, holding hands with them in a circle. They loved him and made him promise to come back. I don't know if he ever did. My father to this day remains the hero of Bettenhausen.

The gangs of forced laborers still roved in Meiningen, breaking into and entering homes and businesses, plundering and mugging. I suppose with the deactivation of the German civil authorities these people thought they could now have free reign. Maintaining order became a major problem for the Allied occupation, not only in Meiningen, but all over occupied Germany. My father told the commandant about his personal experiences with these gangs and the ongoing death threats. Pappi was given a handgun to protect himself, complete with written authorization by the commandant to carry it. He continued to go on runs to intervene and break up civil disobedience; now he was accompanied by the uniformed MP's (military police). These incidents exposed him to the gangs to whom he had become such a familiar face, their most hated man in Meiningen. The death threats continued: "Watch your back. We'll be catching up with you— SOON!"

The new commandant asked my father to stay on indefinitely. Pappi was not only his interpreter, he also became his respected friend. How could he switch his loyalty so suddenly? His loyalty all along had been to the cause of aiding communication, to making the wheels run smoothly between two groups of people who had everything to gain by understanding each other. That was the job he was continuing to do. Another flag was flying, but the communications issues remained the same.

My father was busy each day after the Yanks arrived, getting groups of POW's escorted safely out of town, arranging transports to a staging area in the West, from which they would be flown back to their homelands. When Pappi came home in the evening, he often brought chocolate, chewing gum, coffee, tea, and real sugar. Most of us were still in survival mode; all of these goods represented normalcy. One time Pappi came home with a load of laundry, a pillowcase full of the kind of shirts officers wore with their dress uniforms, to be washed, starched, and ironed. The commandant asked him if he could find a laundry in town that was running. The laundry lady turned out to be my mother, and she was only too happy to do the favor. In return, she was sent all kinds of canned food products, Nescafé, tea, cocoa, K-rations, C-rations, and many cans of SPAM. We were not only eating again, we were dining.

The Germans adored the Americans, finding them open, generous, and happy fellows to be around. We befriended many, and soon the Yanks were coming to our home. I don't recall any officers dropping in, but non-commissioned officers, regular GI's, and my father's driver visited often. The soldiers loved fresh eggs, so my brother would ride along in their Jeeps, visiting farmers in rural areas to barter cigarettes for farm-fresh eggs. American cigarettes would get you anything.

Freddy was fourteen years old, as street smart as they come, and adept at translating. He befriended a communications officer, Captain Russell H. Gunnell, who asked Freddy if he could accompany him as his personal interpreter on his assignment, which was planting new telephone lines to re-establish the communications system in places where the trunk lines had been disrupted or completely destroyed. Captain Gunnell had to communicate with the personnel in charge of the German telephone network, and, because he did not speak German, he had a real problem. Freddy was proud of his language skills and of his ability to earn money. He gave most of his earnings to Mommi.

My girlfriend Sigrid and I would go on Jeep rides, accompanying soldiers who had become family friends, to trade cigarettes and instant coffee for fresh butter and eggs. I got the biggest kick out of the farmers' reactions when they heard me, a little blond, very German looking ten-year-old girl, speaking fluent English with the soldiers, then turning around and communicating their wishes to the farmers, speaking fluent German. The GI's were sweet and delightful with us and returned us home loaded with American treats.

Among the soldiers who befriended our family was an older master sergeant, who had become well acquainted with my father because his duty assignment was in the command station where Pappi worked. He seemed to have a close personal relationship with the commandant, his commanding officer, who was my father's boss. He came by sometimes just to take us for rides in his Jeep, usually when he was on some kind of errand and wanted company. My mother thought it was appropriate that my girlfriend Sigrid, who did not speak English, should accompany us on our excursions. The sergeant was forty-eight years old, career military, from Kansas, and because of his age, all the soldiers called him "Pops." His real name was Harry, but we also called him Pops. He took us to his barracks once to show us where he lived. There were several German ladies there making beds and cleaning the rooms, one of them young and attractive. She and Pops greeted each other in a rather familiar manner. Up to this point my mother hadn't spoken a word to me about grown-ups, sex, or babies. I was a babe in the woods, which is why I never put two and two together. I had no idea this lady was Pops's mistress.

For two-and-a-half months we lived like this, soldiers befriending us, the war winding down, surrender coming on May 7, 1945, V-E Day. Our daily lives were becoming normal, had it just not been for the death threats voiced against Pappi by the forced laborers. Urgent efforts were underway. The Allied occupation moved to enforce the regulations UNRRA (United Nations Relief and Rehabilitation Administration) had stipulated, but getting the program up and running didn't happen overnight.

These people were first of all classified as "displaced persons" (DP's), given subsistence, health care, counseling, and living quarters, albeit in camps, where they awaited further processing. The idea was to get them repatriated to their homelands and reunited with their families if that was their choice or help them find work and be mainstreamed into the post-war economy of a very needy Europe. Many ended up immigrating to the States.

These ambitious plans sounded wonderful for them, and in time, they materialized. But that did not help our situation. My father still lived in daily danger of getting his throat slit or being hung high from the nearest tree by these angry, displaced men, who viewed him as an enemy. They still had a score to settle, a score fueled by the desire for revenge.

More change was in the air. There had been several Big Three conferences. One of them was held as early as February 1945, in Yalta, when the war was still hot. (Yalta Conference, February 11, 1945, attended by Churchill, Roosevelt, and Stalin). We were blissfully unaware that plans for the future of post-war Germany were being designed. The time was rapidly approaching to put the plans into action.

Half of Germany would be handed over to the Russians, the half we lived in. In the early morning hours of July 1, 1945, around 3:00 AM, my mother woke us up with a great deal of urgency. "Come now, come quickly. Here, I'll help you get dressed. Do not put on your shoes. Do not say a word or make any noise. We are leaving!"

She had Freddy and me each grab a packed suitcase, and in silence we tiptoed down the stairwell from our apartment, careful not to slip in our stocking feet. On our way down, we passed American soldiers, also in stocking feet, on their way up to our apartment to pick up our overseas trunks and carry them downstairs. We recognized them in spite of the dark—they were our soldier friends—and as we passed them, they put their fingers to their lips to warn us not to make any sounds of recognition.

When we got downstairs, we were quickly lifted into the rear of a six-ton Army truck. Pappi was already on board and grabbed us. Then Mommi was helped aboard. We were directed to the front, tucked up close to the cab, and ordered to sit down on ammunition crates. Freddy and I were bewildered, not really scared as much as filled with nervous excitement. As our eyes got accustomed to the dark, we saw the driver and next to him, Pops, the good friend of our family. He gave us a quick hello smile and turned back to a map on his lap that he and the driver pointed at. We were getting the hell out of town and Pops was orchestrating our flight. He had become more than a Good Samaritan; he was our savior.

Pappi quickly helped the other two soldiers load our trunks and stack ammunition boxes all around and on top for concealment. Pops yelled one last thing to one of them, something about a chain being securely wrapped underneath the truck, to which the response was "check!" They were then ordered aboard. They tied down the canvas top while our family huddled up front under a tarpaulin. Our two soldiers sat on the rear inside benches of the truck, not under cover, just as they would normally ride in a convoy, acting as escorts on a truck loaded with ammunition.

Our driver turned on the ignition, revved up the engine, and took off driving like a mad man, leaving a deserted Meiningen behind and continuing through a deserted countryside. We drove for about an hour, and it was still dark when we stopped in the village of Themar, and Pops got out to anxiously knock on the door of a house. Out came a lady and small child.

They were quickly helped aboard, along with their few suitcases, and joined our huddle up front. The lady introduced herself as Liesl Weinelt and her five-year-old daughter Hannelore. I immediately recognized her as the lady I saw cleaning the sleeping quarters in the barracks that housed Pops's unit in Meiningen, his mistress.

Our driver looked for a place to turn around in the narrow cobblestone streets when a Jeep with two MPs pulled up alongside and demanded to know, "What are you doing out here by yourself?"

Pops answered, "We had some mechanical trouble," pointing at the chain underneath the truck, "and got separated from our convoy."

"You're also going in the wrong direction!"

"Yes, I'm aware of that, but we're taking a back route, a short cut through the countryside to catch up with the convoy."

"Then go on, and don't waste any time!"

Breathing sighs of relief, we felt the truck lurch forward, and we were on our way again. Thankfully, the loud truck engines were never shut down because the little redheaded brat of Pops's mistress would not stop whining and complaining. Freddy and I wanted to throw a blanket over her head. She could have very easily exposed us all to detection.

Themar was located east of Meiningen and took us almost 60 kilometers out of our way. Although we were speeding through the darkness, this time in the correct south-south-west direction, the Eastern horizon was beginning to show dawning.

We ran into more Jeep patrols. They came up from behind, we were stopped again.

Pops whispered a warning, "Lay low! They can't know you are in here!"

This time the MPs were not as gracious as they had been before, but their message was a gift from God. The axle on our truck was working its way out, and we were about to lose a wheel. The MPs helped fix the axle, as we were hardly breathing under our camouflage tarp. Soon we were on our way. The military policemen provided an escort and kept an eye on our wheels until we reached our departing convoy. Soon we joined its winding line.

It was almost daylight when our convoy slowed to a crawl in the middle of a lot of commotion. Jeeps were stopping and starting, zipping back and forth. Voices shouted commands in English, others in an undistinguishable language. Freddy and I peeked through a tiny opening in the canvas cover. We saw strange military vehicles and military personnel in non-American uniforms. We were passing through some kind of checkpoint. Soon our convoy picked up the pace again. Pops peeked at us through the canvas, indicating an enormous sense of relief, wiping his brow, and mouthing an exaggerated, "Whew!" We had just passed through the newly established border between the American and Russian Zones. We had escaped Russian occupation.

When we got to Wuerzburg, we were in safe territory and left the convoy. Our driver continued through the countryside until Pops directed him to pull off the road so we could all stretch our legs and shake off some of the stress. Even I knew what a close call it had been.

Later we discovered the military knew what the citizens of Meiningen didn't—that on July 1 the city would become part of the Russian zone. Imagine going to bed on the night of June 30, at peace and thankful that the Yanks occupied your territory and waking up the next morning to your worst fears: you were now under Russian occupation.

Imagine having survived the war under a brutal dictatorship, experienced the liberation and precious months of peace, only to end up losing your freedom again, forced to live under an even more brutal system where the KGB replaced the Gestapo. Had the people known, there would have been a mass exodus. As it turned out, thousands escaped anyway, risking their lives to break through or tunnel under the mined and barbed wire borders.

Pops had considerable influence with the military commandant of Meiningen and had arranged *sub rosa* for us to be spirited out. The commandant was not unaware of my father's dilemma and that of his family, should we be left behind.

"I'll make a truck and driver available, but that's as far as I can go," the commandant had told Pops. "You will need some extra help that you will have to recruit yourself. Just remember, all of you are acting without authorization. In fact, you'll be doing something illegal. If you're caught, I know nothing, and all of you will be court-martialed."

Pops, at risk to his military career, had orchestrated our escape and pulled it off. The tree reserved for hanging my father would have to go without its intended victim. Gratitude and relief swept over us.

Pops invited me to come up front, and I gladly came, leaving the others behind. At first I sat between the two men in the noisy front seat of the truck, but then Pops said to me in a voice so loud, I could hear it over the engine and road noise, "Come sit on my lap so you can see better."

I crawled up, and he hugged me in a very spontaneous and fatherly manner, the way Pappi hugged me when something wonderful happened and we were full of joy. Then he began to stroke me in a comforting way, whispering into my ear so nobody else could hear and he patted me on the thigh.

"Aren't we all glad that we're safe? That was a close call back there. I was glad I could help your family. All of you mean a lot to me. You know that, don't you?"

I nodded. There was silence, and his whispering went on.

"You really love your father, don't you? You are your father's pet, his little kitten. You would do anything for him, wouldn't you?"

I nodded vigorously. Of course, I would!

"When we get alone, in a place where you and I can be together, I am going to make love to you."

I looked straight ahead, startled and confused. I was ten years old. What did "make love" mean? What was he saying to me? I had seen movies and recalled words of love spoken by adults, glamorous Hollywood ladies and handsome men kissing. Whatever he meant, I could not relate to the subject, and yet I was aware he was sending me some kind of a message.

It was now full daylight outside of the truck.

"Think of what might have happened," he went on whispering. He detailed frightening scenarios involving Pappi: being seized by mobs, beaten up, hung on the nearest tree branch, or found lying in a ditch with his throat slit. First he scared me, and then he assured me how safe we were and would remain if I would just do this one thing for him. I would really be doing it for Pappi, too, he said.

"Nobody will ever know. It will be our little secret. It has to be."

I grew very apprehensive. What did all of this mean and why was he making me feel beholden to him, using my love for my father to make it seem right? After all, Pops saved us from a fate worse than death, so it had to be all right? Didn't it?

We arrived in Kleinrinderfeld, a village southwest of Wuerzburg. Pops knew exactly where to go, up a little hill to a *Gasthaus* (Inn), which must have been used by the German military to care for retreating soldiers. A regular hospital was nearby. The *Gasthaus* stood eerily empty, but for hospital beds, cots, and mattresses all over the place.

Our driver took a well-deserved rest, while Pappi, Freddy, and the other two soldiers carried our trunks and suitcases inside. My mother and Pops's mistress with her whiny child worked to get us settled into several of the main-floor rooms. Pops found a pretext to have me come upstairs with him and "take a look at the banquet rooms." We found more abandoned hospital beds and cots.

He walked me to a far corner in one of the rooms, where he picked me up, laid me down crosswise on one of the high hospital beds and pulled my panties off. He spread my legs and stood at the edge of the mattress. I had no idea what was going on. Then I felt as if a truck had entered the lower part of my body. It hurt. I started to cry.

"It's all right," he whispered. "Just think of Pappi."

One of his arms was wrapped tightly around my lower body, holding it very close to him. I couldn't move. With his other hand he stroked my face, my hair, my mouth. His heavy breathing was like that of an animal, and all the time he was smiling at me.

When he was done I looked down and saw trickles of blood on the mattress. He held me as you would hold a child, comforting me with little kisses on my forehead. I was sobbing, in shock and sadness.

"Everything will be fine," he assured me. "We are all safe now." He stared into my eyes as he wiped the blood off of me and the mattress with his handkerchief. He pulled something out of his pocket, a little olive green tube that oozed white ointment when he snapped the end off. He squirted that salve inside me, then put some on himself.

"Remember, you'll never have to worry about your father again, and what just happened is our secret forever." He made it sound like a special bond between us.

After a while, he let me get up and took me by the hand, and we went bounding down the steps. He was smiling in a happy-go-lucky way as if nothing had happened. I felt as if in a trance, moving mechanically. In the last twelve hours I had grown up.

Pops bade us good-bye the next morning. He had to rejoin his unit rendezvousing in Coburg. We stood by the truck. He pressed a wad of bills in Pappi's hand.

"I'll be back in six weeks to take you further away to Bavaria to a more suitable location where you can make your new home. In the meantime, you will need some cash to see you through. I want you to take this, and I suggest you keep to yourselves. This stay in Kleinrinderfeld will only be temporary."

He came to hug me and looked deeply in my eyes as a last warning. I had spent a sleepless night, never before so scared or so alone. It took all the courage and self-control I had not to burst into tears. He said good-bye to Liesl Weinelt in an affectionate way, as if to reinforce that he was a GI with a girlfriend. Nothing to worry about, parents. And they smiled as he left, gratefully accepting everything he did, as, of course, they would have. They had no reason to suspect the outrage that had occurred the day before.

I was a girl who had to make an adult decision. My parents could never know of this. Not only had Pops warned me that this was our secret, not only had he saved us and had a power over us that only the conquering can have over the conquered who become friends, but I realized my parents could not stand the shock of what had just happened after all they had been through. I needed to live through this without them. I promised myself they would never know. I would never tell Freddy, either. I would put it away deep inside.

My private life was hellish during our stay in Kleinrinderfeld. Not only was I harboring a dark secret, but having physical trouble. I was a ten-year-old who had been raped by a promiscuous GI, a forty-eight-year-old man with a warped mind, and I seemed to have picked up an infection, ointment or not. I spotted blood for several days, which finally stopped, but a continuous discharge stayed. I led a secret life, washing myself and washing my panties, hoping my mother didn't catch me and ask questions.

While I found myself sadly confused about sex, my brother was discovering it at fourteen in a much different way. He was out and about in the village all the time, and my mother's intuition and watchful eyes made many observations. There was a beautiful blond nurse in her early twenties working in the hospital near our Gasthaus. Freddy used to sit on the windowsill for hours, trying to catch a glimpse of her. She became aware of him, and they connected. Freddy, a handsome, mature-looking fourteen-year-old, became totally infatuated with her. She, a willing participant, became interested in teaching him about the mysteries of sex and illicit love. They would rendezvous at every available opportunity, take walks in the meadows and on the edge of forests, with only one thing in mind.

My mother surmised what was going on and was infuriated. I recall a discussion I overheard between my parents. Pappi didn't seem as steamed up as my mother was. Rather, he had a more boys-will-be-boys attitude and told my mother that every young boy eventually has his first encounter; it is the course of life. But, "that woman" was over ten years older than Freddy! Pappi smiled and assured Mommi we would be leaving this place anyway. Regardless, my mother confronted Freddy and suggested he better get used to the idea as soon as Pops came back we'd be leaving. Freddy said: "I'm not going!"

"Well, we'll just see about that," my mother countered. How I wished my life were so open.

Six weeks to the day, as Pops promised, over an incline in the road through Kleinrinderfeld came a Jeep. "Pops!" my mother screamed with joy. He hit the brakes, surprised to have encountered us taking a walk. Everybody crowded around. It was a bittersweet time for me, but in a strange way I was happy to see him. It meant we would be leaving this place and going on to a new and permanent home. I put on a smiling face for my parents, part of the charade that all was well. But I could not forget what had happened that fateful day.

Pops's mistress, her child, and my family put our belongings into our suitcases and trunks and got back on the six-ton truck that showed up shortly after Pops arrived. The same driver was driving. Another GI who came along to help accompanied him.

We were on our way to Bavaria, not leaving *"bei Nacht und Nebel"* this time (a German expression, "by night and fog"), but in broad daylight for all the world to see. Pops invited us kids to take turns riding in the Jeep with him. Freddy went first. I was glad, but soon had to switch places, which I did so everything looked normal.

On the way Pops asked me if I was okay. I said, "yes" but I thought I might need some more ointment. He said he had some and would give it to me when we got to our new lodgings, at which time he wanted to make love to me again. I couldn't believe what he had said, but he was testing me.

"No," I said firmly. "It is not going to happen again, Pops, and if you try, I will tell my mother." He nodded. Driving on in silence, he stopped after a while to switch kids again. As he pulled over, he reminded me of our secret. He would have faced deep trouble himself for the rape. The other soldiers involved in helping us flee, including the commandant of Meiningen, could also be in trouble. He must have sensed that I would have died before telling anyone of the rape or who had orchestrated our flight. One incident was so knotted to the other, they became one in my own mind.

Six weeks had passed. Lots of time alone to think and sort things out. Not only had I grown up, I had also grown somewhat philosophical. Life had to be lived on its own terms. You had to deal with whatever came your way, sometimes all alone.

I put this incident into the same category as the war. Both were over. We were heading for a new, free life, and our family remained together. I was going to pack the memory of this incident so deep inside that it would eventually go away as though it had never happened. That's what I thought anyway. It worked for a long time.

Collateral damage on the other side of Meiningen from where we lived.

.A POW camp, during the Third Reich. After the Yanks arrived, it became a civilian camp. Third Army was General Patton's.

A very serious Freddy, 14, getting ready to work for the Yanks as a translator.

Yanks parading past the Opera House in Meiningen, April '45.

Above and Below. Pappi's POW camp under Hitler, turned civilian internment camp after the Yanks arrived. Standing next to Pappi is his driver.

Yanks on parade. Germans watching. Meiningen, April/May, 1945.

Pops and I in Meiningen before the flight.

I sit in Pops' Jeep, waiting for the "innocent rides" he took me on.

Kleinrinderfeld after we fled: Freddy and the "older woman" who taught him some things about life.

Pappi's driver.

It was a long hot ride from Kleinrinderfeld to our destination in Bavaria. Our first stop was Nandlstadt, a small town about 55 kilometers north of Munich, where Pops's unit had been temporary-billeted in confiscated housing. He had already scouted Nandlstadt for living quarters, but was unsuccessful in finding anything large enough to accommodate us. So on we rode, scouring village after village for an empty inn. We found one in the village of Attenkirchen. Gasthaus Kettner was a large white building with a *Bierstube* (taproom/restaurant), hotel-size commercial kitchen, butcher shop, upstairs banquet rooms guest rooms and a huge ballroom—all standing empty.

Our family occupied two of the upstairs guestrooms; Liesl Weinelt and her daughter took a third. Pops told us to settle in. This was as permanent as we wanted it to be. For the second time he gave Pappi some money, and they shook hands. We thanked him, said goodbye, and he drove back to Nandlstadt 10 kilometers away to rejoin his unit. He said he'd be back in a few days to see how we were doing. It seemed to be the end of the line for his mission.

Gasthaus Kettner was one component of a family-owned estate. All of its outbuildings nestled around a circular drive, in whose center was a rondelle of green space with picnic tables shaded by a chestnut grove. The wide drive allowed a variety of farm equipment to pass through, everything from teams of horses to huge threshing machines and logging wagons. The surrounding buildings consisted of an adjoining two-story house with living space for extended family, horse barns, an icehouse, a sawmill, a forty-head dairy cattle barn, and numerous open sheds for farm equipment and vehicles. Barns filled with grain, hay, and straw stood in adjacent fields. The entire complex left no doubt in our minds that we had landed in an estate of enormous proportions, a complex of diverse farm industries. It was right in the middle of Attenkirchen next to a Catholic church, surrounded by a centuries-old cemetery.

In addition to the Kettners' own furnishings, the inn was full of desks, library tables, bureaus and office machines. Also lots of telephones, wires, and other kinds of communications equipment. Papers on letterhead with swastikas were all over the desks, which indicated they must have been abandoned in a hurry. It seemed to have been some kind of German military command post as well as an off-site location for the city government of Munich, so the city could function during its capitulation.

We went upstairs to the guestrooms at the farthest end of the second floor, pushed some beds around so we could sleep, and called it a night. The following morning my mother and father walked to the other house on the property and introduced themselves to the Kettner family: Herr und Frau Kettner and their two children, Marielle, six, and Burle, three, the grandfather, the elder Herr Kettner, and one of his daughters and her family. Numerous farm hands and maid servants all lived in quarters on-site, alongside village employees, of whom there were many.

We were a complete mystery family to them. They looked at my parents and offered a reticent handshake. It was not a matter of mistrust, but intense curiosity: Who were we? We spoke German; we spoke English. We were polite, well dressed, and eager to get acquainted. Were we refugees, evacuees, or some kind of family ambassadors connected to the Allied occupation?

All of these questions were answered as best we could, being careful not to divulge too many details. We did not want to trigger an investigation into how we got to the West and get our gang of Good Samaritan Yanks in trouble. My parents didn't lie; they just didn't tell the whole story. It would be a happy time. There were children and animals, and it was summertime with a whole new outdoors to explore. No more sirens, no more running to bunkers. A period of carefree living was about to begin.

As promised, Pops came by a few days after we had settled in to see how we were getting on in our new situation and to inform his girlfriend to pack her things and get ready to move one more time. He had found a small apartment for her and Hannelore in Freising, a small town thirteen kilometers away. Freising was a *Kleinstadt,* a provincial town of between ten- and fifteen-thousand inhabitants, a governmental and marketing hub, which spread out to include Attenkirchen and surrounding rural areas. It lay on the main rail and roadway network, connecting to most of the larger cities in Bavaria, especially to Munich, some thirty 30 kilometers to the south.

Liesl's leaving was no surprise to us, and we parted as good friends who had shared a life-altering adventure. Although my mother and Liesl said they would keep in touch, they never saw each other again. Pops's visits to us became less frequent, inasmuch as the arrangement he had put in place with Liesl afforded them the privacy they needed. I was glad not to see him again.

The younger Kettner family moved back into their upstairs quarters in the inn and worked to reestablish Gasthaus Kettner to its former importance, affording the surrounding population with hospitality services.

Business picked up very rapidly, and many events were booked: everything from church breakfasts and community dinners to private parties and weddings.

Local customs became part of our lives, and the Bavarian wedding celebration was especially interesting. It is performed in rural areas among peasant families and is called a *Bauernhochzeit*. The feasting and merriment could last several days, beginning with the *Buergermeister* performing the legal marriage ceremony in the town hall, like ceremonies performed by a Justice of the Peace. Afterwards, invited guests, usually just the wedding party, are served brunch at a local restaurant, followed by coffee or tea and a pastry buffet, the likes of which would challenge Marie-Antoinette's taste.

The next morning there would be a festive pomp and circumstance procession to the church wedding, after which the bride and groom would proceed to the inn, followed by the wedding party and guests. The daylong feast would begin with a three-course breakfast, a five-course mid-day dinner, afternoon coffee and cake, and, just for good measure, a seven-course evening meal.

Intermingled during the feasting breaks are traditional events: passing of the envelope plate (monetary wedding gifts), speeches by relatives, story-telling by best friends (mostly hilarious exposés), and acknowledgement of guests from far-off places.

As entertaining as this is for the wedding guests, it is a challenging day for the best man, because his expected attentiveness to the bride is diverted by another tradition: bride stealing. He must be watchful that some of his so-called best friends do not steal the bride and spirit her away to a taproom in an adjoining village where drinks are set up for everyone and have to be paid by the best man before the bride is released and he can bring her back. But first he has to find her.

After the last morsel of the evening meal has been served and washed down with beer, wine, and champagne, the brass band strikes up, and dancing begins. Wedding guests who came dressed in the traditional *Lederhosen* and *Dirndls* usually open with a lively *Schuhplattler*, the dance during which the guys slap their hands, thighs, and soles of their feet, while the gals whirl around them. Other folkdances follow deep into the night. At some point, the newlyweds steal away to celebrate their wedding night. In the wee hours of the morning, the weary, but still frolicking wedding guests are sent home, but not before being served yet one last meal: *Bauernfruehstueck* (farmers' breakfast).

My mother was involved in the food preparation for these events. We had become well acquainted with the Kettners, and when they found out about her expertise in food service and her experience in some of the finest houses in Hamburg, they asked her if she would consider helping. Mommi was delighted to do so. She was not only an excellent hotel cook, she also specialized in beautiful food platter presentations. Frau Kettner always referred to my mother as an artist in her craft. The Kettner children, Marielle and Burle, had to be looked after, kept occupied and away from these events. Even though they had a full-time governess, I was asked to help entertain them. As a result of this interaction, we developed a beautiful family-to-family relationship that has lasted through generations. With Liesl Weinelt gone, we had another room upstairs. The extra space went a long way in enabling our two families to live in harmony under one roof.

Pappi went to Freising to seek employment. There were two permanent garrisons in Freising occupied by American troops. One of these posts was named the *Artillerie Kaserne*; the other, the *Vimy Kaserne*. Pappi applied for a position as interpreter at the *Artillerie Kaserne*. He was hired on the spot and began an eight-year-long career in service to the American Occupational Forces.

As we became acquainted with people in the village, our new friends and neighbors approached my father and asked if he would teach them English and Spanish. Soon we had a very active evening school several times a week in one of our rooms. Freddy and I sat in on the classes and spoke English to help with pronunciation and encourage conversation among the students. We had a great time together as our acquaintances became our friends.

It was a mild form of celebrity that we spoke English. Our landlady at the inn, Frau Kettner, would often call on Freddy and me to come downstairs to translate and chat with American soldiers who had stopped by the taproom for a beer or something to eat. Not only could we tell Frau Kettner what they wanted, but she also could boast that here in rural, occupied Bavaria, the small village of Attenkirchen had fluent English-speaking kids.

In late summer my parents enrolled us in the local school systems. Freddy would go to the *Gymnasium* in Freising; I would enter the fifth grade in the *Dorfschule* in Attenkirchen. I was looking forward to going back to school. With every passing day, our lives became more and more normal. I recall my father coming home with his first paycheck from the *Artillerie Kaserne* in Freising and going downstairs to Herr Kettner's office to negotiate the rent, which he felt was his obligation. He was not a man to take advantage and not pay his own way.

We hadn't seen Pops in several weeks, but one afternoon he stopped by for a surprise visit. He informed us he had received his orders to rotate to the USA and would be leaving in a matter of days. He said he had cleaned out his quarters in Nandlstadt and had several boxes of personal effects he wanted us to have. He asked me to go along to pick them up and bring them back, a short one-hour run. I looked at Mommi, and she nodded her okay. She had no reason to think I shouldn't go. I never gave it a second thought.

When we arrived in Nandlstadt, many of the other GI's were also moving out. Pops's entire unit was being transferred and the confiscated housing given back to the local citizenry. We loaded the boxes in the Jeep: two woolen Army blankets and food stuff for my mother, some Army issue for Freddy, and several cartons of cigarettes, tobacco, and a Meerschaum pipe for my father. Then he said he had something for me and asked me to come back inside.

With the door closed, he asked me if I was doing all right. I was determined to feel confident in my life and had little fear. I told him things were going well for us in Attenkirchen, and I liked our home. But I knew he was inquiring about my physical health. I told him I was still having some discharge, and he gave me more tubes of salve.

"Since I am leaving and care about you, let me have one last look to make sure you're okay. I don't want to worry about you," he said.

"One last look?" I was apprehensive, but didn't know how to oppose him. At the same time, I had developed a certain amount of trust again. His concern for my well being seemed sincere. He lay me down, looked at me and began to perform oral sex.

"Pops! This isn't right," I cried. "Don't do this! Take me home!"

With that I ran out and climbed into the front seat of his Jeep. We rode home in total silence. I wept all the way.

Mommi could tell I had been crying. I told her it was because it was hard for me to say good-bye to Pops. He had done so much for us. This was not that far from the truth, but the hurt and disappointment in breaking my new-found trust·in him and ripping open the wounds that had begun to heal was more than I could bear. I couldn't hold back the tears and found myself back where I was in Kleinrinderfeld. Pops said good-bye to my mother, asked her to give his best regards to Pappi, gave me a hug, winked at me, and left. We never saw or heard from him again.

In time I decided to double my resolve to bury this secret even deeper inside me. I knew in my heart Pops was instrumental in saving Pappi's life by bringing us to the West. If this was the part I had to play, it was a sacrifice I could live with. I made up my mind I was going to try to forgive. I had almost accomplished it before and remembered how it eased the burden. I would probably never be able to forget, but I would not go through life permanently scarred or carrying a grudge. I made up my mind never to keep score. The score was settled, and no one would ever find out.

What time was left of that first summer, the summer of 1945, was drawing to a close. School would be starting. For obvious reasons, I spent more time by myself, going on long walks in the meadows, coming home with *Champignons* (edible mushrooms) and bouquets of wild flowers for my mother. I needed time to think and sort things out. But I was getting there.

Thanks to my brother, the days before we had to go back to school were filled with fun and exploration. Freddy made friends with the teenagers in the village a lot quicker than I did. One day he asked me to go with him and some of his friends to a large meadow a short distance outside of Attenkirchen. There the village kids showed us a field strewn with clumps of silvery excelsior, similar to the fine curled wood shavings used for packaging fragile items. But this material was cut from tin foil and was not just interesting, it was unbelievably glittery in the sunshine. In the same area, we discovered large aluminum containers, the size of bathtubs and shaped like fat cigars.

Freddy asked the boys whether there had been a land war in the area when the Yanks came through and was told, "No, there wasn't." Unafraid, Freddy walked into the field, and we followed. The black lettering stenciled on the containers in English indicated they had at one time contained fuel. They turned out to be auxiliary fuel tanks jettisoned by allied aircraft, most likely fighter planes. The curly silvery excelsior was a countermeasure product that would scramble or send out false readings on enemy radar screens.

All of us saw the potential for both finds. I returned the next day with pillowcases and gathered the glittery stuff I thought was so pretty. The boys carried the fuel tanks, which were not heavy, one by one to the village tin-smith and asked him to cut a large opening in the top and turn the sharp edges under. We now had a fleet of canoes. What fun we had on nearby ponds! The canoes were tricky to maneuver and tipped over easily, but that was part of the fun. It was good to be able to swim, even though the ponds were shallow.

In the fall I enrolled in the fifth grade of the small village elementary school, the *Dorfschule*. First through third grades were in one room; fourth through sixth in another; seventh and eighth in another.

I enjoyed geography and the strictly taught math. We drilled on the multiplication tables in German with such routine that their rhythm stuck in my memory. Our teacher, Lehrer Penkert, shot complicated, rapid calculation problems at us first thing every morning as a mental workout to wake up our brains. To this day, when I must add up a bill, I find myself adding, subtracting, dividing, or multiplying in German, then translating the answer.

My teacher had come to Attenkirchen from Prussia and had a serious war injury. He had to swing his injured leg out to one side as he walked, steadying himself with a cane. Like a small child, he had to go up and down steps one at a time. He was very tall and quite handsome. I admired him and made an effort to get top grades to please him. He taught every academic subject, as well as music and art. I dreaded the hour he taught us music appreciation. For his part, he attempted to enhance our cultural sensibilities by playing violin solos and accompanying us as we sang. As he tucked that fiddle under his chin and played, he would grimace, making my friend, Ingrid Wiese, and me break into laughter. We tried to control our laughter but couldn't; and when he glanced in our direction as he fiddled with his funny faces, it made matters even worse. He usually separated us; and when that didn't work, one of us would end up spending the hour out in the hallway.

Meanwhile, Freddy enrolled in a secondary boys' school in Freising. By this time, scheduled public transportation was running, so he and Pappi took the bus to Freising every morning. Freddy was out by mid-afternoon every day, and sometimes he would walk up to the *Artillerie Kaserne* to wait for Pappi to get off. He would hang around the guardhouse and talk to the MPs on duty in English. He told them he was waiting for his father, who worked as a translator inside.

Eventually they became so well acquainted and with the help of his Brooklyn accent, he charmed his way onto the post. One day he walked around until he found the mess hall and followed the music inside. All at once, everything was American again. The atmosphere was relaxed and comfortable; the smell of American food permeated the air, with Frank Sinatra singing "Nancy With The Laughing Face" in the background. He was overwhelmed with a longing to get back to the States. If that were not possible right away, here is where he wanted to be. That night he told my parents he was going to quit school and get a job working for the Yanks. He intended to apply at the *Artillerie Kaserne* the next morning.

Freddy was fourteen, old enough to go to work in Germany after completing the eighth grade. When he announced he was dropping out of school, he put up a pretty good argument. My parents could hardly object. He intended to earn the money to return to the US. Since he was an American citizen, there would be no holding him back. He promised them he would not neglect his education. It would be his top priority. But where would he live? When the time came, he said he would write to Tante Elsie and Onkel Werner in New York and ask if he could move in with them until he was old enough to enlist in the Air Force. The first order of business, however, was to go after the job.

Freddy interviewed with Lieutenant Colonel George R. Quarles, Commanding Officer of the *Artillerie Kaserne* in Freising, where Pappi was employed. Colonel Quarles leaned towards hiring him because of his language skills, and knowledge of the area and local customs, but was apprehensive about his age. He was just so young, really just a boy. Little did he know he had a tiger by the tail! He sent Freddy on to First Lieutenant Mayer, the Commanding Officer of the 689th Field Artillery Battalion, who interviewed him for the second time and hired him under Special Services.

Freddy's job was to accompany a group of soldiers to Munich every morning, leaving at 3:00 AM, to pick up supplies and groceries. Everything the base needed—canned goods, dry goods, small equipment, anything you could possibly think of—was supplied by the US Army Quartermaster Corps. But fresh fruits and vegetables were purchased from the German wholesale produce markets in Munich. They had to be there no later than 4:00 AM for the best selection. Freddy functioned as an interpreter.

They were finished with their work and back in Freising by 8:00 AM. A crew from the mess hall would unload the truck, while Freddy and his GI buddies went to breakfast, served by Army cooks: ham and eggs, toasted white bread, hash brown potatoes, pancakes with butter and maple syrup, and all the ice-cold pasteurized milk and orange juice he could drink.

But Freddy's hours were a problem. There was no public transportation available from Attenkirchen to Freising at two o'clock in the morning, so he was billeted in the barracks, sharing a room with five other GI's, an arrangement he loved.

After breakfast and sleep to make up the hours lost due to his early shift, Freddy's afternoons were usually free. He became, in his own words, a "chief gopher and scrounger," running errands for the officers and non-commissioned officers. Whatever their wishes—where to purchase Bavarian gift items to send home to their families, where to find military souvenirs for the trophy collectors or where the finest, the quaintest or the most out-of-the-way restaurants to enjoy local cuisine and the famously good Bavarian beer were—Freddy came up with the answers. Sometimes he would drop by Gasthaus Kettner in Attenkirchen on the premise of stopping for a beer. He would excuse himself, go upstairs, and come down with his English-speaking mother and kid sister, much to the surprise of his GI companions. We would have a great time together in the taproom and were always delighted with Freddy's spontaneous visits.

My brother and I were leading completely different lives. His lifestyle was totally engulfed in American culture, albeit in a military setting, with very little German social interaction, unless connected with GI's and German girls. My life, on the other hand, was becoming integrated into Bavarian village life. We didn't really grow apart because of this, but as we grew into adulthood, we moved in different directions. Freddy was becoming an American purist. I was developing a strong attachment to the land my parents came from and to its people. I experienced life among them, not the horrid existence during the Third Reich, but life after World War II. The re-birth of the German spirit touched me—the work ethic and dedication to rebuild all that had been destroyed—and I appreciated the natural beauty of Bavaria. I became part of it.

One evening in the summer 1945, Pappi came home with exciting news. He and Freddy had met an English-speaking German gentleman employed as an interpreter at the *Kaserne*. He had been interned in Crystal City, repatriated to Germany, and knew where the Wohlpart family was. These had been our best friends. He told Pappi that the Wohlparts had left the holding camp in Prien-am-Chiemsee shortly after their arrival from Biarritz, and moved to Mr. Wohlpart's parents home in Trunstadt, a village outside the town of Bamberg. They had survived a terrible bombing while traveling through Nurnberg, but made it safely to their destination. After the liberation, Mr. Wohlpart was employed as an interpreter for the Yanks at an Army base in Bamberg.

Mr. Wohlpart had been trained in the restaurant business, specializing in elegant food service and presentation. Coincidentally, the officers' mess hall at the *Artillerie Kaserne* in Freising was looking for just such a professional to upgrade the mess and turn it into a fine dining room. They needed a maitre'd or a headwaiter, someone with training and experience. My father thought Kaspar Wohlpart would be the perfect person and recommended him.

In late summer of 1945, the US Army transferred Wohlpart from Bamberg to Freising, moving the family, belongings and all, just as we were transported in a six-ton Army truck to a comfortable little house with a beautiful garden, protected by a thick hedge from the sights and sounds of Haindlfingerstrasse on the outskirts of Freising.

Kaspar Wohlpart did what he knew best, reorganizing and staffing the officers' mess hall, converting it into a gourmet dining room, refined and elegant. We were so happy to have our good friends, with whom we had experienced so much, within visiting distance.

Time passed, and the seasons in Bavaria were unusually beautiful. Winter was a snow-covered wonderland for kids with natural ski slopes all around our village. A sledding hill known as *Baeckerberg* ("Bakers Hill") started from the center of Attenkirchen and sloped almost all the way down to the nearby village of Weihersdorf at its base. The village bakery and pastry shop was on the main road that ran along the top of the hill from which we began our descent, which is probably how it got its name. It was not only our winter playground; it attracted children from many of the neighboring villages.

My first skis were handmade by the wagon maker, Herr Anneser. Everyone called him "Toni-Papp." They were beautiful, cut of two pieces of wood taller than I and shaped to a point, then soaked and clamped into the proper shape, and allowed to dry by the pot-bellied stove in Toni-Papp's workshop. The soaking and drying process was repeated many times until they finally retained their intended shape at the last unclamping, coming out bowed at the tips and flexible in the center. After lacquering them and attaching the bindings, Toni-Papp taught me how to keep them waxed for maximum speed. The ski wax was best applied in a molten state, then rubbed in by hand. Only my mother could tell you how often I gummed up the plate of her iron in order to melt and even out the lumps of wax on the bottom of my skis.

My first ski boots were also handmade by the village *Schuster*, Herr Blaumoser, custom-made to my foot measurements as I wore two pairs of woolen socks. They were square-toed with chunky, routed-out heels, and I was so proud of them. I clomped around the house for hours, breaking them in and practicing a downhill tuck, so I could figure out just how tight I should lace them up.

The best skier among the girls in the village was Kathi Anneser. She could perform a downhill schuss better than anyone else. We became friends, and soon I was able to keep up with her. I was proud to even keep up with the boys my age. Together we built a little ski jump that would hurl us forward about five or six meters after take-off, our arms thrusting forward as we concentrated on a soft landing with knees bent, then completing the downhill run without wiping out.

I could ski for hours in the freezing temperatures. One day I came home in the evening with what must have been early stages of frostbite. My father knew of an old-time folk remedy and took me through its paces. First he made me run around in a circle barefoot in the freshly fallen snow in front of Gasthaus Kettner. Then he brought me inside for treatment. I had to submerge my feet in warm water while Pappi gently massaged them. Soon my feet started prickling, itching, and turning beet red. For the *piece de resistance*, he swathed lard between my toes and all over my feet and made a poultice of sliced onions, wrapping my feet in strips of sheeting so they looked mummified. That first night I thought I would climb the walls, my bandaged feet keeping me awake with their almost intolerable itching. The pungent smell of onions was annoying and especially strong in bed under the blankets. Pappi made me keep the bandages on for several days and nights until all the itching stopped. After that, I promised to come home while I could still feel my feet.

Although skiing and sledding were our primary winter sports, there was also ice skating, hockey, and *Eisstockschiessen* (a game similar to curling) on small ponds in meadows that belonged to the Kettners. We used the same ponds for our "salvaged canoes" in the summertime. As soon as they froze over with at least a twenty-centimeter thick layer of ice, we'd scrape the hoarfrost off the biggest pond and skate from morning until evening. On weekends we'd watch the men come out with their curling stones, form teams, and get into competitive ice-shooting games.

Eventually Herr Kettner would come to the ponds with sledgehammers and spikes to break up the ice and load huge chunks onto flatbed wagons. He and his helpers would transport it to the two-story icehouse attached to the rear of the inn and hand crank it up a conveyor belt to load the silo-like cavity from the top. When the icehouse was filled to capacity, then insulated with straw topped off with a thick layer of sawdust and sealed, there was enough ice for an entire year to cool the walk-in refrigerator that stored perishable food and meat for the restaurant, butcher shop, and an adjoining cellar designed to lager beer and wine. Kettner certainly put a dent in our ice hockey game when we arrived with our skates and all the ice had been harvested. Sometimes he would leave one of the ponds intact, so the men could continue their curling, but in case of a mild winter, he could not count on the ponds refreezing and forming a fresh layer.

In addition to winter sports, there was indoor entertainment to fill the winter evenings. Twice a month there were free movies, shown in Gasthaus Kettner's upstairs ballroom. It took us kids all afternoon to put up the wooden folding chairs. The projector was set on the stage so the film could be projected on a white sheet, taped to the opposite wall. Even though the films were all talkies, the sound equipment was not the high fidelity stereophonic sound we know today. Most of the films were German, many in an Alpine setting with lots of yodeling between young lovers.

If Freddy just happened to be home to see one of these old-fashioned movies, he could hardly contain himself. Often Pappi had to remind him to mind his manners and hold his laughter. One time they showed a movie called, *Das Zeichen des Zorros!* (*The Sign of Zorro*). It was a Western with German sub-titles. All the younger boys in the village were crazy about Zorro and his exploits and came to me with many questions. Was it really that dangerous to live in the Wild West with all those bad men wielding all those guns? Could Freddy and I ride horses that fast and that good? I hated to disappoint them, but all I could tell them was that we generally rode the subway.

At least once a month there was a dance in Kettner's ballroom. The rhythm of the "oom-pah-pah" band was bouncy most of the time, polkas and marches, but they did have a good repertoire of waltzes, tangos, and foxtrots also. The doors to our rooms were right off the ballroom, so whenever there was a dance, we either had to join in the fun, or stay in our rooms until the last dance was played. There was no quiet to be had until then.

One night when Freddy came home with two or three of his buddies, he said, "Wouldn't we set them back on their heels if we went out there on the dance floor and did the jitter-bug?"

I said: "Let's do it!"

"But what about the music? We need the right beat?" he said.

Toni-Papp, the same fellow who made my skis, happened to be the clarinet-playing leader of the band. The Americanization of Western Germany was already manifesting itself on all levels with American music especially popular. To my surprise, Toni-Papp told me he and his group had already been practicing "Chattanooga Choo Choo," (his pronunciation was hilarious) and he would try to play, if we'd come out and dance. We did, and to make it even more fun, Freddy's two buddies came out on the floor and asked two German ladies for a dance. It turned out to be a delightful German/American mixer.

Our first Christmas in Attenkirchen after the war was magical. There were decorations all over the village. Snow fell on Christmas Eve, and you could hear Christmas carols emanating from the houses. A *Tannenbaum* was glistening in every window. Our family was together, and the war over.

Christmas trees were lit with real candles. There was no such thing as a string of electric lights as in the States, which is probably why families gathered around and watched it all evening long. Freddy and I gave our tree an extra flair. We topped it off with the curly foil excelsior dropped in the meadows by Allied planes, the glittery stuff I had gathered and saved in pillowcases. Our tree looked like something out of *Grimm's Fairy Tales*. My mother cooked *Gluehwein* (hot, spiced, sweetened wine), which we sipped while munching on homemade cookies—*Lebkuchen* (traditional spicy Christmas cookies)—and cinnamon stars.

Herr Rusch, the village barber, who had a knack for the dramatic, brought civic theater to the village. In late winter, while people were still indoors and farm work had not yet begun, he produced and directed shows: dramas, musicals, plays, and folk-comedy skits, many of which he wrote. From early childhood on, I was drawn to the stage. Somehow he found that out and wrote a skit for me. He named it "Der Wiefe Michi" ("Wise Little Mikey"), a solo presentation by a street-smart little Bavarian boy named Michi, who explained the idiosyncrasies and contradictions of adults in a logical and comical manner. I had to dress in *Lederhosen* and wear the traditional Bavarian hat, but most important, I had to speak my lines in Bavarian dialect, which is very difficult for most Germans to understand unless they grew up in Bavaria or Austria. Herr Rusch taught me how to speak the dialect, which has given me much pleasure all my life. I shall be forever grateful for his patience.

My mother and I usually took the bus to Freising on Saturday mornings to go shopping for items we couldn't purchase in Attenkirchen. We had to be done with our errands by 2:00 PM, because all of the shops closed for the weekend. There were no exceptions; only cafes, restaurants, and beer gardens remained open. But another reason we rushed through our morning was my mother's renewed interest in taking a peek into the future. We had to leave sufficient time to keep her appointments with either the palm reader or tarot card lady before we caught the bus back to Attenkirchen.

Part of her peek was her ongoing yearning for all of us to return to the United States as a family. I'm sure when she thought about it realistically and considered Pappi's FBI history, she knew in her heart it was an impossible dream. She could not rid herself of a foreboding that sometime in the not-too-distant future we would be separating again, and so she clung to anything positive her fortune-tellers would forecast. All she wanted to hear were reassurances that in the end we would be together in the America she loved.

After the Wohlpart family moved to Freising, we often stayed in town for the entire day, taking the early evening bus home. My mother would stop at a *Konditorei* (pastry shop) to buy cake, which we took to the Wohlparts when we visited them to enjoy our afternoon *Kaffeeklatsches*. Frau Wohlpart brewed the coffee, and we'd catch up on each other's lives. Invariably, the conversation would turn to going back to America.

It was a foregone conclusion that their oldest daughter Inge would return, as my brother would. The Wohlparts had already set the wheels in motion by making repeated trips to the American Consulate in Munich. Inge was an American, born in New York, and did not have to meet any immigration quotas. Initiating the process for her return merely required completing the paper work. She had to present her birth certificate, prove financial sponsorship and temporary guardianship (she was only fourteen years of age at the time), and apply for her American passport. In August 1946 Inge returned to the States by herself on the military transport ship *Marine Perch*. Imagine the courage of this young fourteen-year-old girl, traveling to another continent by herself.

I did not allow myself to think about anything negative the future might bring. One thing was sure. I was only eleven years old and had no intention of separating from my parents anytime soon. I was having a wonderful, fun-filled summer, riding my bike to nearby villages with friends and swimming in beautiful natural ponds. My best friend, a boy named Pauli Schmidhuber, had a collapsible kayak that we would take on the one-track train that came through our village and ride to the nearby village of Zolling. The river Amper flowed through Zolling, as did the parallel man-made Amperkanal. The canal waters were swift, and we would put in and take turns kayaking and swimming all the way to the village of Haag-an-der-Amper. When we arrived at the spot where the water pooled just before the *Amperwerke* (power generating plant), we would get out, picnic on the banks of the Amperkanal, and wait for the train to come from the other direction to take us back to Attenkirchen.

It was a gloriously exhausting daylong outing, perfectly topped off by the ride home on the *Holledauer Bockerl*, our little train. *Holledau* was the name of the area it serviced; *Bockerl*, a small, stubborn bucking animal, such as a little goat or burro, both words spelled and pronounced in Bavarian dialect. Reminiscent of the train on "Petticoat Junction," it had a steam-powered engine fed by chunks of coal from the tender behind the locomotive. It struggled and chugged uphill, then ran free on the downhill side, happily tooting its horn loud and often. The Yanks who rode it called it the "Toonerville Trolley." We all loved our little *Bockerl*. It laced the villages and its people together all the way from Freising to Mainburg.

The area between Freising and Mainburg is called the Hallertau. Rich soil, combined with the prevailing climate, makes it the perfect environment for hops culture. The flavor of the malt ingredient used in brewing beer is enhanced by the addition of hops blossoms. Acres and acres of hops gardens, dense beyond description, with vines winding themselves around wires strung almost eight meters high, dominate the landscape.

At harvest time when the hops blossoms were ready for picking, our little *Bockerl* brought hundreds of migrant pickers to Hallertau. We were so fortunate to be living in Gasthaus Kettner right in the middle of all the action to experience this happening. In addition to their other endeavors, the Kettners were huge hops growers and housed a large gang of pickers on straw mattresses in their covered sheds. The accommodations were primitive, but that was part of the attraction for the hops pickers that came from far and wide and different walks of life. At the end of the day, after the pickers were served the evening meal in the picnic area in the courtyard, there was much merriment, singing and dancing, with music provided by accordion-playing migrants This wonderful earthy time lasted almost three weeks.

The *Artillerie Kaserne* was scheduled to return to German authority by the end of 1946. Most of the military personnel there would be transferred to other bases in occupied Germany or rotated to the United States for discharge or reassignment. Freising's other Army post, the *Vimy Kaserne*, would absorb remaining personnel. Most of the civilian employees had to seek employment elsewhere.

Freddy was transferred to Moosburg several kilometers to the East, similar in size to Freising. The Army base there held German detainees scheduled to testify at the Nurnberg war crimes trials. He was assigned to translate for a group of American military and civilian events photographers and was billeted with this group, but had to find his own transportation. Pappi helped him buy a used motorcycle, and he was glued to its seat most of the time. It was an easy run to Attenkirchen from Moosburg, and he came home as often as possible and told us of his interesting new assignment.

Pappi found employment as an interpreter with the US Army Quartermaster Corps in Munich, renting a room there. He would leave on our little train at 5:45 AM Monday mornings and return Friday evenings at 7:30 PM. It was a long week for us. My mother busied herself with housekeeping chores and continued working for the Kettners as events demanded her expertise, and there were many. I was involved with the Kettner children, Marielle and Burle. We became one big family. As fall arrived, I went back to the elementary school.

At the conclusion of the Nurnberg trials in February 1947, Freddy was once again transferred, this time to Munich. He would soon be sixteen and felt it was time to initiate the process to return to America. Pappi had already contacted the UNRRA (United Nations Relief and Rehabilitation Administration) and met with the District Administrator, Mr. Berger, an American civilian employed by the United Nations. Berger assisted in obtaining an ID for Freddy. Every person in postwar Germany required a *Pass* (identification) no matter what age or nationality. He also obtained a photostatic copy of Freddy's birth certificate, which he requested from the New York Department of Health. Because Freddy was still under age, a parental consent form and proof of financial sponsorship in the States were also required in preparation for a meeting with the American Consul General in Munich.

Up to this point, Mr. Berger had guided us through the entire process. My mother and I took the train to Munich, meeting Pappi and Freddy, and all of us kept an appointment Berger had arranged with the American Consul General. Everything was falling into place for Freddy to return to America. Tante Elsie and Onkel Werner, acting as sponsors, were looking forward to his coming.

Several months later, my parents received a letter from the American Consulate, asking them to come to Munich to pick up Freddy's passport and his travel instructions. These documents advised him of the date he had to report to Bremerhaven prior to sailing. I was stunned to realize that what had just been a dream of Freddy's was becoming reality.

Freddy stopped working so he could spend a month at home before leaving. Earlier that spring he had brought home a German shepherd puppy for me, and I named the pup "Prinzi." He was supposed to be purebred, but turned out to be quite the opposite, displaying diverse bloodlines as he matured into anything but a proud and statuesque German shepherd. He had floppy ears. That was the worst! We propped them up with popsicle sticks and taped them for days, hoping they would stay. But our efforts were to no avail. No sooner did we remove the wraps, than his ears flopped again, making Prinzi look like a scruffy, overgrown schnauzer. His personality matched his comical looks, and all he wanted to do was play. But he was a precious gift from my brother, and I loved him.

Freddy and I would go on long rides on his motorcycle. We had no particular destination, but usually stopped at a café in some little village and had coffee and cake. We always brought some home for Mommi. We had a good time together, but I could never understand how easy it was for him to leave when it was so hard for me to say good-bye. The thought of saying good-bye to my brother kept me awake many a night. We had been through so much together. My mother dealt with it in her own way, but Pappi understood Freddy completely. He had walked a similar path in his youth.

The morning we said our final farewells at the train station in Attenkirchen, I thought my heart would burst. Pappi accompanied Freddy to Munich and safely transferred him onto the train to Bremerhaven. My mother and I walked home in silence, both of us weeping. Prinzi knew there was something wrong. I hugged him a lot that day, and he licked away my tears.

Freddy sailed on the *Marine Flasher*, formerly in service as a troop transport ship, arriving in New York in July, 1947. Back on American soil, he got down on his knees and kissed the ground.

Freddy's leaving created a huge void in our lives. No more spontaneous visits with this handsome, funny, impulsive brother of mine. No more contact with the GI's who usually accompanied him. Fortunately it was the time of year the hops harvest was about to begin again. My mother kept busy helping the Kettners with food preparation for the hops pickers they housed, and I played in the hops gardens with Burli and Marielle. We even picked blossoms, but didn't stick with it because it took more patience than any of us kids had.

Burli was the ultimate little rascal. He was the youngest and only boy in the household, the little prince of the family and spoiled rotten. He loved his grandfather, the elder Herr Kettner, but no more than he loved my father, "Herr Wiegand." In the case of my father, the feeling was mutual. Pappi got the biggest kick out of the little tyke. When he was still working in Freising and coming home every evening, Burli would be watching for him as he got off the bus, greet him, and invite himself upstairs to our quarters to have a *Schluck Bier* (a swallow of beer). Pappi's transfer to Munich put a stop to this routine, only to make Burli even more watchful when Pappi came home on weekends. No sooner had Pappi arrived than there was a knock. Burli never wore anything but *Lederhosen* and only spoke in Bavarian dialect. Frau Kettner often retrieved him, thinking he would be a pest and apologizing for his behavior. Little did she realize how much we enjoyed this adorable little guy. [1]

In the fall of 1947, I started school in Freising, a 13 kilometer ride on the bus. I had turned 12 that year and was in the sixth grade. I went to the *Oberschule fuer Maedchen* (secondary girls school), a wider experience for me. I could see there were many girls who were already determining what course of study to follow, and thinking about careers. My father wanted me to get an education in literature and the arts, but past that I wasn't focused on my future, other than maintaining and expanding my foreign languages. I knew with these skills I would always find a job.

One of my teachers, Fraeulein Haas, and I were at loggerheads. A fortyish, attractive woman, she taught English. Her pronunciation was very British because she'd spent some time studying in England. My American English irritated to her. I had been keeping myself fluent by reading the *Stars & Stripes* and listening to "AFN," the Armed Forces Network. I listened to the "Hit Parade" and "Hillbilly Gasthaus," a program that came on every weekday at 15:00 hours (3:00 PM) and was hosted by an American DJ who was also a soldier. The program featured country music. I cannot say I was as crazy about country songs as I was the current hits of the Hit Parade, but I did like the variety in American music. It was an antidote to the Bavarian zither, accordion, and jodeling music played on the *Sueddeutscher Rundfunk* (South-German Broadcasting Company).

Fraeulein Haas didn't admire these sorts of English exercises. She took pleasure in correcting my Americanisms, often embarrassing me on purpose. The girls around me were getting private lessons from me anyhow. All they were interested in was being able to talk to the Yanks, and they wanted the groovy American phrases and pronunciation, not the proper British version. "Anneliese, how do you say this?" "How do you say that?" they'd ask after class.

---

[1] Burle grew up to be Dr. Lorenz Kettner, Doctor of Philosophy at the Schyren-Gymnasium in Pfaffenhofen/Ilm, Bavaria. He was appointed to the Ministerium of Culture in Bavaria and authored the book, *Hallertauer Hopfenbau—Geschichte und Gegenwart* (*Hallertauer Hops Culture—History and Today*). This book, published in 1976, was a component of his thesis, which earned him his doctorate. He has since published four more books.

Dr. Kettner directs the theatrical productions of the students of the Schyren-Gymnasium, often assuming an acting role himself. We remain in close touch. His daughter Lena spent a summer with our family in Indiana when she was fourteen years old.

School was out at 2:45 PM Mondays thru Fridays. I usually went straight to study hall, which remained open until 5:00 PM for students with special permission. We were mostly the commuting student population from the surrounding villages. The bus line that served Attenkirchen and villages beyond only made two roundtrips per day. I generally completed all of my homework in study hall before I had to catch the bus at 5:45 PM on the square of the Obere Hauptstrasse (Upper Main Street), a fifteen-minute walk from school. All busses assembled in this busy area and left in ten-minute intervals. If you were late, you got left behind. This was especially challenging during fair weather, when I walked up the Dom Berg, the mountain that rose from downtown Freising and had beautiful gardens with walking paths and benches around the medieval cathedral. It was a lovely place to read and study while enjoying the spectacular panoramic views. Under certain weather conditions, the Alps were visible to the south.

On Saturdays classes were over by noon, and the entire school building shut down until Monday mornings. I had made several girlfriends that lived in Freising, and occasionally they'd invite me to spend the weekend with them. Sometimes I was invited by the Wohlparts, which I especially enjoyed.

One day Mrs. Wohlpart asked me if I'd be interested in being a mannequin. I had never even heard of the word. She explained it was a form of modeling. Live models would assume a freeze position, posing as dressmaker figures displaying clothes, like the figures one passes in the aisles of department stores or in shop windows. She went on to tell me about this entrepreneurial friend who had opened a fashion design business in downtown Freising and wanted to present her clothing designs to the public in this manner. My first reaction was, "How innovative!" If for no other reason than to find out more about freeze modeling, I agreed to meet with Mrs. Wohlpart's lady friend.

Frau Zirzow owned "Modehaus Zirzow" (Fashion House Zirzow). She was a tall, stunning woman who looked a lot like Ingrid Bergman and had a high sense of style. Seamstresses in a back room put her designs into reality. Her salesroom had a corner window fronting on the street that looked more like a stage than a shop window. Here her living vignettes performed.

I had a pleasant interview with Frau Zirzow during which she showed me some of the poses I would have to assume and hold. I posed, and she circled and studied me as I performed my impromptu audition. Then she said, "I would like you to come and be one of our youth models." I was flattered that she asked and delighted to be invited to join her group. I went through a brief training period with one of her older, more experienced models, who shared many tips with me. These included how to focus on an object and relax eye muscles to avoid too much blinking and how to shift your weight internally, so you wouldn't start shaking involuntarily. She also taught me how to breathe properly. There was a lot more to it than I thought. At first I could only hold a pose for ten minutes, but after my training and hours of practice I worked up to fifteen and finally as long as twenty minutes. Frau Zirzow considered freeze modeling an art form.

Finally I was ready. Several other models and I spent many a Friday and Saturday afternoon after school, standing in the shop window of Modehaus Zirzow, concentrating on holding ever so still; sometimes alone, sometimes in a group, wearing Frau Zirzow's originals. It was a tough assignment, but I loved it, and the pocket money I earned was more than worth it. Frau Zirzow made sure I seldom missed the last bus home. If I did, I either stayed with her or with the Wohlparts. She would phone Gasthaus Kettner and leave a message for my mother. It was a wonderful interlude in my life.

In the fall of 1947 my mother and I went to the American Consulate in Munich to begin another series of appointments. My parents knew all along the day would come when my mother would have to return to the United States to reside for a prescribed period of time to maintain her American citizenship. It was a foregone conclusion that I would go with her.

A file was opened on her case. Our caseworker was a lovely American lady by the name of Miss Schroeder, who had already served years in the Diplomatic Corps and was an aide to the American Consul General in Munich. Because of the many twists and turns in our history, Miss Schroeder with her many years experience was assigned our case.

My mother presented Miss Schroeder with the original naturalization document, which established that she became an American citizen in 1938. Furthermore, she could prove we had maintained our legal and primary residence in the USA five years later (1943). Under normal circumstances, that would have been the end of the story, and my mother would return to the States in 1948 to reside a minimum of six months. At that time, a naturalized American citizen could only reside outside the country for five years. My mother's deadline was rapidly approaching. It would soon be 1948, but Schroeder, in performing her routine background search, discovered that in 1943 my mother had told the FBI she would relinquish her American citizenship if that was the only issue holding back her request to be interned with my father in a family internment camp after he was arrested. Furthermore, there was still a warrant out for her arrest as a danger-

HWS:bm
100-123329

Mr. C. E. Rhetts   November 1, 1945
Acting Head, War Division
John Edgar Hoover - Director, Federal Bureau of Investigation

ALMA WIEGAND
DENATURALIZATION PROCEEDINGS - G

     Reference is made to your memorandum dated October 13, 1942, transmitting two copies of a presidential warrant for the apprehension of the above captioned person.

     Information has now been received that the above captioned person with her husband an alien enemy of German nationality, Otto Karl Wiegand, were repatriated to Germany on February 15, 1944.

     A review of the Bureau files failed to reflect any information that Alma Wiegand was denaturalized before her departure, and I would appreciate being advised of the facts in this matter.

     Unless advised to the contrary, the presidential warrant previously referred to is being cancelled.

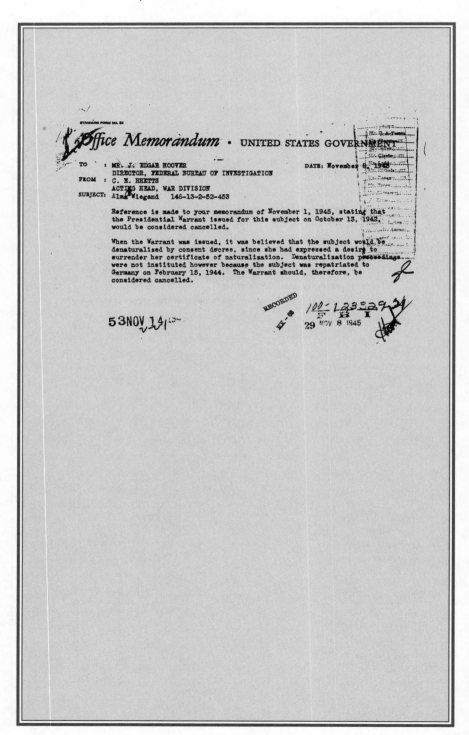

STANDARD FORM NO. 64

Office Memorandum • UNITED STATES GOVERNMENT

TO   : MR. J. EDGAR HOOVER   DATE: November 8, 1945
        DIRECTOR, FEDERAL BUREAU OF INVESTIGATION
FROM : C. E. RHETTS
        ACTING HEAD, WAR DIVISION
SUBJECT: Alma Wiegand   146-13-2-52-453

Reference is made to your memorandum of November 1, 1945, stating that
the Presidential Warrant issued for this subject on October 13, 1942,
would be considered cancelled.

When the Warrant was issued, it was believed that the subject would be
denaturalized by consent decree, since she had expressed a desire to
surrender her certificate of naturalization. Denaturalization proceedings
were not instituted however because the subject was repatriated to
Germany on February 15, 1944. The Warrant should, therefore, be
considered cancelled.

RECORDED

EX - 8

100- 123329

F B I

29 NOV 8 1945

53 NOV 14 1945

ous enemy alien, which had to be investigated.

We had developed a pleasing rapport with Miss Schroeder, and my mother did not hold back any information. But Schroeder had no other recourse but to investigate these discoveries. Members of her family were also German immigrants at one time, and this fact gave her compassion for our case, but didn't alter the procedures she had to follow. Still, she was kind in dealing with us, never letting us go home without the reassurances that things would surely work out and my mother's American citizenship would not be in jeopardy.

The long period, as we waited to hear from Schroeder was unnerving, especially for my mother. During this time, every Saturday her path led her straight to the tarot-card lady or the palm reader in Freising. While she was there, I'd be freeze modeling in Modehaus Zirzow's shop window. The news had gotten around to some of my schoolmates as well as friends from our village. Boys who knew me and were supposed to be my friends stood outside the window trying their best to break my concentration and make me laugh. Busses parked nearby; this was a great sport to pass the time while waiting for the bus to Attenkirchen. It was all in good fun, and I knew that.

We exchanged letters with Freddy almost every week. Things were going well for him, and he was not turning Tante Elsie and Onkel Werner's household on its ear. On the contrary, according to the notes my aunt and uncle penned on the bottom of Freddy's letters, he was a Godsend. He had arrived at a time when Elsie and Werner were in the throes of a family crisis.

As soon as the war was over, they had set the wheels in motion to get their daughter, my cousin Marianne, out of occupied Germany and back to New York, where she was born. Raised by her grandparents and a doting aunt in upper-class circumstances since she was left with them in 1938, this little Princess of Privilege was now facing a life-changing move to America, returning to live with parents she knew of, but really didn't know.

Werdau, the small town Marianne was about to leave, was located in Saxony and did not suffer much damage during the war, but was now in the middle of the Russian Zone, the same area from which our family had so dramatically escaped. Negotiating with the Soviets to get Marianne out was an arduous and lengthy ordeal, with one even having to negotiate diplomatic channels. It took almost a year and a half to complete the process, but finally Marianne returned to her parents. She arrived in New York in late 1946. Just twelve, she was another little girl traveling halfway around the world by herself and speaking only German.

What was to be a happy reunion with her parents turned out to be a traumatic event for Marianne, moving from the lovely small hotel her grandparents owned in provincial Germany, albeit under Russian occupation, to a fifth-floor walk-up apartment, with its only view a brick wall with dirty windows belonging to the building next door. It was a view framed by fire escapes and clotheslines stretching across every floor of the dingy buildings, revealing a filthy, garbage-strewn alley below.

Marianne developed a severe case of *Heimweh* (homesickness). There were times she just couldn't stop crying, and she would withdraw to her room, not just for hours at a time, but for days. This was not what Elsie and Werner had envisioned. They wanted only the best for Marianne, the opportunity to be a family again, learn to love each other and give Marianne a life in America. Her room had been redecorated with new furniture, carpeting, and happy wallpaper. Her closet and dresser drawers were filled with the things a budding teenager's heart would desire. All of this didn't matter, Marianne had *Heimweh*, and for the moment there was no antidote short of sending her back. Tante Elsie and Onkel Werner were disappointed, frustrated, and very sad.

With the help of German friends, they managed to muddle through, day-by-day, week-by-week, slowly introducing, then integrating, Marianne into their lifestyle, which encompassed the German/American society of Yorkville. Marianne had to learn English, and my aunt and uncle had to get back to work. They both had careers.

Then Freddy arrived, bringing the breath of fresh air everyone needed. He was ready to re-start his own life with energy and enthusiasm and swept everyone into the happy, "Let's all go forward" atmosphere he created. He recognized Marianne's emotional needs right away and became her surrogate brother. Tante Elsie had enrolled her in a private school that offered accelerated English language classes; but Marianne was struggling and Freddy grasped the opportunity to help her with her courses and homework.

My aunt and uncle enjoyed an active social life, singing with the *Liederkranz*, a German/American chorale group, acting and singing with the *Baeckermeisters*, another German vocational group. There were many concerts, banquets, and dances to attend. They would go as a family, and Marianne was delighted to have Freddy around as a dancing partner, at least for part of the evening. After all, she was only twelve and Freddy almost seventeen. Before the evening was over, he had a way of disappearing, giving Onkel Werner the kind of worries he had never experienced before. They were normal worries every father can identify with, responsible for a teenager whose hormones were running rampant. In a way it was payback time. Many years earlier my parents had their hands full when my father's younger and free-spirited sister Elsie came to live with them. Perhaps Werner could remember what he was like in his youth and identify with his nephew.

Freddy stuck to his promise to my father to continue his education, but he had to make adjustments to the plan because his lifestyle demanded money. He found a job with a butcher within walking distance and worked all day, attending school at night. He also went to the gym, worked out, and swam several times a week. Chasing girls was a way of life with Freddy, and he still found time to date. His energy was boundless, but on Sundays he slept around the clock. My aunt often checked on him to make sure he was still breathing. On Monday mornings, he would arise, refreshed, and begin the same schedule all over again. For Freddy the weeks flew by.

In Attenkirchen, however, time was dragging. Occasionally my mother would check with Miss Schroeder at the American Consulate in Munich, inquiring whether there was any movement in her case regarding the status of her citizenship. Miss Schroeder told her to continue to be patient. News would be forthcoming, and she would call the moment she received a response from the State Department. As for my nationality, it never came into question. The laws of both lands protected me. At that time in Germany, if you were under age, you were the same nationality as your father. That made me a German. American law is that you are the nationality of the country of your birth. That made me an American. I always felt fortunate and proud, too, that I had dual citizenship. It offered me the best of both worlds. I chose what I thought were the finest attributes of both countries and made them my own.

We continued to wait, and it was during this period that my mother began turning towards her faith for strength and direction, rather than relying on the tarot cards. I saw her reading her Bible again. Her return to spirituality was perhaps triggered when a Lutheran minister, sponsored by the Missouri Synod, began visiting our village once a month. We were Evangelical Lutheran and were joined by a small minority of other Lutherans who had fled from East Prussia, Poland, and the Sudetenland (German speaking area of Czechoslovakia) during the war and lived in and around Attenkirchen.

There were mostly Catholic churches in Bavaria. The population at that time was over ninety percent Catholic, and in the rural areas among the parishioners there was a certain amount of distrust directed towards Protestants. In my opinion, the distrust was linked to the fact that most of the Protestants were relocated families, transplanted because of the war. They were still strangers and not quite accepted. This attitude was more pronounced in rural areas; larger towns and cities absorbed outlanders more easily. But opening their sanctuaries for another denomination's service was out of the question. Our services had to be held in one of the larger class-rooms of our elementary school.

I often attended the Catholic church in Attenkirchen with my girl-friends and sat with them in the choir loft. Sometimes we would climb the ladder into the belfry, where we were almost able to touch the bells. They were not automated as they are now, and it was fun watching the bell-ringer manipulate three different ropes attached to three different-sized bells and ring out a carillon. The sound of bells tolling off in the distance, coming from churches in the small villages all over Bavaria will forever be a part of my memories of Germany, stirring a longing in me, a wish to go back to those wonderful days of my childhood. Now the bells are comput-erized, and much of the nostalgia has been lost. Though the bells still sound the same, they are programmed to stop on command. You cannot hear them fade away as they used to when the bell-ringer had to hang onto the rope and use his body as a counterweight to make them stop, as he was pulled off his feet before he could silence the largest.

Finally, the day came when our postman delivered a letter from the American Consulate. It was the one we had been waiting for and brought the good news we had been praying for. My mother was advised her Ameri-can citizenship was intact. An appointment was to be scheduled with Miss Schroeder, and we were instructed to bring along duplicate prints of regu-lation size black-and-white photographs of both of us, so our passports could be ordered.

When we walked into Schroeder's office, she came towards us, hands outstretched, beaming. She confessed she made it a point not to get emo-tionally involved in any of her cases, but for some reason she could not avoid being openly delighted that my mother had retained her citizenship. Because of the fact that we were repatriated, de-naturalization proceedings had never been instituted. The presidential warrant for her arrest was still out there, but it had never been executed. It was cancelled by order of the Attorney General. Repatriation did have an upside! All we had to do now was wait for our passports. Schroeder assured us it would be a short wait.

※ ※ ※

Christmas, 1947 was not the same. Freddy was not with us, and I missed him. To make matters worse, he wrote unbelievably sentimental letters. His Christmas card that year was signed, "I'll be home for Christmas, if only in my dreams—forever, Freddy." I found out later he borrowed that line from a Frank Sinatra song. But knowing him as I did, I knew it came from the heart and expressed his emotions exactly. No doubt he could have written these words himself. I still have the card.

Soon after the New Year, our passports were ready. We were on our way to Munich on the next train. To my mother's surprise, aside from the passports, there was an entire package prepared for us, which contained sailing dates, travel instructions, baggage tags, meal coupons, customs information, and much more. We had approximately thirty days to prepare before we were scheduled to leave. Our plans were speeding forward at a dizzying pace.

The first time my mother had inquired about immigration quotas for German nationals (my father) was in 1945 when she visited the Consulate several months after the war was over. She was told that none existed, and there was no point in filing an application. Over two years had passed since then, and this time she asked Miss Schroeder whether any quotas had opened up in the meantime. She said yes, but the criteria was so restrictive she feared an immigration application filed by my father at this time would not be considered. Nonetheless, she would be willing to try. She would reopen his file and submit a request to have his case reviewed. Response time would take six weeks at the very least.

This meant we would be leaving Germany without any knowledge of Pappi's status. My mother simply could not live with this notion and asked Miss Schroeder whether she could somehow extend our exit date. Schroeder, speaking off the record, told my mother to have her family doctor send a letter to the Consulate, advising against her traveling at this time, due to some health condition. He'd have to figure out a believable problem.

Fortunately, my mother had been treated and monitored for a nerve infection in one of her legs earlier that year, and our family doctor in Attenkirchen had no problem issuing a statement, declaring that it had flared up again and she was currently under treatment. We got a sixty-day extension.

My mother was relieved. I was ecstatic! The thought of leaving Pappi behind in Germany by himself had been gnawing at me for some time. Having a window of time after all of our plans came to a head so quickly made it easier for me to cope.

My mother, very focused, packed all of our personal effects and most of our household goods. She had collected three original oil paintings in addition to the one given to her by Frau Segelke in Meiningen after the war, and they were not going to be left behind. One she particularly loved was a large painting of the old Nymphenburger Allee (a street in Munich leading to the Castle Nymphenburg) from a bygone era, which she had seen displayed by the living artist (Loichen) in a bank window in Freising. After inquiring, she discovered it was for sale, but high priced. She didn't give up, convincing a bank manager to contact the artist and ask whether he would consider a payment plan.

He did, as long as it remained on display until it was paid off. Once a week after school I dropped off an envelope with the pin money she had squeezed out of our household budget. For her birthday Pappi matched the modeling money I had saved, and together we were able to bring the remaining balance down considerably. It took almost a year, but she finally brought it home. For all I know, my mother might have introduced the German post-war economy to the good old American easy payment plan.

Now that painting was coming off the wall, along with the others. She packed as though we were going to America for good. Jokingly, Pappi asked her to please leave him *einen Topf und einen Kochloeffel* (one pot and one wooden cook spoon) so he could warm up some soup for himself when he came home from Munich on weekends.

It was hard to think of leaving Germany, and I put off thinking about the inevitable. We had established our place in the village, school was going well, and I was having a fine time on weekends with all of my friends. There was always a dance in some nearby village we could bike to. Like other Germans fond of dancing, none of our crowd had attended dancing school. We taught each other. I learned to dance the Viennese waltz, the English (slow) waltz, tango, polka, and many folk dances, of which my favorite one was the "Rheinlaender." In turn, I taught my friends how to do the jitterbug, the lindy hop, and how the boys were supposed to swing the girls around to the lively boogie-woogie beat. On Sunday afternoons we would often go on long bike rides through the countryside and stop at a café for coffee and cake; and as the weather warmed up, there were soccer games in every village.

Some of the girls in my social group, the older ones, were starting to get around a little and seemed to be damaging their reputations to one degree or another. In a small village everyone knows everyone else's business: who is seeing whom and who is rumored to be in trouble. I didn't allow that for myself, not only because I was the youngest of the girls, but because I had experienced too much in my early childhood and was still putting traumatic memories to rest. I had no problem holding hands with a boy as he escorted me home, even a goodnight kiss at the front door was all right, but that was it. If you really wanted to get my attention, you would have had to share an interest in sports. Skiing, ice-skating, swimming, biking, or dancing, and we would be best friends, but expect nothing more.

The news came that Pappi was again denied access to current quotas for Germans. It was not a flat-out "No," but for the time being, he did not qualify to immigrate to the United States.

My father's FBI files reveal a considerable amount of correspondence between the FBI, the Special Intelligence Service/European Desk, the 303rd CIC Detachment/Headquarters Third US Army, and the US Army Intelligence Center/United States Forces European Theater. This mountain of correspondence, all in the form of interoffice memoranda, was generated after my father applied for his first job as interpreter for the Allied Occupation Forces in Freising in late summer 1945, and a routine security check was performed on him. Referencing the fact that he requested repatriation to Germany, a quote from one of the memoranda reads as follows: "The Army's attitude toward the employment of such repatriates as these has never been completely clear. Naturally, we and our colleagues in CIC view them with extreme suspicion. However many of them are no worse security dangers than other German civilians whom the Army employs, and it therefore appears that inquiry into the background of each individual is necessary."

After this information came to light as the reason my father's application was denied again, Miss Schroeder advised my mother not to procrastinate, but return to the States to retain her American citizenship. It was of the utmost importance. It had been recommended that my father reapply sometime in the future, and my mother could then work the system from the other side and try to get the INS (Immigration & Naturalization Service) to reconsider and realize the advantage of allowing my father to immigrate and support a family that might otherwise become a financial burden to the United States government. The plan made sense, and we stayed the course.

It was a depressingly gray morning when Pappi walked us to the train station in Attenkirchen. He held my hand in his. It felt warm and moist as it always did. In my other hand I was holding onto Prinzi's leash. He was a happy dog, enjoying a surprise early morning walk with the whole family. My girlfriend Ingrid came along to take the dog back home after I gave him one last hug. When the moment came, he didn't understand why she was taking him away and we weren't coming along, so he kept turning around, tugging at the leash. I couldn't look anymore; my tears blurred everything. I vaguely made out the Kettner family as they waved to us from atop the hill a short distance away. It had also been a tearful good-bye, and they promised to look after Pappi when he was home on weekends.

Pappi rode on the train with us to Munich. Mercifully, we had little time before we had to board the next train to Bremerhaven. Sadly, but bravely, we said our tearful good-byes. One word from my father to that effect, and I would have turned around. My mother was an iron woman in her resolve; she was on a mission. I was secretly clinging to the hope that after six months residence in the US we could come back. I would survive.

Leaving Pappi was the hardest thing I ever had to do. As the train pulled out, and he disappeared in a crowd of travelers on the platform, I worried about what would become of him. He was so attached to me, and I to him. Little Burli Kettner had promised me that he would continue to visit Pappi every Saturday afternoon and drink beer with him. It was of no comfort to me at that moment, but later in life I came to cherish that heart-felt promise made to me by this adorable four-year-old boy in *Lederhosen*.

The trip from Bremerhaven to New York was uneventful. Our crossing took twelve days on a converted troop ship named the *Marine Tiger*. My mother was seasick all the way and relieved when American shores appeared on the horizon. Entering New York harbor and passing the Statue of Liberty is always a moving experience, no matter who you are. For us, it was especially emotional, bringing back memories of the countless ferry rides we took, cutting through the same harbor waters to neighboring Ellis Island to visit Pappi.

We arrived in March, 1948. Everybody was there to welcome us: Freddy, Tante Elsie, Onkel Werner, and my cousin Marianne. Our reunion was a happy one. Freddy had matured even more and was as handsome as ever. His hair was combed in a deeply waved pompadour, the "in" style of the moment for young men.

After passing through immigration and having our passports checked, we took a taxi uptown to Elsie and Werner's apartment, where a beautifully set table and a festive meal prepared by Onkel Werner welcomed us. But first Freddy popped the cork off of a bottle of champagne, and we clinked the glasses with a loud celebratory *"PROSIT!"* ("CHEERS!") Our stay with them was brief. Their apartment at 1704 First Avenue, just off of 86th Street in Yorkville, was small, especially now that Marianne was back. Within a week we moved across the street to 1685 First Avenue, a partly furnished apartment in a walkup, four-story brownstone.

Yorkville was familiar to my mother from earlier times. Eighty-Sixth

A United States Governments office memorandum indicates a security check was filed by the United States Armed Forces in the European Theater on subject: OTTO WIEGAND.

This security check was most likely performed when my father was hired as an interpreter at the Artillerie Kaserne Army Post in Freising, late summer, 1945, shortly after we arrived in Attenkirchen. Security checks of this kind were routinely performed on all applicants seeking employment with the US Occupation; whether they were Germans or other nationalities, such as refugees from East European coutries, as long as they could identify themselves.

Note, this memorandum is dated February 25, 1946. My father was hired the day he applied in late 1945. He did not have to wait until this memorandum gave him fficial clearance.

Author's note: In the second paragraph of the memo, there is a significant error. It states that Wiegand was "repatriated" on September 30, 1942. Incorrect. That is the date he was "interned." We were repatriated on February 15, 1944.

STANDARD FORM NO. 64

Office Memorandum · UNITED STATES GOVERNMENT

to   : Mr. D. M. Ladd

FROM : J. C. Strickland

SUBJECT: OTTO WIEGAND
ALIEN ENEMY CONTROL - G

DATE: February 25, 1946

Reference is made to the memorandum from Mr. E. G. Fitch of the Liaison Section dated January 31, 1946, furnishing information concerning Otto Wiegand, which information was received from the United States Forces in the European Theater.

A review of the Bureau files reflects that Wiegand was apprehended by this Bureau, interned, and subsequently repatriated on September 30, 1942. There is no information contained in the file indicating that Wiegand is presently wanted by this Bureau.

RECOMMENDATION:

It is suggested this memorandum be transmitted to the Liaison Section who in turn can notify the Army that the Bureau has no interest in Wiegand at this time.

HWS:ka

b7C

58 MAR 28 1946

Street was our main drag. It was not only our shopping street, but where we socialized with many other Germans living in this predominantly German section of Manhattan. My mother introduced me to Café Heidelberg, Café Rheinland, Kramer's German Bakery, Schaller & Weber Quality Meats, the German Movie House, and my favorite place, Café Geiger, which featured the most decadent pastries and tortes, served with whipped-cream topped cups of aromatic coffee. Live Viennese music completed the atmosphere. When you entered this place, you were taken to Munich, Salzburg, or Vienna. I felt very much at home.

Flower and fruit stands spilled out onto the sidewalks of 86th Street, and, walking by, you could hear as much German spoken as English, if not more. I loved it, and I could tell my mother was happy to be back. It was certainly a change, this *Grossstadtleben* (city life), compared to our laid-back lifestyle in Attenkirchen.

When our household goods were delivered, my mother gave our apartment her personal touches: familiar bedcovers, photos, doilies, and her beloved oil paintings on the walls. Mommi could turn the dingiest hole-in-the-wall into a cozy, even elegant, New York apartment. But we had not returned to New York to enjoy the German-American life. We were there on a mission: to get our family established and forward the process of getting Pappi back over and all of us permanently residing in the United States again.

My mother found work immediately at a nearby luncheonette, Kurtz's Bakery & Luncheonette on York Avenue. Freddy worked the same job he had since returning the year before and continued going to night school. I was responsible for all of the housekeeping chores, in addition to going back to school. I started in class 8BR in Junior High School #96, at York Avenue and 81st Street. According to the report card I still have, the second term, 8B, began on February 4, 1948. My admission date was Monday, April 5, ten days after our arrival. The "R" in "8BR" stood for "Rapids," denoting a class for accelerated students. Just exactly why I was placed in the accelerated class I don't know but surmise it might have been because of the languages, living history, and current events I could share.

It was an interesting adjustment, and I made it fairly quickly. I had not been to an American school since I was a young child and really knew only the German educational system, regimented and strict. I loved the more informal atmosphere and warmth of American schools, as opposed to the formal practices of schooling in Germany. JHS #96 was an-all girls school, like the one I had attended in Freising, but unlike the cool reception my German classmates gave me at first, the American girls were welcoming and wanted to know all about me.

The teachers were people you could approach, and they related to students as human beings. Miss Helen Klug was my homeroom teacher. She was also our eighth grade social studies teacher and was interested in the fact that I could give a firsthand account of Germany now and my family's experiences throughout the war. I was often asked by Miss Klug to get up in front of the class after a lesson on current events and answer questions. Miss Klug was Jewish and especially interested in what our lives were like living in Hitler's Third Reich. At one point, I was invited to speak and answer questions at a faculty meeting in the teachers' lounge. Persons of authority had never treated me with more respect. I never forgot.

English was a bit of a problem. The biggest challenge was catching up on literature assignments. I had to cram works by Edgar Allen Poe and Robert Louis Stevenson, as well as the *Odyssey* and the *Iliad* by Homer. *Ivanhoe* was a struggle. I had always spoken English fluently and kept my spelling up in Germany by reading the *Stars & Stripes*, occasional magazines, and comic books Freddy brought home. But I had trouble with grammar. I had to be taught to pick out verbs, adverbs, and conjunctions and how to diagram a sentence. I didn't have any patience with all that parsing.

Math, science, geography, gym, music, art, and drama class—all were wonderful, and I caught up quickly and kept in stride. I got involved in drama, and at the end of the term we had a variety show in which I played a little Italian girl (I wore a dark wig) and sang a solo, "Return to Sorrento."

I quickly fit in with a group of girls in my class. They were very kind in bringing me up to speed in all my subjects. I'd say we were the poster children of our time in the melting pot of New York; the American-born generation of immigrant parents and grandparents. Annina Comforti was Italian; Alice Horowitz (our brain child) was Jewish, as was Myrna Manoff, both of whose ancestors came from Eastern Europe. Hildegard Singer was a fellow German; Elinor Hansen, Scandanavian; and Leslie Bingham was British.

Our out-of-school activities were primarily school projects, work we had to complete as part of our homework. Leslie Bingham always had permission to invite us to her house, and I loved going there. She lived in a private, three-story brownstone on East 87th Street. We never got to go all the way upstairs, as her mother had her artist studio on the top floor and her mother's boyfriend had his writing cubicle somewhere on the second floor. He was an author and wrote columns for magazines. There was always something so romantically mysterious about Leslie's "parents." Occasionally one or the other would come downstairs to say hello and offer us a

Coke. I was intrigued by their avant-garde lifestyle.

When we were done with our homework, we usually walked to the eastern end of 87th Street, just a few houses past Leslie's, where Gracie Mansion, New York's mayoral residence, was nestled in the luscious green of Carl Schurz Park along the East River. A short walk through the park to 86th Street, and we would break up and head for home. Some of the girls would invite me to stop at an ice cream parlor, but I was always in a hurry. I had household responsibilities. It was always surprising to me that my girlfriends had such freedom from chores. To the best of my knowledge, they never had to pitch in at home; several of them didn't even have to clean their own rooms. And they had so much spending money. Their parents gave them an "allowance." I had never even heard of the word.

When I needed or wanted something and could justify it, my mother gave me the money, but I certainly didn't ask for any of her hard-earned money to spend frivolously on myself. Freddy always slipped me a couple of bucks, but I usually saved that for something I had my eye on. Therefore, I felt I could not afford to go to the movies with them because that was only the beginning. Afterwards they'd go for hotdogs at Nedick's or to White Castle for hamburgers, then Revlon lipstick-and-nail polish-shopping at Walgreens. Finally, a stop at a nearby newsstand for the latest *Seventeen* magazine and two or three movie magazines. A few Milky Way and Almond Joy candy bars tossed in for nibbling. All of that was out of reach for me. The only thing I could participate in, and thoroughly enjoyed, was when Myrna Manoff invited us over to watch Ed Sullivan's "Toast of the Town" show on television. Myrna's family was the only family I knew in the neighborhood that had a television set. It had a magnificent fourteen-inch, black-and-white screen, encased in a walnut cabinet.

My cousin Marianne was never really a part of my circle. She was still attending private school and working hard to get rid of her German accent. She had been invited to join us several times, even accepted, but felt out of place. She had made enormous strides in adjusting to her new life, and by the time Mommi and I arrived on the scene, she had gotten over her bouts of homesickness and was well on her way to becoming an American teenager. Much of the credit has to go to Freddy. I had no problem adjusting and became an American teenager overnight. I just didn't have the funds to live the teenagers' dream.

By nature, Marianne was much more serious than I. She would never be a free spirit, but I understood her, and we were the best of pals, even though we would get mad at each other and make up again. We had lived through the ravages of war—fear, hunger, death, and destruction—and there is no denying the sobering effect these experiences have on children. This was our common bond though we rarely talked about our past.

We both had to keep our apartments clean. We went to the laundromat together when it came time to do the weekly laundry, so why couldn't we clean our flats together? Mine first, of course, since it was my idea. Marianne agreed to the plan, and we picked "my day" and "your day." Our mothers were okay with it, just so the work got done towards the end of the week and not on weekends.

Marianne came over immediately after school, and I assigned her the kitchen and bathroom.

I took the two bedrooms and hallway. We'd meet in the living room and do it together. I was done with my end long before she was; so rather than get a head start in the living room, I poured myself a glass of my mother's favorite Mission Bell port wine, lit one of my brother's cigarettes, flopped down on the couch, trying to look slinky, and called her. As she appeared, I puffed. "What a dump! What's keeping you so long? When are you going to come in here and clean this place up?"

Marianne was so predictable. I got exactly the reaction I was looking for. She was shocked, indignant, and at a loss for words! The nerve of it all! I rolled back and forth on the couch, my laughter making me fall to the floor. She stomped around not knowing what to do: walk off the job angry, or join me in the fun I was having at her expense. She finally decided the joke I played on her was funny, but had to have time to get over my chutzpah. I put on a stack of Freddy's records, and we danced in between dusting and vacuuming. I was teaching the lindy and the jitterbug again, this time to my cousin.

Onkel Werner was cut of the same somber cloth as Marianne. It was hard to get a belly laugh out of him. Soon Marianne was getting used to my love of practical jokes. I had even talked her into participating. Our goal was to get Werner laughing. He was the headwaiter at the Madison Avenue Grille, a high-end eatery in a posh Madison, Park, and Fifth Avenue neighborhood. His hours were split, so that he'd have to be at work late mornings to work the lunch crowd, come home by 3:00 PM, rest, then go back to work in time to serve evening dinner guests, before he finally came home between ten and eleven o'clock at night.

He had his routine when he came home for his mid-afternoon rest. He would take off his clothes, slip into pajamas, sit down at the kitchen table, and have a bottle of Pabst Blue Ribbon. Then he would smoke a cigarette, go into the bedroom, close the door, pull down the room-darkening shades, and slip under the covers.

It all started on a day we were cleaning their apartment. We began by stripping the sheets. As we were making the beds, the thought struck me: wouldn't it be funny to short-sheet Onkel Werner's bed? I had to show Marianne how to do it, but she wasn't sure he'd consider it funny. I assured her he would because we'd be doing other things to lead up to it. So we basted the hems of his pajama bottoms shut. Then we exchanged half of his beer with cream soda and recapped it.

Marianne was nervous, and I was giggly as we finished cleaning the bedroom, listening for the key turning the lock in the front door. Finally he came, and his routine began. Soon we heard him grumbling in the bedroom, then in German, *"Was ist denn hier los?"* (What's going on here?) "Marianne!" We had been suppressing our laughter, then burst out as we saw him sitting on the edge of the bed in his boxer shorts trying to get into his pajama bottoms. He was not overcome with laughter, instead he said, "Okay girls, you've had your fun, now let me have my beer in peace!" Marianne and I just looked at each other.

A sip of the beer, and then "Anneliese, *das ist ganz bestimmt deine Arbeit!"* (This is your work, for sure!) We were all laughing as he went into the bedroom assuring us how much fun this was, but enough now. I could hardly wait for the final act. Marianne on the other hand was ready to escape. We heard the room darkening shades drop and shortly thereafter, *"War der Teufel los!"* (The devil was loose!—A German expression for all heck breaking out). I thought it was hilarious, picturing him all wound up in his sheets, fumbling around in the dark.

"Marianne, Anneliese! *Was stellt Ihr zwei Spassvoegel bloss mit mir an?"* (What are you two jokesters doing with me?) At that point we dissolved in laughter and assured him our comedy had come to an end, that the short-sheeting trick was our final act. Onkel Werner told that story more times than I can remember.

With the exception of school activities, Marianne and I were always together. Our social lives were based in her mother's involvement with a number of German/American organizations. Tante Elsie took memberships seriously and did not shy away from hours of volunteer work. She never belonged to an organization where she didn't go through the chairs in one capacity or another. She could organize, she could lead, but above all, she loved to sing and act. For years one of her closest friends was the society editor of *Die Staats Zeitung*, the German language newspaper published in New York. We always kidded Tante Elsie about having her own publicity agent, a fact that was probably more truth than fiction!

Almost every German in Yorkville knew Elsie Knoch. She and my

Onkel Werner were very involved in the café society there, frequenting many of the German bars and cafés on 86th Street. Their favorite hangouts were Café Rheinland and the Heidelberg Restaurant and Bar on Second Avenue just off of 86th Street. There they would meet after Werner's work and Elsie's evening *Liederkranz* rehearsals to have a nightcap and enjoy some *Gemuetlichkeit* (geniality) with friends. Werner would have his favorite cocktail, a Perfect Manhattan, and Elsie would have a Bull Shot, (a shot of rye whiskey and a beer chaser).

Marianne and I were swept into this lifestyle, not the drinking, but the fellowship and the German ambiance. We joined in with our favorite, a cherry Coke, the Dr. Pepper of our generation; but Europeans really don't make a big deal out of young people having some wine anyway, or beer on occasion. It's part of the culture.

To my disappointment, my mother never joined us for a drink at a neighborhood bar. She was for the most part a tea-totaler though she poured an occasional glass of her favorite port when company came. She could not bring herself to enjoy this pleasure, knowing Pappi was alone in Bavaria.

She initiated a new investigation of my father's case shortly after we arrived. The American Consulate in New York established a file and proceeded to research his history, as well as to review our current family status in regards to demographics, health, and financial needs. The system was overburdened with the huge wave of DPs (displaced persons) immigrating from Europe, and it was very slow going for us. But we remained persistent in our quest.

Pappi was always interested in my progress in school, encouraging me to reach for more and more knowledge. "What you learn, no one can take from you," he wrote in one of his many letters. We corresponded weekly, and the more detailed my letters were, the more he enjoyed them. I told him how much I liked my school, the American educational system, and all about the wonderful teacher I had in Miss Klug.

I was thirteen years old and hadn't attended an American school in almost six years, practically all of the elementary school years. Upon returning from war-torn Europe, I was so inspired by Klug and so idealistic, I wrote a poem in Social Studies class and dedicated it to her. It is simple, the best I could do at the time, considering my limited literary skills, but it tells exactly how I felt:

– This is America –
Isn't America a nation for all?
There is no such thing as a separating wall

All races and religions live together here,
Everyone is free—no one has fear.
Let it be Mohammidan, Christian or Jew,
We're all alike, just as a ship's crew.
Though our skin be dark or white,
Though we be short or tall,
It makes no difference, for God made us all!
Since the birth of our country,
We fought many a war,
But we always won, because we were decent,
Determined and strong to the core.
May the sons of our nation grow straight and tall—
We're all for one and one for all!

I was stunned when Klug read it aloud in assembly at the end of the school year. Our entire 8B-R class was promoted to 9A-R. Not one of our accelerated students was moved out of the rapids program and moved to regular 9-A, and Klug remained as our social studies and homeroom teacher. I was very happy and proud of our achievements.

The hot, humid summer of 1948 brought with it a frightening public health problem. Polio was threatening the lives of countless children and young adults, reaching epidemic proportions. Hundreds of new cases were diagnosed in the New York area on a daily basis. I sought all the information I could to educate myself, my mother, and Freddy as to how the virus was spread and how to avoid being vulnerable. The more I learned about this dreadful disease, the more it scared me, and I was grateful when my aunt and uncle invited me to join them and Marianne on their summer vacation in the Catskills. Three weeks out of the city was a tremendous relief although I was terribly worried about Mommi and Freddy.

Meanwhile, the effort to get Pappi to the US continued. The American Consulate in New York asked my mother to obtain personal references from people living in the States who knew my father during the years prior to his internment. This was a tall order. Personal references given by relatives didn't count, and most of our friends had also been repatriated. Pastor Greber's ministry was no longer active, and he, along with any other business and organizational contacts of my father, had moved away.

My mother took the subway back to our old Brooklyn neighborhood in search of former neighbors, but they, too, had either moved away or died, and the neighborhood stores had changed ownership or closed. She was hard-pressed to find someone who remembered my father in a favorable light since most probably remembered him as the German butcher on the corner arrested by the FBI, if they remembered him at all.

The day my mother went to Brooklyn was a terrible one. I recall her sitting at our kitchen table, arms folded on the tabletop, her head face down, buried in her arms, crying. Our young family's life, when we were all together in Brooklyn passed before her. The loss of it all, and everything that had happened since then, was more than she could bear. Freddy came home, and for a while we all hurt together. We could not ignore the facts. Maybe we should be heading back to Germany after all. It was not what we wanted. "Let's keep going. Let's try harder. We're not giving up, not yet!" we told her.

We rededicated our efforts to working hard, saving money, and getting our educations. My parents were remarkable in their ability to save. My father had been leading a frugal existence in Bavaria and surprised us with a copy of a bank report that reflected an extraordinary combined savings balance spread over four accounts. He had opened an account in his own name, as well as accounts for my mother, Freddy, and me. My mother's account carried the largest balance, so she would have funds available for transfer to establish a more permanent home if and when Pappi came, or have the money to buy our tickets back to Germany if that was our destiny.

For the immediate future, we stayed the course. I was happy when school started. Ninth grade. Lots of work lay ahead and decisions had to be made. Did I want to take entrance exams for special high schools? I would have to defer my decision until I got my call from the guidance office.

Marianne and I started confirmation class and joined the choir at Immanuel Evangelical Lutheran Church on the corner of Lexington Avenue and 88th Street, a three-block walk. It was the same church where we were both baptized as infants in 1935. We started going regularly, not because we suddenly got religion, but because as future confirmants, church attendance was mandatory. Of greater importance to us was the opportunity to hang out with boys.

We always dressed in our Sunday best back then—suits and coats, heels and hose, white gloves, and hats—although Marianne and I usually only wore hats on Easter. Often we would sneak out of church after our junior choir sang and walk the three blocks to Central Park with some boys while our pastor delivered his boring sermon, then hurry back in time to be seen when church services were over. Afterwards we would walk down 86th Street, where I could never resist teasing my cousin with one of my favorite Marianne embarrassments. In heels and hose and dressed to the nines, I would leap frog over every fire hydrant on 86th Street from Lexington Avenue all the way to First Avenue. Sometimes she would act as though she didn't know me; other times she would cross the street, which didn't help much since there were fire hydrants on that side too.

The news coming out of West Germany was both bad and good. The good news according to my father was that the Marshall Plan, also known as the European Recovery Plan, was succeeding, and the morale of the German people was optimistic. Everyone was working and focused on rebuilding their lives. The bad news was that the Soviets under the direction of Joseph Stalin were constantly stirring the pot and bringing the Cold War to a boil. On June 24, 1948, Stalin shut down all routes into Berlin, halting overland traffic in and out of the city. On June 26th the first C-47 aircraft took off from Rhein/Main Air Force Base, loaded with milk, medicine, and flour, and landed at Tempelhof Flughafen, Berlin. (Tempelhof airport.) The Berlin Airlift had begun. For the next sixteen months the Allies landed cargo airships at the rate of one every three minutes to keep the city and its residents supplied.

Miss Klug treated me as though I was a fountainhead of firsthand information on what was going on. I tried my best to tell her everything I knew and often let her read portions of my father's letters. What really astounded her once had nothing to do with the airlift, but rather the revelation that I still had two uncles (my father's brothers Karl and Willi) in Russia, three years after the war was over. The family knew Karl was still alive, but held prisoner in some gulag with no release date in sight. Willi had not been heard from since his capture on the Russian front in early 1944.

My cousin Marlene, her sister Ulla, and her mother, Tante Lisbeth (Karl's family), received authorization in October 1945, to move back to Berlin from Bettenhausen. They were fortunate in getting their old apartment back and doubly fortunate that it was located in the American sector.

Marlene vividly recalls the *Luftbruecke* (air-bridge), which we called the Berlin Airlift. As a child she remembers looking skyward with her playmates and calling the incoming cargo planes *Rosinenbomber* (raisin-bombers), a nickname given to these cargo planes as a result of their crews throwing candy bars and packages of chewing gum to the children below as they were on their final approach, flying low over the city. The cargo plane that was the first to land at the onset of the airlift is on permanent display at Templehof Airfield and open for public viewing.

Stories of these topical events and the connection I would make with the people living them enchanted Miss Klug. I shared as many as I could with her; sometimes I could even show pictures. More often than I can recall, these accounts became the subject of our social studies class.

One day we received a letter from Pappi with a list of addresses of all of our relatives living in the Russian Zone. My mother's sister, who lived in Hamburg in the British Zone, was included on the list, as were family friends, who never escaped as we did and were now stranded in the Russian Zone. He asked that we send all of them a Care package for the oncoming holidays. Whatever the cost, it didn't matter. They were not needy, but they were all deprived of goodies, and this was just something he wanted us to do.

What a project! Our apartment looked like the staging area of a mail-order house. I recall our packing sixteen or seventeen large, heavy-duty cardboard boxes with coffee, tea, cocoa, tobacco, spices, bar soap, and facial cream for the women; shaving cream and aftershave for the men; and choco-late bars and candied fruit for the children. The accompanying paper work alone (customs declarations) was a job. "Care package" was a familiar term on both sides of the ocean, but with special meaning to the recipients on the other side. We got our gift boxes off by early October. They would be en route to their destinations for eight to ten weeks, and, we hoped, would arrive in time for the holidays.

Christmas, 1948. Our family was still was not together. Pappi sent pictures that were taken when he was invited to the homes of friends. I felt so cheated when I saw him in the midst of other families. He didn't belong there; he belonged with us, but he looked good, better than Mommi did. Disappointments were beginning to wear on her. She was only forty-five, but at times she looked older than her years, especially when she was tired and her make-up was not fresh. She was always so beautiful; I didn't want her to change.

My brother brightened our holidays by taking us to see the Rockettes at Radio City Music Hall for their Christmas show. Then he surprised me with the one gift I had been wishing for: a new pair of figure skates. And tucked inside one of them was a pair of white woolen socks that held a season pass to the ice skating rink at Rockefeller Center, a gift from my mother. I was overwhelmed. If tears of joy could freeze, I would have al-ready been standing on a patch of ice.

The New Year came, 1949, and we found ourselves making impor-tant decisions. Freddy told my mother that regardless of what happened—whether we wound up living in the States or went back to Germany—he intended to finish his high school equivalency and enlist in the Air Force. Armed with this information, my mother visited the American consulate and went on record.

If Freddy decided to enlist early, we would lose the earnings he contributed to our household and leave my mother as the sole support of our family. Perhaps they would give some consideration to the added burden this loss would place on her. And wouldn't Freddy's desire to join the Armed Forces reflect positively on our family? Surely this new information could even move my father's case forward. "We'll take it under consideration," they said.

My father was also making some decisions back in Germany. Although he was building his nest egg, he was getting impatient and felt he was going nowhere. He was not satisfied with just having his money accrue in a bank account. He wanted to invest it and make it work for him.

He had the opportunity to purchase some acreage in a great location at the edge of Attenkirchen and he made an offer. It was accepted, and the property was ours. Thus he had put down family roots in Bavaria, and the Wiegand family became legitimate residents of Attenkirchen. It was something he had to do.

As soon as the weather broke, he bought around eighty *Zwetschgenbaeume* (Damson plum trees.) He was a happy man, coming home from Munich on Friday evenings and having something constructive to do. He spent the rest of his spring and early summer weekends planting trees. It was good news that Pappi was doing so well, and yet I was dubious. Deep inside of me that old feeling of "what does this mean for our future?" crept into my thoughts. I dismissed it and kept going. I had my own decisions to make.

My guidance counselor and teachers encouraged me to apply for the High School of Music and Art. I decided to drop my plans to test for Bronx Science and concentrated on my portfolio. I had to submit at least eight pieces of artwork. My application was sent in by our school administration along with a letter of recommendation from a member of the faculty and a transcript of my grades. I was delighted when Miss Klug told me she would be writing the letter. Others sometimes said I was her pet, but I felt she sincerely wanted to further my chances for a higher education and do everything she could to help me get into the school of my choice.

Testing for Music and Art was a two-day process. On the first testing day, we had to submit our portfolios and go through a one-on-one personal evaluation, which included a review of our academic status. I was a B+ student. Then a panel of directors of the various art departments questioned us as to where our main interests lay and in what direction we saw ourselves going: graphic arts, fashion design, textiles, backdrops for the performing arts, cartooning, animation, and so on. An unbelievable smorgasbord of courses was offered after the sophomore year, which was pretty basic.

The second day began with a brief art history quiz, followed by demonstrations of our artistic talent. A poem was read, which we had to illustrate. Then we had to do a contour pencil drawing of a live model sitting on a stool. After that we had to choose one of three still-lifes the teacher had arranged on tabletops and draw it three-dimensionally in pastels. After lunch we broke into teams and collectively painted backdrops for the scene of a play that was read. Finally, we were instructed to sketch something from imagination, using the medium of our choice: Pastels, charcoal, watercolor, pencil, ink, and so on, but no oils. It was an exhausting day. I came home feeling positive about my contour rendering of the model on the stool. Something worked for me that day, and I knew I nailed it.

Several hundred students from the five burroughs of New York applied for Music and Art. Only four classes were taken in at the beginning of every school year. Two students from our school were accepted: my classmate, Diana Land, and I. We were ecstatic when Klug informed us.

On graduation day we were introduced in assembly, along with other students who had passed the entrance exams to Bronx Science and the High School of Performing Arts. There was one girl who had been accepted into the Institute of Fashion Design. It was a defining moment in our lives.

The summer of 1949 was unbelievably difficult for me. All I wanted to do was get through it. Polio was not only reaching epidemic proportions again, but was predicted to be twice as virulent as the summer before.[2] I was absolutely paranoid about catching the virus and holed up in our apartment, avoiding almost all contact with the outside world. Marianne and I were members of the New York *Turnverein*, an athletic club on 85th Street and Third Avenue, where we worked out every Thursday evening. I didn't go anymore. I dropped out of choir practice for the summer and stayed

---

[2] Public Health statistics later revealed there were 27,726 reported cases of Poliomyelitis (paralytic and non-paralytic) in the summer of 1948, and 42,033 in the summer of 1949. The worst recorded polio epidemic in US history took place in the summer of 1952 when 57,628, mostly children and young adults, fell victim.

away from movie houses. I did, however, go swimming with Freddy as often as possible. The pool at the St. George Hotel, which was open to members of the New York *Turnverein* on designated evenings, was loaded with chlorine. Occasionally my mother and I would take a walk up and down 86th Street on cool, clear evenings. The only fresh air I got otherwise was when I would go out on the roof of our building late at night. That became an important part of my routine, along with writing letters, reading, studying art books, and keeping house.

I was concerned about Freddy and Mommi, as they had intensive contact with the public at the workplace, especially my mother, who was in food service. I made her promise to wash her hands often. After that she always smelled like Clorox when she got home. Freddy thought I was turning into a nut-case, but I did not come this far to wind up inside an iron lung. Not if I could help it. It would be the ultimate tragedy for my family and myself. I finally convinced him, and he practiced good hygiene.

It was an exciting day for me in September when I started at my special school. I had to catch the 86th Street cross-town bus, which went through Central Park to Amsterdam Avenue on the West Side. From there I rode the subway to the 137th Street station. A short walk took me back to 135th Street and Convent Avenue, and there was my school, the High School of Music and Art in the middle of St. Nicholas Park. It was an idyllic setting, which got my creative juices flowing.

My mother had gathered a beautiful back-to-school wardrobe for me. She purchased all my clothes, except for lingerie, shoes, and hose, from thrift shops along Second Avenue. She had befriended many of the shop owners and, whenever the Fifth Avenue ladies dropped things off the owners thought my mother would like, they held them for her. Although mostly conservative in style preference, I was one of the best-dressed girls in the sophomore class. My clothes had some fancy labels in them and were of impeccable quality, but much to my mother's chagrin, my favorite piece was the white smock we had to wear in our art classes. These cover-ups became pieces of art in their own right after months of paint splatters, autographs, and cartoons were painted on them by fellow students. I started out with a sparkling white lab coat, which soon turned into wearable art.

Our High School of Music and Art, as well as the High School of Performing Arts, received tickets to matinees of Broadway shows. The first musical I ever attended was "South Pacific" with Mary Martin and Ezio Pinza. It had opened earlier that year, April, 1949, and was the hottest ticket in town. After the show, we students were invited backstage to meet the stars. I discovered what it meant to be star-struck. How I loved my school for affording us such an extraordinary opportunity!

My letters to Pappi were filled with news of my accomplishments and goals for the future. I shared my dream with him, which was to earn at the very least a partial scholarship to Cornell. In his responses he told me how proud he was of me, but he started to omit his usual phrases, such as "when I come" or "when we're together again in the States." Instead, he told us about having hired an architect. Together they were drafting plans for a combination farm building/garage. Construction was scheduled to begin as soon as approval by the local building authority was secured. Plans for the future addition of the main house residence were also being drawn up, but held for submission. He had already received authorization from the zoning board to fence in the property, following a non-remonstrance sign-off by adjoining owners.

Did Pappi know something we didn't? Or was he merely putting two and two together, figuring the stalling tactics by the INS meant they were signaling a "no" to the possibility of his immigrating?

My mother called the American consulate and insisted on an appointment with the consul general. It was time. We had tried everything; nothing was working. She was angry about having been put off time after time and prevailed in obtaining an audience with him. He said he had reviewed my father's file, even consulted with the INS, but my father's history was so suspect that his case did not warrant further consideration. Not at this time. "Maybe some day, but not in the foreseeable future," she was told.

We had just repeated our annual Christmas Care package project, shipping over a dozen boxes to relatives in Germany. The holidays came and went. Afterwards my mother got those damned overseas trunks out of storage, and we started packing again. She told me we were going to return to Germany. Pappi could not join us, and we needed to be together. That was it. She booked passage for two on the *Queen Mary*, New York to Cherbourg, Tourist Class, scheduled to sail February 16, 1950.

Freddy was not coming. His plans were set, and he had arranged to move in with a boyfriend for a few months until the time came to enlist. I probably could have stayed on, continuing my special school and living with Elsie and Werner, but Marianne and I had taken different paths as far as education was concerned. Although I did love my aunt and uncle dearly, their lifestyle was not mine. But the truth was I simply wasn't ready to separate from my parents.

The final disappointment came when my mother received a letter from the Dean of the High School of Music and Art several days before our departure. It was dated February 10, 1950, and stated I had attained a 90 percent or more average in all major subjects in this challenging school.

I left many good friends behind, old and new, as well as a boyfriend, who came to the pier with flowers. He was the president of our Junior Walther League at church, a Lutheran Youth Service Group, and we were just getting to know and like each other. We had met on a daytrip up the Hudson River to Bear Mountain, a church-sponsored outing for our youth group. After that we had gone to the movies several times and had a few Coke dates after Walther League meetings. Already a junior in high school, his name was Ronnie Riemenschneider. As the name would imply, he was of German heritage.

The crossing on the *Queen Mary* took five days. Our cabin was on E deck, home of the tourist class. We were fortunate to have a porthole. I made friends on the upper decks, easily slipping through First and Second Class, getting fresh air and exercise by walking around the ship on the promenade deck with teenage sons and daughters of the more affluent passengers.

We had a smooth crossing on this magnificent ship with clear but cold weather. We teenagers discovered an inside swimming pool on one of the lower decks. I suspect it was there for the ship's crew inasmuch as we were the only ones who ever used it, and there were no lifeguards. We dove and splashed to our heart's content for hours at a time.

My mother became acquainted with an elderly gentleman, a single traveler. He befriended us and asked if he could join us in the dining room. We were assigned to the first seating, and there were extra places at our table, so we welcomed him. By the time we arrived in Cherbourg and disembarked, he had appointed himself our personal helpmate.

We boarded the train from Cherbourg to Paris, and he joined us in the same compartment.

"Have you ever been to Paris?" he asked

"Of course not," we replied. He offered to take us on a sightseeing tour. My mother, squeaky clean as she was, worried about how it might look to be traveling with a man we had just met.

"How it might look to whom?" I asked. I thought it was just fine. She and I would be together in one room, and the gentleman, although in the same hotel, was on a different floor. I saw no problem. My mother agreed, but insisted on paying our own way for everything we did.

After we checked in and freshened up a bit, we went out for dinner somewhere on the Left Bank. It was obvious our gentleman friend knew his way around. After dinner he hailed a taxi, and we took in a late performance at the famed Moulin Rouge. All I remember is how bawdy and boisterous the women on stage were and how loudly the audience participated and responded to their whooping it up. Long legs were all over the place, kicking and twirling from ruffled skirts, and all I could think of was how our Rockettes kicked just as high, but performed with so much more precision.

The next day we had just enough time to go up the Eiffel Tower and visit Notre Dame before our friend helped us into a taxi, and we were on our way to Gare de L'Est, where we boarded the Orient Express to Munich.

I cannot remember the name of the gentleman who became our traveling companion, helper, tour guide, and protective escort in Paris. Where did he come from? Where was he going? My mother and I never talked about him again. He was one of those souls who passes through your life, enriching it, leaving a mark, and before you realize—that person is gone again.

Our reunion with Pappi at the station in Munich was very emotional. He couldn't hold back his feelings. His big expressive eyes were swollen from shedding so many tears. I couldn't let loose of him, and he couldn't believe we were back. It was dark when we finally arrived in Attenkirchen. The Kettner family, the owners of the inn where we would still be living, welcomed us like family. Prinzi, my dog, was curious at first. Then all at once it clicked in, he recognized me, and it was obvious how happy he was.

The next morning the Kettners had a beautiful *Bauernfruehstueck* (farmers' breakfast) prepared for us, and we ate together. Then it was time to view our new property and everything Pappi had accomplished. It was truly amazing. A flat-roofed concrete building, already in place, would be our home until the main house could be built in two or three years. A chicken house attached to the south side of the existing building, designed to hold several hundred laying hens, was under construction. A generous front yard was already fenced and waiting for the arrival of the pullets he would order come springtime.

The plum trees Pappi had planted stood in perfect rows. The rest of the acreage was being readied for cultivation. A large pile of organic material had been dumped nearby, which the farmer my father hired would plow under the furrows in readiness for the first 10,000 strawberry plants on order. A second shipment of another 10,000 plants would arrive as soon as my father acquired the adjoining acreage, on which he had an option-to-buy. Water was discovered when a gentleman from the village walked around holding his divining rod until he felt a strong earthward pull, indicating the presence of a freshwater vein. A well was dug, a cistern installed, and a manual pump with its handle standing high was ready for action.

My father had built a chicken house for egg production, planted a plum orchard and started a strawberry farm. Now all he needed was manpower. But all he got was womanpower. Fortunately, it was still winter and there was time to finish the inside of our quarters before we moved out of our post-war haven, Gasthaus Kettner.

Our house did not look like much from the outside, but it was charming inside. My mother was nesting again. Oil paintings went back onto the walls, pillows were tucked cozily on the couches, and fresh flowers sat on the table. The Kettners let us take the furniture we had in our rooms at the inn, which was stuff the German army had left behind when they were quartered there. Frau Kettner furnished beds and mattresses, for which my mother gave her the last of our Lady Pepperell sheet stash, minus one or two which she would use to sew ruffled tie-back curtains.

My father had accomplished much during our absence. One only had to speak to anyone in the village to hear how much Herr Wiegand was respected. He had provided well for his family.

I was happy to be with Pappi again, this father whom I adored. I reflected on our wonderful *Wiedersehen* (reunion) at the Munich station and I felt maybe, just maybe, we got it right this time. To return to Bavaria to live permanently, might have been the best decision after all. For the moment, all was well with the Wiegand family. We knew in our hearts that Freddy would find a way to Germany as a member of the US occupation and be stationed at some Air Force base nearby.

My mother was adjusting to life in Germany, a life that by all appearances was going to be permanently rooted in Bavaria. It was tough for her at first, considering how much she loved America. She had lived in New York for the last two years and experienced all the German cultural and some of the social activities in Yorkville and was now facing a list of farm chores each day in tiny Attenkirchen. But this was my parents' first opportunity to build a future together. Since Pappi couldn't immigrate, this was the side of the ocean on which they would have to cast their lot. They had been through so much; this new venture was just another challenge, but with one major difference: they were in charge of their lives. They embraced hard work and, as always, they were devoted to each other. That's all that mattered to move on to a new life.

The realization of having walked away from everything I had accomplished in junior high and as a sophomore in high school was setting in, and it was at best bitter-sweet. There was no point in going back to the girls' school in Freising I had left two years prior. No sooner would I re-enroll, than the current school year would be over. Besides, I could not see myself going back to a school where there was so much focus on discipline, and the faculty was so rigid. Not after having attended an American co-educational high school, such as my High School of Music and Art, where the atmosphere was free and easy, and the focus was on creativity. I needed time to think.

Pappi was reading me. "Mutzi," he said, "We need to see to your future. You are no longer in the art school you loved so much. But let me assure you that you will play a most important role in the family business we have started. We are going to be the biggest and best strawberry farm in the area and the supplier of fine fruit and fruit products all over Bavaria. You will be our American-style marketing genius and design artist."

It sounded good to me although a bit pie-in-the-sky. To prepare for the career move, I was to go to a private business school in Munich, a fine economics school still respected today, Private Handelschule Sabel. I would enroll in September and live in a boarding house there. Pappi would pay my tuition and housing as compensation for working at home all summer. After graduation, until our strawberry enterprise could justify a marketing director, I would take advantage of the placement service Private Handelschule Sabel offered. Pappi thought it would be especially advantageous for me to gather experience in the real business world.

He gave me a lot to think about. I had an entire spring and summer to digest all of Pappi's plans for me and formulate some of my own. I reconnected with my old friends very quickly. We had matured, and our former playful pastimes were just that, past times. Everyone was focused on continuing his or her education, working jobs or serving apprenticeships. But going dancing on weekends and stopping at cafes and coffee houses for those wonderful, chatty visits would continue.

I visited our good friends in Freising, the Wohlparts, and stopped to see my fashion mentor, Frau Zirzow. She asked me if I would be available to participate in her fashion shows. "Freeze modeling?" I asked somewhat reluctantly.

"No," she said. Her fashion house was now well established, and she had developed steady clientele. She was now presenting her seasonal designs on the runway.

Zirzow announced her fashion shows in newspapers, on the radio, and with American-style posters all over the surrounding towns where she presented her line. She would set up her runway in inns, hotels, and sometimes in the officer's clubs of US Army and Air Force bases in the area. Most of the officers and NCOs brought their dependants to Germany to live with them off base in requisitioned housing. We could always count on great attendance by the American ladies, no matter which location. When we performed in the Hotel Bayrischer Hof in Freising, the classiest hotel in town, most of the fashion-conscious women of Freising were also there.

Photographers would be hired whenever Frau Zirzow premiered a new collection. Photos of the models on the runway or chatting with customers at tables were incorporated in future advertising campaigns. She was a marketing genius. I asked her for copies of myself at work, and this time I wasn't wearing the traditional *Sound of Music* folk dress. I had grown and physically developed, and was showing smart Chanel style suits, glamorous gowns, and aprés-ski furs. I sent copies of the photos back to Freddy, and he showed them to his buddies. He was surprised to see how his kid sister was growing up.

I mentioned to Frau Zirzow that I had brought back many pairs of shoes from the States. All were high heels, the latest styles and in every color imaginable. I offered to wear them and share them with other models. She was delighted. Great looking shoes, especially chic high heels, were not yet available in Germany. After every show we got as many inquiries on my shoes as on her clothes.

Newspapers were full of dramatic occurrences in Germany. Every day there were stories about people escaping from the Russian Zone by digging tunnels underneath the death strip the Russians had created. Others tried their luck by making a run for it, hoping they would make it through the barb-wired minefield. We read stories of German guards, loyal to the other side, following shoot-to-kill orders given by the Russians. These guards were the infamous "VoPos," the *Volkspolizei* (Peoples' Police), openly despised by all West Germans, and secretly hated and feared by those in the East. Imagine those unfortunate Germans—having lived through the Gestapo years when you couldn't trust your own brother or your best friend—after the war, being subjected to the same atrocities by fellow Germans—not in Hitler's Third Reich, but in a Communist police state. The VoPos were referred to as *Schweinehunde* (pig-dogs).

In early spring of 1950 we received an envelope delivered by courier. Inside was a letter from my father's youngest brother Willi. He was back in Bettenhausen, having returned from Russia where he was held prisoner since 1944.

His war history was fascinating. He was twenty-one years old in 1942 and had not been drafted into the Wehrmacht. People were whispering. He was working for an uncle who owned a slaughter house and meat-packing plant in Naumburg-an-der-Saale. His job as butcher was considered critical to the war effort to keep food supplied to the front lines. The general population, who had sons, brothers, and fathers, many of them older than Willi, fighting against the Russians, expressed their contempt. They asked why this young single fellow was still at home while others were dying, leaving widows and orphans behind. The pressure on him became so unbearable that he volunteered for service with the *Panzers* (Tank Corps).

He fought on the Eastern Front until captured by Russian guards on the Russian/Rumanian border in the summer of 1944 and transported to a POW hard-labor camp in the coalmine district of deepest Siberia. The work and the living conditions were brutal. The harsh winter came early, and many men died from the cold, malnutrition, and blacklung disease. Willi escaped and made his way westward, only to be recaptured and sent to a gulag in Vladivostock, one of the easternmost towns in Russia, located on the Sea of Japan. It was so far away, beyond Manchuria and a few kilometers north of Korea, it defied your imagination, which no doubt made his captors feel secure that he would never attempt another escape.

They didn't know Willi. However, some of them would get to know him well. He became one of the chief cooks and food handlers. Accompanied by Russian guards, he would leave camp to buy food from farmers or open-air markets. He was a likable fellow and befriended the guards, sending them home with bags of food for their families. A little bribery moved these friendships along nicely. Soon they would make connections for him, dropping him off in town for the night and returning him in the wee hours to assume his duties.

This lifestyle continued for years until he arranged his successful escape. Underneath many kilos of garbage, his guard/friends smuggled him out and dropped him off in Vladivostock at the home of a newfound Russian friend, where he stayed under the nose of his captors for many more months. When the dust had settled, he again took off for points west. He had become fluent in Russian in these years, and it served him well. This time he made it. Thought to be missing in action, never to be heard from again, he arrived in Bettenhausen in the dead of winter, late January 1949.

Willi's letter arrived intact. Had it been sent via the German Post and not by courier, it would have been censored and subjected to many cutouts. It would have been like trying to read a piece of mail that had gone through a paper shredder. In his letter he told us of plans to escape to the West. He could not say when, only that it would be soon, and would it be okay if he showed up on our doorstep? If we didn't reply, he would take that as a "yes," asking for regrets only. We didn't respond.

Recently I found out how Willi escaped from the Russian Zone: My father's oldest sister Lydia lived in the village of Wilmars in the American Zone, a mere 3 kilometers from the Russian border. She had lived there most of her adult life with her husband, Edwin Kirchner, and their two sons, Guenther and Winfried. Onkel Edwin was a *Jaegermeister* (Chief Forest Ranger). He knew practically every tree in the wooded area he controlled, as well as the area east of Wilmars. It had been under his jurisdiction prior to the newly drawn border and now extended into the Russian Zone all the way to Bettenhausen. By virtue of his profession as forester, he had contact with the border guards, accompanied by their German shepherd attack dogs. He befriended several of them, who turned out to be loyal to the West and risked their lives to help people slip through. It was arranged that on a night with no moon when the dogs had passed, a friendly guard and a good brother-in-law would guide Willi through the death strip. Ever so carefully they picked their way through the mine field and sent him on his way to freedom.

Gasthaus Kettner in Attenkirchen. We lived upstairs, the last three windows.

The Wohlpart family (with Pappi, behind them) visiting us in Attenkirchen.

Frau Kettner, two-year-old *Burle* ("little boy" in Bavarian) and sister Marille (5).

Pappi's plum trees in the snow.

Our train station at Attenkirchen.

Toni "Papp" the village cabinet maker who also led the village band. He made my first skis.

The P-51 flying over Germany dropped its extra fuel tanks; we children picked them up to make canoes.

The *Holledauer Bockerl* train as it crossed the bridge over the Amper River.

Our last family picture before Freddy left for the USA, taken in Kettners' fruit tree garden. Spring, 1947.

My Onkel Willi, Pappi's youngest brother, after he had made his escape from Russia and the Russian Zone, then came to live with us.

Willi, later in life with his wife, Emmi, picking hops. From the book *Attenkirchen* published by that village.

Pappi spent his Christmas in '48 alone—invited into the Ganzenmueller family celebration. Pappi is far right.

But we had Christmas together without him, in New York.

Cousin Marianne and I, New York teenagers.

Marianne's parents, Elsie and Werner, still enjoyed a lusty social life in Yorkville in the city. Werner lifts his glass, upper right. Elsie, second from left at the bar, also raises her glass.

1949. Portrait with Freddy in New York. Taken on the occasion of my confirmation.

This water-damaged photo is of the graduation from Junior High School #96. I was headed for the High School of Music and Art. I'm bottom row, second from right.

Queen Mary ship.

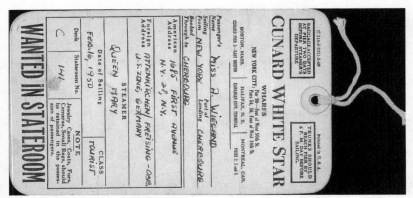

The luggage tag.

Our passport picture.

It must have been on a weekend because Pappi was at home. I remember there was no knock. The door just opened and there he stood.

Had he been a young boy or a teenager, I would have said, "Uh-oh, Mommi, here comes trouble!" Instead, there stood a young man with dashingly good looks, an engaging smile, somewhat short in stature, whose eyes were a dead giveaway. The *Wiegands-Augen*—he had 'em! Those big, bulgy, expressive eyes that linked the whole Wiegand family together. I could have easily picked him out of a crowd.

Willi had arrived. Now the fun would begin. My father, the oldest brother, Willi, the youngest, greeted each other more like a father welcoming his son home from war, than two brothers who might have greeted each other with "Hey bro, what took you so long?" It was emotional. My mother, on the other hand, gave him a lusty welcoming hug, and they must have whispered into each other's ears because they were both laughing when they unclenched. I had no doubt they were back in the old groove where they had left off in 1937. The kidding around, needling, and teasing had begun.

Willi and I clicked right away. He was more than an uncle. He was to become my best friend and my surrogate brother. I missed Freddy, even though a string of girl friends had taken him away when Mommi and I were in New York. Now he just wasn't around at all. Willi filled a void in my life similar to the void Freddy had filled in Marianne's. This young relative of ours needed to recoup the years spent in Russia as a prisoner of war, missing out on the best years of his life. He had a lot of catching up to do.

"Willi," I asked, "can you dance?"

My father continued to work for the US Army Quartermaster Corps in Munich. During the week he roomed with a family named Ganzenmueller, related to friends in Attenkirchen. My mother and I rarely traveled to Munich since we had no business at the American Consulate and our shopping trips were few. But when we did go, we would visit Pappi's host family. They were kind to him and would often invite him into their living room for the evening. Their six-year-old daughter Helga loved to sit with my child-loving father as he drew animals, told stories, and taught her how to count to ten in English and Spanish. But Pappi lived for Friday nights when he could go straight to the train station from work and come home for the weekend. He was looking forward to the day he would become a full-time fruit farmer and dreamed of a bright future in farming for us all. For the time being, however, he needed the steady income his regular job provided.

Pappi caught the train back to Munich at 5:45 AM every Monday morning. His ritual on Sunday evenings was to write out the week's work schedule for Mommi, Willi, and me, to which we would never fail to give him a you've-got-to-be-kidding reaction.

It was too early in the season for the outside work, but inside our little house was a separate storage room at the far end that still had an earthen floor. Without batting an eye, he instructed Willi and me to pour a concrete floor. And when we were done with that—while we were still in the cement mixing mode—we could start pouring as many cement fence posts as we had pre-built wooden forms for. And when we were done with that, we could start building the forms for the cement entry into the storage room and order gravel for the bottom layer. My father could be a slave driver.

Willi was hilarious to work with, his conversation a running barrage of one-liners. He would complain loudly and needle my father about his forced labor tactics. He said he came to the West to begin a new life, not necessarily a life of leisure, but certainly not to work harder than he did in the Russian POW camps. When Willi carried his grumbling too far, Pappi would needle him back. With his arm around his shoulders, tongue in cheek, he would say, "*Bruederlein, Arbeit macht frei!*" (Little brother, work shall make you free.) Since the slogan that was posted at Auschwitz, Pappi was indulging in his own brand of black humor.

Willi could live with us indefinitely cost-free. He would help as much as he could. But Pappi also realized Willi would need an income. When a major public works project was about to begin in Attenkirchen, he encouraged Willi to answer the call for sign-ups. It paid well. The project involved moving the old cemetery from the church in the village's center to a spacious farmland area at the edge of town. Headstones and monuments had already been moved and set in place at the top of freshly-dug graves, into which remains would be transferred. It was not a job for the faint of heart.

Willi accepted. My mother was shocked by his callousness about the matter. "It's just a job, they're coming across with good paychecks, and I've got to sock some money away for my future. It couldn't be any worse than some of the things I saw during the war," he said.

Willi discovered what he had signed up for went beyond grave digging. For centuries the dear departed had been placed in the same family plots of the increasingly crowded graveyard. Most family plots had multiple graves, but some were just single. It had always been the practice to bury the dead in a wooden casket, so body, box and all would eventually decompose. It had also been the practice that after sufficient time had passed and another member of the same family died, the grave was re-opened, and the newly departed laid to rest in the same grave.

The time came for Willi and his crew to dig up the remains of all of the folks buried layer upon layer, giving no consideration to how long they had been interred. Regardless of the many stages of decomposition, all remains had to be exhumed, identified, and placed into a new wooden casket with the correct nameplate on the lid. Another crew would pick up the boxes and transport them to the gravesites in the new cemetery, where they would be laid to rest. Willi's phase was the grizzliest work.

When he came home at the end of the day, my mother would meet him outside, demanding he strip off his clothes and hose down his boots, his hands, and his hair to rid himself of the dust of the dead. I'm sure had she not thrown him some towels, he would have walked into the house totally naked.

One memorable evening as we sat at the dinner table, Willi, leaning on one elbow and mischief written all over his face, said to my mother, *"Heute haben wir den alten Kettner ausgebuddelt. Weisst Du was? Der hat garnicht gut ausgesehen!"* (Today we dug up old man Kettner. You know what? He didn't look too good!)

My mother dropped her knife and fork and said, *"Willi! Wie kannst Du nur sowas entsetzliches sagen, und das noch beim Essen!"* (How can you say something so atrocious, and that while we are eating?)" Willi dissolved in laughter, as he thoroughly enjoyed getting the reaction he was looking for.

We spent the summer digging postholes, stringing chain-link fence, tending the 300 pullets that arrived in late spring and were beginning to lay eggs, and preparing the strawberry fields. There was no end to our workload.

When the first 10,000 strawberry plants arrived, we were overwhelmed. Pappi took a week of his vacation. Mommi hired as many women as she could find to help us plant.

As soon as the work was assigned in the morning, Pappi and I were relegated to the kitchen. He was a magnificent cook of hearty soups and goulash, a throwback to his days at sea. I was his helper. Cooking was an activity we shared and enjoyed over a lifetime. My father was the earthy cook; my mother taught me gourmet cooking and the fine art of food presentation. On this occasion, however, we had to cook substantial meals to fill hungry bellies.

The main meal in most European countries is at noon. When I served Pappi's goulash, our hired help really dug in, wiping their plates and bowls clean with thick slices of black bread and unsalted, snow-white butter. My father had already developed a reputation as an ambitious man, a teacher of foreign languages, and a budding fruit farmer, and now he revealed his talent as a cook. We didn't have much of a harvest that first summer, although we delivered fresh eggs and plums to market. But when it came time to re-hire the same women as strawberry pickers and packers in ensuing years, they never failed to inquire if Herr Wiegand would be cooking again?

We had two neighbors close by. Herr Gruenwald across the street had a heavy machine repair shop and did a lot of welding. His was a noisy operation, especially when he was road-testing the equipment. He was also an amateur middleweight boxer, whose sought-after victories always seemed to be "KO's." You could tell by his beatup nose and cauliflower ears, he had taken a lot of punches in his time. He had a flamboyant wife, probably the first liberated woman I ever knew. She had her own BMW - 750, a monster of a motorcycle. This at a time when women were just beginning to think about getting a driver's license or upgrading from a bicycle to a motorized Vespa. They were an interesting couple, but I felt sorry for their young children who had to fend for themselves most of the time. The kids were often sent home from school because they had lice. When they were young teenagers, we would give them summer jobs. As the oldest daughter grew into womanhood, she turned into a lovely, silky-haired brunette and eventually married into our family.

The other neighbors were just as interesting. Herr Mueller and Frau Bauer, a forty-ish significant other couple, another first for me, purchased the bakery and pastry shop next door and were doing a fine job establishing themselves. We were their first customers every morning as soon as the aroma of *frische Semmel* (freshly baked hard-crusted breakfast rolls) drifted over the fence and into our kitchen window. They were also the only house close by that had a private telephone. Not only did they let us use it, they didn't mind yelling from their kitchen window if a call came in for us. Consequently, they knew everything going on in our lives.

Like my parents, who were in their forties at this point, the Mueller/ Bauers were ambitious and soon added a small café with several tables on an outdoor terrace. One afternoon Frau Bauer was standing at the fence, calling for my mother. An American soldier, accompanied by his lady friend, had stopped at their café. They didn't speak German. Frau Bauer didn't speak English, but she figured they were interested in the fields in our area with large poles and long vines. They had never seen hops gardens before, and Frau Bauer was unable to explain.

My mother came to the fence, smiling knowingly, aware of their dilemma, and greeted them in fluent English. They couldn't believe their ears. A whole new series of questions spilled forth: How, what, where, why, who are you, how come you're living out here in the "boonies" of Bavaria, and on and on.

Frau Bauer excused herself. My mother invited the couple over, and we spent the rest of the afternoon sitting at our kitchen table getting acquainted. It was an instant mutual admiration society. That's how we met Captain Peter James Mulligan and his wife Naomi. Mommi invited them back the following Sunday afternoon for *Kaffeeklatsch* to meet Pappi and Willi. A lifelong friendship that spanned oceans and generations had begun.

The summer of 1950 was jam-packed. Willi and I played as hard as we worked. There were folk festivals all around, and most *Biergartens* had outdoor dance floors with live Bavarian music. Soccer games abounded. Every village had a team and participated in league play against neighboring villages. The victories would be celebrated with brimming steins of beer and a hearty *"Prosit!"* (Cheers!) The defeats, the same way. Our bicycles were our mode of transportation, and the only thing I insisted on when we went dancing was that we would go with a group of friends so I would not be coming home alone in the dark. Willi had a way of disappearing occasionally.

The Mulligans paid us weekly visits, usually on Saturdays. We were on a first name basis, and, even though they were older than my parents, I called them "Pete" and "Naomi." Chess was Pete's passion. No sooner would he arrive when the chessboard he traveled with was set up on the kitchen table. My father knew chess, but didn't have the patience to play when so much work beckoned on the outside. If you wanted to play Pappi's game, you had to pick up a garden hoe and work alongside him in the strawberry fields. It became a Saturday afternoon ritual that I would play chess with Pete.

One special Saturday, Pete and Naomi invited me to drive to Munich for dinner. "Munich for dinner and then what?" I asked.

"Just for dinner, and then we'll bring you back home," they said. I could not believe people did that. Germans at that time would not have dreamed of driving such a distance just to go to dinner.

They took me to the renowned Hotel Koenigshof situated on the Karlsplatz in the center of Munich. How often my mother and I stood in front of this magnificent hotel in an area called am Stachus, waiting for the trolley to take us to the American Consulate. Above the hotel entrance was a sumptuous, glass-enclosed restaurant overlooking the teeming square below and the Karlstor in the distance. The Karlstor reminded me of the Arc de Triomphe in Paris. Passing through the Karlstor would take you into the Alt Stadt (old town Munich). It was a beautiful part of the city. I can remember watching the diners and fantasizing about where in the world all of these rich and famous people might have come from. And to think I was now seated at one of those tables with Pete and Naomi, gazing down at the world at my feet. I thought I was living a dream.

Pete said he would order for the three of us. Dinner arrived in chafing dishes on teacarts, served by uniformed waiters. I had never had lobster. I recalled my mother talking about *Hummer* and how delicious it was. It was a menu item in every restaurant in Hamburg, but unaffordable for most of us.

For dessert Pete ordered a *Koenigsbecher* (kings cup). This turned out to be an enormous crystal goblet filled with fruit and scoops of ice cream in assorted flavors, brimming over with a mountain of whipped cream set aflame with grand marnier. It was an impressive presentation. We were each handed a long-handled silver spoon and dug in. The hotel's name Koenigshof means "King's Court." That evening Pete and Naomi wined and dined me like a princess.

Pappi, his eye on my future as his marketing manager, had submitted my application to Private Handelsschule Sabel, the business school in Munich he had heard so much about. Soon my letter of acceptance arrived, accompanied by a comprehensive informational package. They offered an intensive one-year course in business administration, marketing, accounting, international banking and exchanges, business correspondence, and such basic office skills as stenography, typing, bookkeeping (including current tax structure), and penmanship. It was considered business etiquette that employment applications and resumes be submitted in one's own hand-writing. Prospective employers considered it a component of their first impression of the applicant. The school also offered language courses in the evening, and I elected to continue studying French, which I had already studied in junior high school and high school in the States. I intended to be at least tri-lingual by the time I entered the business world in Germany. Pappi didn't know I had my own agenda in addition to the plans he had for me. I kept my plans to myself.

School started on September 1, 1950. Through a friend I acquired lodging at the large apartment of Frau Bumberger, a typical bourgeois *Muenchnerin* (citizen of Munich). She never had any children of her own. Her student boarders filled this void, and she really cared about us. We called her our "Bum-Mama." She was widowed too soon after her husband retired from his lifelong career as a *Schaffner* (conductor) with the Munich trolley car system, and she kept his memory alive with her storytelling. The time-honored profession of *Trambahnschaffner* (tram-conductor) was an institution throughout the city, but it did not come without a checkered reputation. These fellows were known to shower the passengers with insults, boss them around, and be downright rude. Or, they could be hilariously entertaining and funny. Munich residents expected this outlandish behavior, while visitors were warned.

Bum-Mama's rules were strict. No male visitors inside her apartment. We could be picked up and dropped off at the downstairs door, but it would be locked after 10:30 PM. She expected us to be settled in by 11:00 PM, lights out, radio off, and no late night baths. The running water would disturb residents in the apartments above and below. No food in the room, only fruit. She gave us a little space in the pantry where we could keep snack food, which we either took to school or consumed in the kitchen. She would cook breakfast and supper five days a week.

On weekends she expected us to go home, but if we stayed in town, we were on our own as far as food was concerned. Her curfew still applied. She did no laundry. So on Fridays I had to take my suitcase full of soiled clothes to school with me and place it next to everyone else's luggage in the back of our homeroom. I was shocked and embarrassed one afternoon when my girlfriend and I came in from lunch and some smart guys got into my suitcase and draped all of my unmentionables over the tops of the windows. After that incident, all suitcases for commuting students were placed in the administrative offices.

Our student body was made up of young adults of varying ages who were seeking a quick path into the business world, as well as older men and women in need of re-schooling to acquire the skills and certification to enter the job market. Most students commuted, but a few lived in Munich and surrounding suburbs. Among them was my schoolmate, Marie-Louise Schneppenhorst. I called her "Marlou," and we became best friends.

I generally went home on weekends, that is, until the snow started falling in the mountains. Sometimes friends from school and I would journey into the Alps and ski—a sport I had learned as a young girl and still loved. Boys and girls traveled innocently together in those days. We stayed in youth hostels, and it was exciting and fun.

A few weeks after I moved to Munich, my parents received a letter from Freddy, postmarked, "Lackland AFB, San Antonio, Texas." He informed us he was in basic training. He had enlisted in the Air Force on September 22, 1950, at a recruiting station in Times Square. He was nineteen years old.

Freddy and I were setting the course for our futures. Willi made a change, too. After all the strawberry fieldwork was done, he wanted to find a job in Munich. My father suggested he apply at the Quartermaster Corps, the same place where he worked. The hours were good, the wages also, and he might find an opening in on-site barracks housing. There were so many single male DP's after the war, the US Occupation provided some housing along with a job if the men had no place to stay. It was designed to be short-term, and not every facility had it; but luckily everything fell into place for Willi, and he joined the rest of us weekly commuters.

Having Willi living in Munich turned out to be great fun for me. Instead of going home on Friday evenings, we would meet at the *Hauptbahnhof* (main train station) for a night on the town. We would put our carry-ons and my book bag in a locker after I slipped into my New York high heels, then head for a restaurant. While there, I would go to the ladies' lounge and unbraid and comb out my hair, pile on more make-up and—voila!—I was Willi's date for the evening. Who would know he was my uncle? I could have fun, stay away from trouble, and see Munich at night in safe company.

He for his part could look at girls, dance with them, and with a little bit of luck get their names and addresses for later on in the week. I pretended to be unaware of what he was doing. Sometimes we would go to a midnight movie or take the trolley to a section in the northern part, called "Schwabing," known for its comedy clubs and cabarets. If I got carded, I would flash my American Passport, and for the most part, that's all it took to be allowed inside. We would end our night with a hearty breakfast before catching the trolley back to the Hauptbahnhof, where we'd return to the locker, collect our belongings, and board the morning train to Attenkirchen.

We would come home dead tired and my parents weren't happy, even though they knew beforehand that we'd be partying all night. Much to their relief, it didn't happen often. Willi quickly filled his little black book with the names and addresses of available young ladies in Munich, and before long he met one that took up about all of his nights. Her name was Emmi.

After I had commuted for some months, I found strange faces soon became familiar. Frequent fellow travelers became acquaintances. We had an especially jolly group of passengers that collected in the last car of the *Holledauer Bockerl* as it made stops in all the villages along the Mainburg to Freising line. I had to catch the train at 5:45 AM Monday mornings and the only good thing about that ungodly hour was joining friends who were having a good time on the train.

One day a young man sat down next to me and asked, "May I have this seat?"

I had noticed him before because I often caught him looking at me. He seemed popular with his own crowd, always laughing and joking around, but on this day, I could see he intended to get acquainted. His name was Friedl, tall and handsome, with dark eyes and hair. He was always dressed in business attire, rather than the leisurely turtleneck sweaters and loose jackets we wore. He was obviously not a student.

I judged Friedl to be in his mid-to-late twenties. He had polished manners and was a smooth conversationalist. He spoke *Bavarian Hochdeutsch*, high standard German, with an accent that meant he was either Bavarian or Austrian. He told me he was originally from Vienna and had moved to a nearby village with his family after the war. He worked as an accountant for a brewery in Freising and traveled a lot, visiting his brewery's distributors to audit their books. It sounded like an important job, but I was aware he wanted to impress me. That was about the extent of our first conversation. His village was the last stop before we changed trains to connect to either Freising or Munich, which made the time we were able to chat on the same train short.

We saw each other on the train only once a week, sometimes less often, depending on whether he was out of town or I had weekend plans with friends in Munich and didn't come home. One day he suggested I take an earlier train from Munich so we could meet in Freising at a coffee-house. That way we would have time to talk and still catch the evening train home. I told him that would not be possible because my class schedule was full on Fridays, but I sometimes spent Saturdays in Freising, modeling for Modehaus Zirzow. To meet on one of those occasions might be possible, as I always stayed over with Frau Zirzow or the Wohlpart family.

Not too long afterwards, there was a style show in the Hotel Bayrischer Hof in Freising, and, as I came off the runway greeting people and answering questions regarding the design I was modeling, I spotted Friedl at a table off in the corner. I was surprised to see him and stopped to say hello.

"Could we meet after the show?" he asked.

I had a two-hour window of time before we had a second showing at the Officer's Club inside the Army base. We could get something to eat, but I had to watch the clock. I dared not be late. After the late showing, Zirzow's driver would be taking me to the Wohlparts to spend the night. They would be expecting me.

Little by little Friedl and I got to know each other, and I liked him because he treated me like an adult. We talked about my education and what plans I had for the future. I told my parents about him. He sent postcards and letters from places his job took him, always describing the natural beauty of the area in great detail. Mommi saved his letters until I got home on weekends, and we sat down and read them together. Occasionally he sent pictures, once including a studio portrait of himself. I sent the picture to Freddy.

Freddy sent it back—with some brotherly advice: "Be careful, Anneliese, there's something about this fellow I don't like. Don't trust him."

I didn't heed my brother's advice. He didn't know Friedl as I did, nor how flattered I was by his attention. Our friendship was strictly intellectual, nothing beyond that.

There were several occasions when we went out in Munich during the week. It was after school and quite casual, a café date, followed by an early movie. He knew I had to be in by 10:30 PM, and by the time the streetcar reached my stop, we were already running late. Bum-Mama had to throw the keys down to me from her kitchen window, so I could unlock the door and let myself in. Friedl accompanied me upstairs to apologize. She was not happy with me. The second time it happened, she let me know in no uncertain terms, "One more time," and I would have to find another place to live. I was terribly embarrassed and apologized profusely. But I also told her not to read things into my friendship with Friedl that didn't exist.

He started to come to Attenkirchen on the Sunday afternoon train for friendly visits with my family. My parents thought he was a nice young man, yet Willi, like Freddy, didn't like him and told me so. One day he showed up on a brand-new motorcycle, and we started to go for regular rides through the countryside, always stopping at a café for *Kaffee und Kuchen*. Friedl would order a *Schlagober*, the Austrian version of espresso. I suppose it was the Viennese in him. I enjoyed it, too.

"Have you ever been to the Alps in springtime?" he asked one day. "Nature is wondrous in spring. Why don't we take a tour on my motor-cycle?"

I didn't think my father would allow that, but I would ask. To my surprise, Pappi was not totally against the idea, but would only allow me to go if we had a definite plan, a destination and the assurance we would not travel after dark. He suggested we look up the Breitenberger family. Mr. Breitenberger was one of my father's closest comrades during his intern-ment years, and in the Crystal City family camp they were on the same men's soccer team. They had repeatedly invited our family to spend a week-end with them after they found out we were in Attenkirchen. Pappi told me I could get their address, phone number, and exact directions to their house from the Wohlparts, who had already visited them.

I got in touch with the Breitenbergers, and much to my delight they wanted us to come as soon as we could. We'd be welcome anytime. "Bring the whole family," they said. They lived in Herrsching-am-Ammersee, a picturesque small town on an alpine lake southwest of Munich. We arrived on a Saturday, just in time for *Kaffeeklatsch*, and were heartily welcomed. We sat around the coffee table and reminisced over Crystal City Intern-ment Camp for hours, sharing whatever information we had about mutual friends.

Friedl had excused himself from the table, and I thought he was go-ing to the bathroom, but he didn't return. Herr Breitenberger suggested we get up, stretch our limbs, and follow another one of those German rituals, going on a *Spaziergang* (taking a walk). When we got outside, there sat Friedl like a bump on a log, pouting and looking bored.

The Breitenbergers lived in a typical Bavarian chalet on the side of a hill. From the upstairs front balcony you could see the Ammersee with a magnificent view of the Alps in the background. We walked downhill to the docks, and Herr Breitenberger showed us his boat. Friedl was disinter-ested and downright rude. He behaved like a brat and as soon as I could, I quietly told him so. I got an inkling that the trip was not working out the way he wanted it to. He had a different agenda, and I saw a side of him I had never experienced before. The fact that Mausi, the Breitenbergers slightly retarded daughter, was clinging to me like a toddler to its mother didn't help matters. She was getting in his way.

We stopped at a *Gasthaus* for a beer and an *Imbiss* (light snack). Mausi squeezed herself in next to me. She functioned on the level of a child much younger than her years, but was very sweet. It was evident she had been raised with love. When I told her we were staying over, she was delighted and made me promise to stay with her.

The following morning at breakfast Herr Breitenberger gave Friedl the keys to unchain his boat, inviting us to take it out on the lake. It was an oversized, flat-bottom rowboat, and no instructions were needed. Oars and safety gear were aboard. I don't know where Friedl spent the night. Frau Breitenberger invited him to sleep on the couch downstairs, but, if that proved too uncomfortable, there were guestrooms at the *Gasthaus* where we ate supper. At least he was in a happy mood, and we were looking forward to a boat ride. It was a new day, and the weather was perfect.

Friedl rowed around several coves, getting used to manipulating the heavy oars, and then he headed for open water. We were out of sight of Breitenberger's chalet and quite a distance from the shore when he stopped rowing and let the boat drift. He came to sit on the bench beside me, making the boat wobble quite a bit. He put his arm around my shoulder, and we talked about the overwhelming beauty of nature, the crystal-clear lake, and the magestic snow-capped Alps in the distance.

Suddenly, he started putting his hands on me as he had never done before. He was getting amorous and kissed me as never before. A goodnight kiss after a date was nothing compared to how he was coming on to me now.

Then he said, "*Darf ich dich beruehren?*" He was asking permission to touch me? It didn't take me long to figure out this was his way of asking to make love to me. I told him I would not, I could not, be intimate with him, and I was not just alarmed, but angry at his attempt to take advantage of me under the circumstances. I asked him to please control his emotions and take me back. He acted as though he had me trapped and didn't stop his groping. I grabbed the life preserver and threw it overboard, yelling at him to pick up the oars and start rowing or I'd be next. If he thought I couldn't swim the distance, he was mistaken.

He got up and made his way back to the bench with the oars hooked to its sides, acting as though he was going to tip the boat over. He sat there and glowered at me until he started laughing in a crazy, almost hysterical, manner. Finally he picked up the oars, and we rowed back in silence. I didn't look at him for fear he would see how scared I was.

The Breitenbergers were in the midst of preparing Sunday dinner when we got back. We put on smiling faces and thanked them for letting us use their boat and allowing us to indulge in the beauty of their lake, but it was now time for us to go. We wanted to take a different route home, so we could tour more of the area and get back to Attenkirchen before dark, or so we said. They were disappointed we didn't stay to eat, but understood our desire to get on the road. We said our good-byes and expressed our thanks for their hospitality, promising to come back and at the same time extending invitations for them to visit us.

We started back on the motorcycle, tense and unhappy. I told Friedl I wanted to go straight home. He said yes, but we'd have to stop somewhere to fill up the gas tank. This we did, and he asked me if I was hungry. I told him I had no appetite. As we got back on the motorcycle, he cheerfully said, "*Appetit kommt beim Essen*" (Your appetite will return as we eat). I guess he wanted to lighten up the atmosphere. We rode for some time. Rounding a bend, we spotted a *Gasthaus* that looked inviting, tucked against a wooded area halfway up the mountain.

"Let's go there, and stop to rest for a few minutes and go inside for a snack if you feel like it," he said. Warily I agreed and watched apprehensively as we headed up the narrow road.

He pulled off onto the grass, parked the bike, and asked me to sit down beside him. He wanted to talk. He began by apologizing in a gentle way and asked why I was so adamant about his touching me. No other girls had ever been so unresponsive to him, and here I was beginning to tremble. He told me he had fallen in love with me, as he went from holding my hands to putting his arms around me and began smothering me again.

"I simply can't do this, Friedl. I'm not ready, and by forcing yourself on me, you are ruining everything," I said.

I pushed him away. I could tell he was hurt. He told me, had I not been as mature as I was, far beyond my young years, his friendship with me and ultimate desire would have never reached this point. I was crying and pleading with him to stop talking to me this way.

He gave me his promise to give our relationship more time. But he was convinced there was more going on inside of me. Was there? Was there anything he could do to help me? He felt I was at some kind of emotional breaking point, and I was. Would it always be like this for me? He had kindly asked me a question. I wanted to respond to what seemed to be his new, considerate behavior. Should I answer it?

Yes, I said, there was a reason I did not welcome advances. I had had traumatic experiences as a ten-year-old with an American soldier, and I ended up telling him the entire story about Pops.

He seemed so solicitous. "Please may I hold you as I try to apologize again? I am so sorry you've been through such a terrible personal ordeal. I cannot tell you how I regret pushing you. Never will I do that again."

I was shaken, everything had been said; there was nothing more. We reboarded the motorcycle and headed out onto the main road. I felt a little more at ease putting my arms around his waist to hang on, which was not the case when we left the Breitenbergers earlier.

He took me home, and we both lied to my parents and said we'd had a wonderful time. I even felt okay when Friedl said a very correct good-bye. The incident was over. I'd been able to explain myself to a friend who seemed to understand, but the events of that day left me totally drained.

We saw each other only briefly on the train the following morning. He was anxious to know if I felt all right. I assured him I was fine. He told me his work would be taking him away for ten days, perhaps two weeks, but he would write often. That gave me time to sort things out, and before long I began to want to free myself from this burdensome relationship.

The ugly incident on the rowboat, his rude and childish behavior towards my friends, our host family, and the reopening of old wounds—all conspired to change my feelings towards Friedl forever. Our relationship was shattered, regardless of the declarations of love he wrote to me. I took all of his letters to Munich because he had made slight references to the Pops story in one of them, and I had to keep this from my parents.

He came to Attenkirchen sooner than I had expected. Less than a week later, on a Friday evening, he showed up, having come directly from the town in which his work assignment was. I was extremely uneasy. I wanted him and the memories he stirred out of my life. He suggested we take a walk.

"I've missed you as never before this past week. Please forget what happened. I love you and will not relent until I know you've forgiven me."

"Friedl, it's over. I forgive you, and in time I will forget, but I can't see you anymore."

A dark look crossed his face. "I can't live with that answer," he said. "I must have you, and I will not rest until you want me just as much!"

My intentions had been to part as friends, but he only made me dislike him even more. He left in a dither. My mother knew something was wrong and asked what was going on, "I told him I didn't want to see him anymore, and he didn't like it."

Two days later I heard his motorcycle pull up. Pete and Naomi Mulligan had stopped in to visit my parents, and we were sitting around the coffee table as usual on any given Sunday afternoon. Friedl came in, pleasant and smiling. I introduced him to Pete and Naomi, but didn't ask him to sit down with us. Instead, I excused myself, and we went outside.

"I think I have come to realize that I created these bad feelings you have towards me now, and I am willing to accept the responsibility for having done so. Let us have one more motorcycle ride to our favorite café in Au, and for old times' sake, have coffee and cake as friends and go our separate ways."

That is exactly what I wanted. I agreed and went inside to fetch my purse and say a quick good-bye. I got on the back seat of the motorcycle, all the while thinking, "This will soon be over, once and for all."

But Friedl had his own plan. He speeded up as we were leaving and veered off to the left onto a country road, instead of following the main road to Au. "You're going the wrong way!" I shouted, "And you're going much too fast!" The road was narrow with deep ruts full of gravel.

"Slow down, Friedl! You're going to cause us to wreck," I screamed, pounding on his back.

He was acting like a madman, going faster and faster. I knew I was in terrible trouble. I believed he was willing to harm or even kill me—or us. I saw Guetlsdorf, the next village, off in the distance, and as we approached, he had to maneuver through a sweeping S-curve. Miraculously, a passenger car appeared around the curve and slowed down to let us safely pass each other. Friedl had no choice but to also slow down; and before we cleared the other vehicle, I made the split-second decision to take my chance for life, and I jumped off.

I rolled down the berm into a ditch with tall grass and took off running into a hops garden. The hops garden with its full-grown, leafy, blossom-laden vines swallowed me up. I zigzagged through the rows of vines until I found a deep furrow into which I dropped to the ground. I lay still, hardly breathing as I thanked God and prayed He would stay with me for a while longer. I could hear Friedl running his bike back and forth, stopping frequently to call my name. I heard him walking and started belly-crawling away from his voice behind me. I continued crawling, and soon I heard him re-start the motorcycle.

The hops garden was about three kilometers from my home. I knew exactly where I was, but I would have to skirt the village through open fields, and I didn't want to risk being seen. I would have to wait until dusk. I could still hear the muffled roar of Friedl's motorcycle as he continued to make passes.

Finally darkness came, and I started for home. As I neared our house, I saw him pull out of the driveway, and I could hear sobbing screams coming from within. It was my mother, frantic with fear, hysterically calling my name. Pappi had taken the Sunday evening train for his work week, unaware of what had happened. My poor mother was living this nightmare all by herself.

"Mommi," I told her silently, "I know I am giving you one of the worst evenings of your life, but it will soon be over."

She was near collapse when she saw me. She was crying hysterically, but thankful and relieved I was all right. Mud had soiled my clothes, my hair, my feet. I was a frightful mess from top to bottom. I told her what had happened.

"You are not going to Munich tomorrow morning," she said. "I will not let you board the same train that madman is on. I fear for your safety."

"No, I have to go to school," I said. "What can he do on a train in broad daylight?"

I promised to not only avoid him, but I would surround myself with my traveling companions. If I don't stick with my routine, I said, he'll know he could intimidate me and I was not going to let that happen. I had to go on with my life.

It was mid-week when I came home from school one evening, and Bum-Mama met me in the entry of the apartment. She was visibly upset.

"There's someone here to see you," she said. "He's in the kitchen."

"Who is it?" I asked.

"Your gentleman friend, the one who brought you home late from the cinema several times. I just want you to know I am going to the milk store on the corner and expect him to be gone when I return!"

I was shocked when I saw Friedl sitting there. "Why are you here?" I asked. "How did you get past Bum-Mama?"

"She remembered me, and I told her I had some important information to give to you and would leave immediately afterwards. She let me come in and wait for you."

Why on earth did Bum-Mama leave us alone in the apartment? Friedl was capable of crazy mood swings when he didn't get his way. I was terrified of him. He stood up, and in an authoritarian manner, he said, "I am going to go to the German court authorities and file a legal complaint against your American master sergeant, informing the court about your incident. I also intend to report him to the judicial arm of the Occupation Forces, as I am sure they, too, will be very interested in hearing about this."

I could not believe what I had just heard and struggled to remain calm. His threat was aimed at me, but to turn on me with such a hateful act of betrayal! What a monster Friedl had turned out to be. I began hyperventilating and feeling faint. I knew I was going to get sick and ran past him down the hall into the bathroom, locking the door. I threw up in the toilet.

A short while later, I heard his footsteps coming down the hall, hesitating for a moment, and then I heard him say, "Don't bother looking for my letters and pictures. I found them in the top drawer of your nightstand, and I am taking them with me." The ultimate *Schweinehund!* I didn't come out of the bathroom until I heard Bum-Mama's key in the door. Friedl was gone.

I didn't go to school the next day. I went home. My mother was stunned when I walked in the door and instinctively knew something was wrong. I told her Friedl had been to see me at Bum-Mama's in Munich and was threatening me with a court action. She was already hostile towards him but she naturally asked on what grounds?

And so the time had come. Events kept in secret, probably much too long, needed to be told. I had to reveal the truth about the much-respected savior of our family, Pops. I began to tell her what happened during that tumultuous time six years ago when the Allies entered our area in Thuringia, of the aid the American soldiers rendered, and of Pops's truly heroic action in spiriting us out of what was to become the Eastern Zone just before the Russians took over. As difficult as it was for me to continue, I went on to tell my mother about his subsequent betrayal of a ten-year-old girl who felt nothing but gratitude for his saving her father and who trusted him, was violated, and then determined to protect her parents from the knowledge.

Mommi's reaction was predictable, and we embraced each other in a flood of tears. But her steely nature took charge, and she became angry, as angry at Friedl as she was at Pops.

"Dieses falsche Biest!" (This deceitful beast!) "How dare he exploit the confidence and betray the innermost revelations of a girl who had told him such a private story? The story of a little girl's nightmare that he pressured her into telling him."

As she spewed out her anger, the enormity of the incident began to register: the tragedy that had befallen me, the awesome burden of keeping it to myself, and the unbelievable disappointment in a cherished friend. We finally calmed down, realizing we had our biggest challenge ahead of us—telling Pappi.

Ever since the motorcycle incident and my flight across the fields, my father had detested Friedl. He would only hear his name, and it would send him into a tailspin. My mother decided it would be best if she told him while I was away. Yes, I nodded sadly. I took the early train to Munich from the Heart's Closet

the next morning and went back to school for the rest of the week.

I decided to take the Saturday mid-day train to Attenkirchen, rather than ride home as usual on Friday evenings. I didn't want to chance an encounter with Friedl, any of his friends, or any of mine. I was usually in a happy weekend mood by the end of the week, but I just wanted to be left alone.

Arriving at our station, I descended the steps, and there stood my Pappi. This was most unusual. He never met me at the train! My heart was pounding. I will never forget the stricken look, the devastation it conveyed, and how his face twisted into an emotional grimace when he saw me. I ran into his outstretched arms.

We clung to each other. Neither of us could say a word. There was nothing to say. When Pappi cried, his shoulders heaved and he did this now. He quieted down and started breathing normally. He held me at arms length and said, *"Mein Mutzi, mein Mutzi—komm, wir geh'n heim"* (My Mutzi, my Mutzi, come, we're going home).

Hand in hand we walked home on the grassy path that would take us the back way. We had to walk up a little rise, where we could see our modest house a short distance away and look back and see the train station and our *Holledauer Bockerl* choo-chooing through fields of hops gardens toward Nandlstadt. Pappi hesitated a moment and turned me towards him.

With tearful eyes he looked at me, his head shaking slowly from side to side, and said, *"Wie hast Du nur gelitten, mein liebes Mutzilein—und so ganz alleine"* (How you must have suffered, my dear little Mutzi, and so all alone).

It had been a long time since we hugged so tightly. I remembered a game he used to play with me as a child. He'd ask me, "How much do you love me?" I would spread my arms so far apart I'd almost be doing a backbend to show him how much.

He would say, "And now let me show you how much I love you!" That was my cue to start running away, knowing he would catch me, sweep me up into his arms, and say, "Here, I'll show you!" Then he would squeeze until I yelled, "I give up. I give up. I believe you!"

My father was my teddy bear. He felt so warm to me, and the fruity fragrance of rum and maple pipe tobacco was as much a part of him, as my mother's favorite Tosca perfume was of her.

How crushed he must have been. He would for the rest of his life carry a burden even larger than the one I had. We spoke quietly over the weekend, revisiting details. By this time I had processed all of the experience of fleeing and being raped by someone I trusted, someone we all trusted, and had become matter-of-fact about it. For my parents, however, it renewed the feelings of the time when they were hidden under a canvas, afraid for their lives and the lives of their children. And there was guilt for never having noticed their little girl's predicament in that time of *Todesangst* (mortal terror), so preoccupied with surviving were they.

My parents had to put it to rest as well. Most of all, they were proud of that little girl, who so long ago had the courage to protect them at such personal cost. Time would heal them too.

Now this other swine was planning to exploit our tragedy. Shock and mourning turned to anger. My mother's fiery nature asserted itself again.

"No, he will never get away with it! Never! I will report him to the Austrian Embassy. I will go to the American authorities before he ever gets a chance. I will get to the German courts and give them an even better story about how he repeatedly endangered the life of my daughter and how he tried to maim, perhaps even kill her by risking a motorcycle accident. I will tell them everything! He will rue the day!" Etc., etc., etcetera.

My mother was on a roll! Pappi and I stood there and took it all in. I know we both felt the same way. We thought she was amusing. As happened so often in our family when things got tragic and you'd think we could bear no more, we would turn to our sense of humor for relief.

I looked at Mommi and said, "You know, that Friedl is damn lucky he isn't here right now, or he'd be dead meat. One more barrage of verbal punches like the ones you just threw, and he'd be picking himself up off the floor!"

Pappi, the quiet man who never spoke before he thought, convinced her there was nothing to gain by going to the authorities. We would hold our peace and see what happened. It wasn't likely anything would come of Friedl's ranting and raving to the authorities. It was bombast.

And nothing did occur. We put it to rest to the best of our ability. We were not going to keep score. We were not going to waste any more energy. As we always did, we moved forward. I felt an enormous load had dropped away and I felt like dancing.

And I did—with my Pappi.

Pete and Naomi were Air Force friends from Germany to the US for fifty years. Here, in a picture in later years, they are at their eternal chess game.

Annelie modeling for Modelhaus Zirzow in the Hotel Bayrischer Hof in Freising.

Hotel Bayrischer Hof in Freising.

I was recovering from my nightmare with Friedl and turned my attention to Private Handelschule Sabel. My goal was to end my study year with a strong finish. Accomplishing this, I earned a spot on the list of eligibility for graduates who qualified for immediate placement.

Our class and several teachers chartered a bus and planned a sort of senior trip, as in American schools. We wanted to say our good-byes and make lasting memories. The school year had been productive. We were a happy group, having spent many weekends together, skiing and hiking in the Alps and getting to know each other. Lasting friendships were formed.

We traveled to Lindau, a resort town on the Bodensee, also known as Lake Constance. It is a huge lake southwest of Munich, bordered by Germany to the north, Austria to the east, and Switzerland to the south. The Rhine river flows out of the Bodensee at the lower west end, and legend has it that it cleanses itself near the Swiss town of Schaffhausen in a dramatic display of powerful, "ripping" waterfalls. The area around the Bodensee is one of the most beautiful in Germany and the surrounding Alpine countries.

As most farewells go, saying good-bye to my schoolmates was bittersweet, and many of us promised to stay in touch. My girlfriend Marlou and I did just that. We corresponded and visited each other for years.

All of us were focused on our futures and anxious to get started. I applied for a position with KLM airlines at their human resources office in Munich. After filling out a lengthy application, I attached a copy of my brand new business diploma, as well as documentation certifying fluency in English, German, and conversational French. I also wrote a cover letter in longhand, explaining my desire to enter their stewardess-training program.

Following a brief perusal of my application and support papers, I was asked to return that afternoon for an interview.

A dignified gentleman received me in his office, and my file was on his desk. As he was leafing through the pages, I noticed check marks on my application, along with some answers underlined. Someone had thoroughly checked out all the information. He began by complimenting me on my fine *Zeugnis* (School report, which in Germany includes personal observations and recommendations by various instructors). He went on to say I was highly qualified to be considered not only to enter their stewardess training program, but for a job at one of their ground stations. He then became condescending, almost fatherly, and continued in German (up to this point we had been conversing in English) *"aber Fraeulein Wiegand,"* he said, *"kommen Sie bitte in zwei Jahren zurueck"* ("But Miss Wiegand, please come back in two years").

I had been foolish to think I could stretch the truth about my age, changing the year of my birth and making myself two years older. He said he would keep my file current and all but assured me of a position when I returned at age eighteen. So much for getting my wings clipped by KLM. I never told Pappi. In time, he would find out I would not be content to stay in the little village forever. The same wanderlust of his youth was burning inside me.

For now, I stayed the course and met with Sabel's placement consultant after graduation and told her I needed to take a few months off before seeking employment. Our first big strawberry harvest was coming in, and I had to help out at home. I would contact her in late August, asking for assistance in finding a job in Munich that fit my qualifications and utilized my language skills.

I was home for the summer and enjoyed the peace and security of our little house, my parents, friends, the strawberry fields, the orchards, and last but not least, those clucking chickens, whose coop my father had enlarged to run the length of the house. Our roosters, who used to irritate me with their crowing at first light, didn't bother me anymore. Their cock-a-doodle-doos had become music to my ears.

Willi, still living in Munich, spent his spare time with Emmi, but took his vacation as soon as the strawberries began to ripen and came home for several weeks to help during the harvest. Our workload was unbelievable. Pappi hired about thirty pickers and packers, the same women who helped us with the planting. Despite such a large group of workers, we could hardly keep up with the ripening strawberries.

Every little square box had to be packed and weighed with the finest berries reserved for the top layer and arranged so that all blossom ends were facing in the same direction. My mother would then wrap the boxes in cellophane, secure them with a rubber band, and stick our "Produce Grower's" label (which I spent evenings hand-printing) on top. She was again in her element, reaching back into her early food service training, where presentation meant everything. She would delight in viewing a crate of finished product and often said, "See, they look like newborn babies!"

At two o'clock in the morning, Willi and I would load the day's harvest onto the pre-war, rickety pick-up truck Pappi had leased from our neighbor, who owned the equipment repair garage across the road. Parts of it were wired together, which didn't make it look very roadworthy. But Herr Gruenwald assured us a careful driver would get us where we had to go and back. Willi was that driver, and he kept me in stitches with his stream of one-liners.

Chidingly, he said, "Should the brakes fail on a downhill run, get ready to stick your foot out and drag it on the ground. I'll do the same on my side, and if we're lucky, we'll bring this old crate to a stop."

Loaded and ready to go, we headed out for the wholesale produce halls and the famous *Viktualienmarkt* in Munich. We had to be there by 4:00 AM to make sure we would sell all of our strawberries to the retailers that came to buy that early. On the way home, we would deliver reserved crates to the mess halls inside the Army bases in Freising and Erding.

We never had a problem selling our entire load because our product had so much eye-appeal. My parents were keen on packaging the berries the same way American housewives bought them in supermarkets all over the United States, and the small German retailers liked that. However, on one occasion we returned to Attenkirchen with an entire day's load. My father thought he was seeing things.

We had experienced a day of heavy rainfall midway through the harvest, and many of the strawberries were lying in mud, despite our having bedded the stocks in straw prior to ripening to prevent this from happening. We had to soak the mud off of the affected berries, which not only made them appear juicier, but also increased their weight. This worked in our favor when we sold our berries in bulk and by the pound to customers right off of the farm on the same day they were picked and soaked. But my father came up with the idea to soak the berries before we packed them for delivery. It backfired! By the time Willi and I got to Munich, having driven over the washboard roads that connected us to the asphalt highway, our produce was reduced to a mushy mess.

Pappi learned his lesson, but all was not lost. My mother cooked enough strawberry preserves to supply the entire village and Pappi started four 20-liter jugs of wine with the berries that had been reduced to mash.

I was sorry to see my Uncle Willi return to Munich near the end of the harvest. Work or play, his sense of humor and comedic behavior made everyone's job more like fun than the hard work it really was. Farm work was never ending, but the urgency of having to pick the ripening strawberries was behind us, and we had our weekends back.

Pete and Naomi Mulligan had returned from Lyon, France, where he'd been assigned to temporary duty, and their delightful Sunday afternoon visits picked up again. Pete was a captain when he left on assignment. Upon his return, he proudly re-introduced himself as "Major" Peter James Mulligan. He was a slight man, only about five-feet seven-inches tall, but when he walked in our door that Sunday afternoon, he was ten feet tall. He had been promoted to the permanent rank of major and re-assigned to his former base in Erding, where he was to serve out his final tour of duty as Chief Base Financial Officer. It was quite an honor, and we all went next-door to the café and celebrated. Many neighbors who had gotten acquainted with the Mulligans joined in the fun and congratulated him as well.

There was also a formal dance at the Officer's Club following the installation of promoted officers and a medals ceremony. Pete and Naomi invited me for the weekend. Did I have a formal to wear to the dance? they asked. "Of course not," I told them. But I had an idea.

I had visited Frau Zirzow earlier that summer to let her know I was out of school and would be living at home for several months and could participate in some of her showings until I went job-hunting in Munich come September. We had become good friends over time, and I had no problem asking her for a favor. Was there a gown in one of her collections or in the sample room that I could borrow for the dance? I told her friends stationed at Erding Air Force Base had invited me to a formal dance. It was to be held in the ballroom of the Officer's Club. She was familiar with the site. Coincidentally it was the same room we had shown her collections on prior occasions.

I attended the dance in a pale-blue, tea-length gown, which made me feel very special all evening. Almost like Cinderella. Pete turned out to be quite the dancer. He told me as soon as the band struck up one of his favorite beats, a fast swing, we'd go out on the dance floor and cut a rug!

Pete was in his early fifties, which at the time seemed ancient to me, but on the dance floor he was a youngster, a wild man at that.

Pete and Naomi originally met at a USO Club dance many years ago in Washington, D.C., when he was a young second lieutenant working at the Pentagon, and she a registered nurse at Walter Reed Army Hospital. Pete loved to play chess, Naomi was an avid bridge player. They married, but never had children. Pete was career military, and soon after he was transferred overseas, Naomi gave up her career and followed him around the world, often volunteering at base hospitals and living on the economy of whatever country he was stationed in because military housing was not always available for dependants.

When the band started playing the Charleston, they got up and treated the audience to an amazing display. Years of dancing together became most evident. It was as though all of their joints became disconnected, so loose and yet combined were their moves. The rest of the dancers backed away and made a large circle to give them the floor. They finished to rousing applause. Their performance was great, and I was so impressed. It was the energy of the dance and their exuberance that struck me as very American in the manner of the roaring twenties. The next day I made them teach me the Charleston.

In addition to that wild and wooly dance, Pete was dedicated to showing me how to drive. He had a small green Fiat, a four-on-the-floor stick shift, and he took me to one of the large parking lots on base and let me jerk that little car around until I learned how to step on the clutch, shift gears, slowly release the clutch and simultaneously step on the accelerator. He was unbelievably patient with me as I alternated between grinding the gears and killing the engine of his car. But I got the hang of it, which delighted us both. I spent several more weekends with them that summer and had the opportunity to practice. Eventually I became a good driver.

When I returned the gown to Frau Zirzow, she asked me what my plans were for the future. She had become my mentor of sorts. I told her I would be contacting the placement counselor at my school and going on job interviews. She offered me a position with her firm. Modeling would only be a part of it. She was mainly interested in bringing me into the business as her assistant to learn it from the ground up. If I decided to accept her offer, I could start any time, the sooner the better. She would also provide an automobile for me to drive as soon as I was old enough to obtain a license.

It was difficult for me to turn down such an opportunity, but it didn't take me far enough away. I could not work in Freising, where Friedl worked. The town was small, and he would eventually discover me. He could find me any time he desired, and I felt this put me at risk for possible future encounters. We had spotted each other on the train several times after that last traumatic incident, and I avoided him like the plague. I would catch him staring at me, sometimes with a crazy grin, and although nothing ever came of his threats to go to the authorities, I would always be terrified.

I thanked Frau Zirzow for honoring me in such a way. I told her how much I appreciated her offer, but I was committed to finding a job in Munich in which I could use my languages. That was all I told her, never confiding the real reason I had to decline.

My placement counselor instructed me to write to the firm of Haacke & Hinrichsen, an import-export company on Dachauerstrasse, Munich, and attach my curriculum vitae and a passport-picture size photograph. A copy of my diploma along with a letter of recommendation from Private Handelschule Sabel had preceded my correspondence.

Several days later I was contacted by Herr Haacke, asked to come in and then I was hired on the spot as his corresponding secretary in English. The position paid well and when I told him I would be commuting, he picked up the cost of a monthly train ticket from Attenkirchen to Munich, unlimited roundtrips, weekdays only.

It was a good offer, more than I had expected, and I accepted, even though I had some trepidation. The location of the firm was all right, within a fifteen-minute brisk walk to the train station, but the building was old and foreboding. A dark, creaky stairway led up to offices that occupied the second floor, laid out railroad-car fashion, typical of old European inner city architecture. Buildings were narrow along the street side, with even narrower driveways separating them, but extending quite deep, usually ending with a small courtyard that backed up to the courtyard of a similar building on the opposite block. Although efficient in the use of space, the amount of sunshine these buildings would allow through was pitiful.

On my first day at Haacke & Hinrichsen, Monday September 17, 1951, my heart was in my throat as I climbed the steps to the second floor. I had met Herr Haacke on my interview, and found him to be direct, rather abrupt, and domineering. I perceived nothing gentle about him, but didn't let it bother me. I could be wrong. My fellow workers, on the other hand, whom I met that morning beginning with the office manager, Herr Bueger, were very friendly. Bueger had my application lying in full sight and was pointing to my picture as the rest of the personnel gathered around and said: "Yes, yes, that's her! That's the one we picked!" They then introduced themselves to me and made me feel welcome.

My daily commute was rugged. I had to get up early enough to catch the 5:45 AM train from Attenkirchen to Freising. In Freising I transferred to the *D-Zug* (express train), which took me into midtown Munich. Following that, a no-dallying walk in all kinds of weather, and I would make it to my desk with ten minutes to spare before the business began at 8:00 AM. At the end of the day, my commuter schedule reversed itself. I didn't dare leave the office later than 17:30 to catch the 18:05 express train back to Freising. If I missed it, I would also miss my connection to Attenkirchen. I'd make it home by 20:30 in the evening. Had it not been for the opportunity to snooze on the train, chat with fellow commuters, or read, it would have been a grind. Frankly, at times it was. But I made up my mind I would stick it out until I reached my eighteenth birthday when I planned to reapply at KLM, when a whole new world would open up.

In the meantime, there was Haacke & Hinrichsen, and I wanted to do well, increasing my vocabulary in business English as it applied to the import/export trade. Although my goal was earning and stashing cash, I was going to prove to Haacke that I was the best English corresponding secretary he could have hired.

Our company exported scrap metal (and post war Germany abounded in scrap metal) selling huge amounts to other countries, especially to Syria. A firm in Switzerland, Domeisen in der Schweiz, acted as our agent handling all of the international transfer, transportation, and tariff papers. They generated lots of our correspondence, both in French and English. A lady in our organization came from Alsace/Lorraine and was fluent in French. She handled all of the French translations, as well as functioning as Haacke's private secretary.

I judged Herr Haacke to be in his mid-fifties, and he was not a candidate for Boss of the Year award. He ran the office like a Prussian overlord. Our office manager, on the other hand, was a kind and quietly efficient gentleman, first on the job every morning to receive and sort the mail. The rest of us arrived by 8:00 AM and spent the first half hour chatting, smoking, and working at ease, until we heard the screech of the tires, the slamming of the car door and the door downstairs, signaling that Haacke had arrived.

He came in, grouchy as always, and with a booming voice announced, *"Morgen!"* instead of *"Guten Morgen"* (Good Morning), as he marched through the offices to the last one, which was his and had a view of the courtyard. In my mind's eye I imagined him goose-stepping like the German *Wehrmacht* on parade. Then a few minutes later (it was the same every morning) *"Fraeulein Schaadt! Kommen sie 'rein!"* Off she'd go with an armful of mail given to her by Herr Bueger, dutifully taking her place at her secretarial desk, which Herr Haacke insisted on having in the corner of his large office. Then it was work, work, and more work in the grim atmosphere he created.

He ordered us around in feudal tones, but we were amused when his young blonde wife arrived with their pre-school, spoiled-rotten brat of a little boy and turned him into the subservient husband. Then timidly, it was, *"Ja, mein Schatz, was immer Du wuenschest!"* (Yes, my sweetheart, whatever you wish). This from a man who had thrown a typewriter out of a fourth-floor window when he was an officer in Berlin during the war, a man whose voice could be heard through the walls screaming at suppliers.

I made every effort to have my English correspondence, translations attached and in the folder, on his desk by noon. I brown-bagged my lunch to give myself extra time if I needed it. After he came back from lunch, he could count on my work being there. Then I had to wait for him to order me into his office for dictation while I busied myself with whatever Herr Bueger gave me to do, filing, etc.

If Herr Haacke didn't call me by 2:30, I got very nervous. If he wanted his responses to go out that day, I needed sufficient time to get them translated, into the signature folder and back on his desk before it was time for me to leave. I often had to remind him of my commuter schedule. One time he got so irritated at me that he came stomping into my area and asked if it was convenient for me to take dictation now! If so, *"Dann kommen Sie mit!"* (Then come with me!) He was a most difficult man, and my only motivation to stick with my job was the good pay for someone my age.

Another and probably more important issue that kept me from walking out was the fact that it was not a good idea in Germany to develop a reputation as a person who moved from job to job. Especially in my case, inasmuch as Private Handelschule Sabel's placement counselor worked through the *Industrie und Handelskammer* (Industry & Chamber of Commerce) in Munich, and any new employer could track my record.

I settled into a routine; it was the first component of my long-range plan. My mother, on the other hand, was not doing as well on her version of the plan—Pappi's plan. She was trying her best to be a farmer's wife, looking at Pappi's daily to-do list that he left as he walked out the door on his way to work.

"Hoe ten rows of strawberries every day. Call the tree pruner and cultivate the plum trees. Don't forget to feed and water the chickens. The egg man comes on Thursdays." And on and on.

She did her chores dutifully, but it was grueling and taking its toll on her. She would look overtired when I came home in the evening, and after we ate supper together we were ready to go to bed immediately.

Pete and Naomi started stopping by during the week to visit Mommi. In a way this complicated matters. They knew she was alone a lot and wanted to brighten her day by taking her out, but she was held captive by her chores and could only manage an hour or two away from home, barely long enough to go for coffee and cake. Their well-intended visits continuously exposed her to the richness and the interests of American life, and memories of long ago stirred the yearning within her to come back to the country she loved most.

Together my parents had again achieved so much, yet by this time I realized Mommi did not see a future in Germany in the strawberry fields. Not the future she wanted. She had made a cozy home for us in that garage/chicken house, a home my father promised would only be temporary. We slept under Lady Pepperell sheets and snuggly feather ticks. We had oil paintings on the wall and wonderful food with crystal glasses to drink out of. I was taking a chunk out of my salary to make payments on twelve place settings of fine Hutschenreuther porcelain dinnerware, which I planned to give her for Christmas. When I told Pappi about my intended gift, he said, "No, we're not going to wait that long. I want her to have it now." He helped me pay it off early, and, as expected, she was very happy when a huge wooden crate arrived, a total surprise. She was a nester at heart.

As the weather got colder, the outside work eased up, as did my mother's workload. My father, on the other hand, added to his. He took on a second job as sales representative for a company in Munich, Eugen Wolf Waeschefabrik, selling custom-made bed and table linens door to door in the evening. Once he got started, he worked by appointment only and was remarkably successful. The timing seemed to be just right. The war was over. Regionally manufactured consumer goods were beginning to hit the marketplace. People started to earn money again, and German housewives were ready to buy the beautiful bed and table linens they had been deprived of for so many years.

Pappi earned commissions only with a small travel allowance, which he never used up. He confined his calls to areas within Munich and those suburbs he could reach by streetcar. He kept his full-time job with the US Occupation and continued living in Munich during the week. There were often weekends he'd only be able to spend Sundays at home, due to having his Saturdays filled with sales appointments. Pappi was earning a fine living for his family, though his hours were endless.

Back in the States, Freddy was moving upward in his Air Force career. His letters kept us informed of his progress. He loved being in the military. After completing basic training at Lackland Air Force Base in San Antonio, he was transferred to Keesler Air Force Base, Biloxi, Mississippi, where he began his training as a radar operator. His ultimate goal, however, was to become an airborne radio operator and achieve flying status.

After completing his training at Keesler, Freddy and some of his graduating class were transferred to Selfridge Air Force Base, Mt. Clemens, Michigan. Selfridge was the Division Headquarters of the 30th Air Defense Command, from which the newly trained radar operators received their duty assignments. At that time these duty assignments could have been Korea, England, Germany or any air base inside or outside the continental United States. Freddy was reassigned to Lockbourne Air Force Base in Ohio, a massive radar site where his training could be put into actual use. Several months later he was picked as part of a group of airmen assigned temporary duty (TDY) at Willow Run Air Force Base, Ypsilanti, Michigan, which was designated a P-1 Radar Site and had to be upgraded and integrated into the North American early warning system. Freddy's group had orders to ready the site and prepare for installation of equipment. On his way to his TDY assignment, he was required to check in with Division Headquarters at Selfridge.

Much to Freddy's surprise, the personnel clerk he checked in with was an airman who had originally been with him at radar school when both were stationed at Keesler. Delighted by this chance meeting, they promised each other to get together after Freddy was settled at his new duty station and catch up on each other's military lives and off-base conquests. The airman's name was Joe Krauter. His home was near Fort Wayne, Indiana, where he grew up on a farm, the youngest of seven children. He had six older sisters.

Freddy and Joe met several times. Together they would hitch a ride into nearby Mt. Clemens and hang out in some of the GI beer joints, doing what soldiers do when they're out for a night on the town. During the course of these evenings, they became acquainted with each other's backgrounds and family demographics and shared the latest photographs from home. They became good friends.

On one occasion Freddy came into town to meet Joe and found him bubbling over with excitement. "I'm going to Germany!" he said.

"You lucky dog!" said Freddy. "How did you manage that?" Joe went on to explain that he had typed a manifest the day before, listing airmen from the pool of military personnel available whose AFSC numbers (Air Force Special Classification Code) matched the AFSC codes of the slots that had to be filled for overseas duty, European Theater of Operations. Joe realized he had an opportunity to control his own destiny as he spotted an opening for a personnel clerk matching his AFSC classification. On the spur of the moment, he made up his mind to add his name to the manifest and ship himself overseas. Germany or England would be good assignments, far better than hot Korea.

"Joe," Freddy exclaimed, "you must send me there too! Here's my AFSC classification, radar operator, see if there's matching slot for me. My folks and my kid sister live in Bavaria; it's my home too." And with that he pulled out the most recent photos of my work, modeling for Modehaus Zirzow, and showed them to Joe. "Please see what you can do."

The orders for Germany had been cut, but copies had not yet been run off on the mimeograph machine, nor had the orders been implemented. Joe promised Freddy he would see what he could do first thing in the morning. He seemed very interested in the photos. Joe went into the office early the next day and found a slot for a radar operator on the manifest with the same classification as Freddy's. He scratched the previously assigned soldier's name off and inserted "Corporal Frederick O.C. Wiegand." None of us could have imagined how life-altering Joe's simple act of accommodating a friend's fervent wish would turn out for the Family Wiegand.

Freddy's letter with the news that he was being transferred to Germany arrived in late October of 1951. He didn't know the exact date, but it would be soon. He didn't know exactly where he would be stationed, but it didn't matter. He'd be on our side of the pond, and that's all we cared about. Freddy would find a way to come home if all he had was roller skates.

The private bedroom I had been pleading for finally became reality. No longer would I have to sleep on Pappi's side of my parents' double bed when he wasn't home or on the sofa in the tiny living area when he was.

A generous portion of one end of the chicken house was walled off, finished out, painted, carpeted, and furnished with a bed, nightstand, wardrobe, and desk. A large picture window with southern exposure allowed lots of sunshine, and the room had its own door to the outside. From inside, it was accessible through the living area. Mommi added her decorative touch, making the room cozy and glamorous, in spite of the thin walls, through which I could hear the hens moving about, scratching and rearranging the bedding in their nests, getting ready to lay eggs. I was so pleased to have my own bedroom and eager to let Freddy use it when he came. Now all we had to do was wait for news of his arrival.

Freddy and Joe received their formal orders in November, which authorized them to take two weeks leave prior to reporting to Camp Kilmer, New Jersey, on December 11, 1951. Joe didn't have far to get back home to Sidney, Indiana, to visit his parents. The timing was perfect: Thanksgiving on the farm, and the entire family coming home. It was a festive, if somewhat bittersweet occasion, seeing Joe before they said their good-byes and wished him well as he left for overseas.

Freddy went to New York and spent the Thanksgiving holidays with Tante Elsie, Onkel Werner, and Marianne. He had invited Joe to come and spend time with him, seeing the sights and experiencing life as he knew it, both day and night. Freddy had arranged to use his friend Fritz's apartment. Fritz just happened to be out of town for a month.

Joe took the Greyhound bus from Fort Wayne, Indiana, to New York, an overnight ride, arriving in Grand Central at high noon on December 1. Freddy was to meet him, but as usual, he was late. This gave Joe the opportunity to step outside and get his first glimpse of the Big Apple as he stared skyward in awe, until a tap on the shoulder and a voice said: "Hey, Buddy, I'm here! Welcome to my town."

Freddy had called all of his friends to let them know he would be in New York until December 11, the date he had to report to Camp Kilmer to ship out to Germany. He had invited a fellow soldier along, his Air Force buddy, Joe. It was party time, and the phone rang off the hook. Joe experienced New York around the clock. He saw sights of booze and broads and merrymaking, as presented by Freddy and his old crowd. Gathering from their reminiscences in later years, their last days in New York were one big blast.

They sailed on December 20 aboard the troop ship General HMS *Hahn*, transporting over four-thousand troops and a full crew. Far from being the uneventful crossing they had expected, they encountered stormy weather, which by Christmas day was so severe they were tossed about like a toy boat in hurricane-driven waves and currents, the waves so tall, Freddy couldn't see the sky when he looked outside. Most of the passengers were seasick and scared out of their wits. Outside decks were off limits to everyone except the crew, and they had to be tethered. Finally they made it into the calmer waters of the English Channel and sailed on to Bremerhaven, arriving on December 30. Not so fortunate was the American freighter, *The Flying Enterprise*, which could not withstand the force and broke apart off of the coast of southern England.

Back in Attenkirchen, we were unaware of this drama on the high seas. All I remember is being called to the phone by our neighbor, Frau Bauer, and hearing Freddy's voice. He spoke hurriedly, just long enough to let us know he was on German soil.

After disembarking, troops were ordered to board the train on the siding next to the pier, which would take them to their destinations. From Bremerhaven in the North to Sonthofen in the deep Southwest, the train ride through Germany took all night and most of the next day. Army troops were dropped at various points along the way until only airmen were left to be off-loaded and trucked to a facility that had served as a Hitler Youth Camp. The camp was situated in the highlands outside of Sonthofen on a stunningly beautiful plateau surrounded by towering, snow-covered Alpine peaks. Here and there mountain lakes dotted the landscape. The beauty of the area overwhelmed Freddy and Joe. The camp commander welcomed the arrivals and extended an invitation to attend the New Year's Day dinner in the main dining room. Processing and reassignments would commence the following day.

Joe was ordered to report to Personnel/Group Headquarters, 433rd Troop Carrier Wing, Rhein/Main Air Force Base near Frankfurt. Freddy reported to the 604th AC & W Squadron, a radar site in Haindlfing, on the outskirts of Freising, less than 13 kilometers from Attenkirchen.

Our lives had been infused with so much excitement as we looked forward to Freddy's home-coming that we started decorating the house for Christmas early. Even if he didn't make it home by the December 24, it wouldn't matter. That year Christmas would happen when Freddy walked in the door. We always kept our decorations up until February 3 anyway. That was my birthday, and since childhood I had insisted on keeping the Christmas tree up until then. Pappi's birthday was on January 29 and we always celebrated our birthdays together.

Freddy arrived in early January, 1952. I cannot recall the exact date, but there he was, bigger than life and more handsome than ever in his dashing uniform. He amazed me with his ability to dream of plans for the future and turn them into reality. As I looked at him, I saw he was living his dream. Our *Wiedersehen* was part it.

My life had become very routine as far as my work in Munich was concerned, my daily commute, downright boring. I lived for weekends, especially now that Freddy was stationed so close by. He seemed to find plenty of Air Force buddies to bring home, and it was up to me to gather up girlfriends willing to go out with them on Saturday nights. The service club in Freising saw a good deal of us.

There were weekends in between when I didn't come home. Frau Holzer, the bookkeeper at Haacke & Hinrichsen, and I became good friends. She was a lovely fortyish woman, very athletic, married but childless. She and her husband were the ultimate ski-buffs, and when the slightest amount of fresh powder fell in the Alps, they were off on a skiing weekend. They invited me to come on one of their trips to learn all about *Langlauf* (cross-country skiing). We drove to a town nestled in the Austrian Alps called Hintersee. I had never been to a more picturesque area.

I discovered cross-country skiing to be much more fun than down-hill. There is something spiritual about *Langlauf* as you glide through the serenity and magnificence of nature's snow-covered beauty. We followed trails that took us along the banks of Lake Hintersee in the pancake-flat valley, and then rose gently towards the highlands. We followed ski tracks through forests of towering fir trees until the path opened to a panoramic view of snow-capped Alps. We would stop often to drink in nature's majesty. After my first cross-country skiing experience, I was hooked and hoped the Holzers would ask me again.

Freddy started to bring up the subject of his buddy, Joe Krauter. He said he wanted the two of us to meet and would try to set something up. Other than that, all he could tell me was that he was a nice guy, tall, dark, and handsome, and that he grew up on a farm in Indiana. Freddy had no pictures to show me. Indiana was about as foreign to me as another country, so I didn't get excited. As time passed and nothing happened, I dismissed the whole thing from my mind.

Frau Zirzow was getting ready to show her spring and summer collection and asked me to stop in for fittings on my way home, usually on Friday evenings. If I could reach Freddy, he would pick me up afterwards and take me home. If he were nowhere to be found, I'd stay over at Frau Zirzow's and catch the noon train the next day. We had become close over the years. She had been both widowed and divorced during the war years, but remained childless. Perhaps I filled a void in her life. We recognized many similar character traits in each other. I admired her creativity and worldliness, and she enjoyed my youthful energy and the fact that I always had plans for my future.

On Saturday, March 8, 1952, everything changed. I got off the train in Attenkirchen in the early afternoon. Much to my surprise, Major Mulligan, "Pete," was parked in his green Fiat, engine running, waiting to pick me up. I was delighted to see him. We chatted on the way home, exchanging small talk, when he said, "By the way, Freddy's home." That meant we'd be going out that night, and I was looking forward to an evening of fun.

Everything was quiet when we got to the house, but I knew where to find Freddy. He was in the feathers, always catching up on the sleep he had lost the night before or banking some sleep for the night of partying ahead. I took off my loden cape, went straight to my parents' bed, and threw myself on top of the feather tick on my mother's side and started tickling and wrestling with my brother. Since early childhood, it was our practice to romp with each other, much as puppies carry on with their littermates.

It wasn't until Freddy overpowered me and tossed me to the other side of the bed that I discovered there was another person there. He had the covers pulled up to his nose as he watched Freddy and me having our sibling fun. Stunned, I managed, "Oh, you must be, uh, I know, you're the guy my brother was going to bring home. Wait a minute, you are …"

"I'm Joe," he said, smiling sheepishly. "Hello."

"Hello," I stammered. "I'm Annelie."

I extricated myself as gracefully as anybody could from a feather tick, blushing and confused as to what I should say next. Not only was I taken back, I was overwhelmed by his good looks. I had never seen a man so handsome in my entire life. Thank goodness Pete had already set up the chessboard on the kitchen table. Usually it was a pain in the neck to have to sit down with him right away and play chess, but in this instance it was a welcome diversion. I just could not concentrate, and Pete knew it as he smiled at me knowingly.

Freddy had our evening planned. I didn't have to dig up a girlfriend; he already had his date lined up. She was a gorgeous blonde American girl named Vlosta, visiting her sister and brother-in-law, First Lieutenant Kibbick and his wife. Kibbick was an officer in Freddy's squadron. It obviously hadn't taken Freddy long to make the connection. We went to dinner at a German *Gasthaus* and had a pleasant time in our all American company. I didn't feel quite as nervous as earlier, but there was no denying Joe and I were aware of each other.

After going to the movies, Lieutenant Kibbick and his wife Pat invited us to their house to play cards. The men brought out the pinochle deck. I spent the time half-heartedly chatting, watching Joe. I observed his every move. How charmingly he interacted with everyone! I studied his looks and facial expressions. We caught ourselves eyeing each other, and there seemed to be some chemistry there. He smiled easily and often. His porcelain blue eyes were rimmed with thick, long lashes; his hair, immaculately groomed, was so black it shone blue. He reminded me of my two favorite actors, Robert Taylor and Gregory Peck, and I wondered what kind of a person he was inside. I liked him.

Not surprisingly, by the end of the evening, Freddy had split. That meant we were on our own and would have to call a taxi to get back to Attenkirchen. It was after midnight, and we had to make several phone calls before we finally found a driver who agreed to take us so far outside of Freising. He would have to charge twenty D-Marks one-way. If the soldier wanted to come back to Freising with him, it would be thirty for the roundtrip. We squeezed into the backseat of his Volkswagen.

We arrived in Attenkirchen, and as we got out in front of our driveway, the taxi driver asked if he should wait. I didn't realize that Joe had
already spent the previous night at home with Freddy and invited him to
stay. I told him I was sure my mother would agree to his staying, if he didn't
mind sleeping on the couch. I was positive Freddy would show up some
time the next day to take him back to Freising. With that Joe dismissed the
driver, handing him his twenty D-Marks.

Joe had had his arm around me in the back of the Volkswagon taxi
because of the tight space, and, much as I wanted to, I didn't attach much
meaning to that. But now we were walking down the driveway together
and he took my hand in his. It could not have been a more romantic night.
We looked up at the full moon shining down from a star-studded sky. Joe
stopped and turned me towards him, holding me at arms length. We just
stood there, looking at each other in the moonlight.

"Something very special seems to be happening tonight," he said. "Do
you feel it too?" I agreed there was something magical. He thanked me for
the wonderful evening he had had and wondered out loud if he could be
living a dream, for he believed he had found that someone he could spend
his life with.

My heart took a leap! Did I just hear what I thought I heard? For a
moment I couldn't collect my thoughts. This was all happening too fast. I
knew I desperately wanted to believe him, for I felt the same way, and yet I
was wary. I was afraid to trust, much less speak my own feelings. I wanted
his words to be true, and at the same time I was afraid they might not be.
Then Joe kissed me, a gentle first kiss, followed by a beautiful passionate
kiss and another and another. I liked the way he held me, strong, willful,
and confident. He stroked my hair and my face and traced my lips. He
made me feel protected, as though he was never going to let go.

We walked over to the garden pump and sat down on the well housing. Neither was ready to go inside even though it was quite chilly. I nestled
into Joe's arm, my head resting on his shoulder. He held my hands in his.
He had huge hands, soft and warm. It was as though we didn't want it to
end, whatever it was that was happening.

"Freddy had shown me pictures of you back in the States," he said.
"Do you believe in love at first sight?" I said I had heard of it and read about
it in novels, but I just didn't know how one could be sure.

"Do you believe what I told you is true, and that I sincerely meant
every word?" I was so touched that he had opened up his heart to me in

such a gentle and yet direct way. I felt I, too, was rapidly losing my heart. I just didn't want to lose my head.

"Joe," I said, "I want you to know I am deeply drawn to you by your beautiful words. Still, the moon is casting its glow on the mystique of this moment, and we've had a fabulous evening. Tomorrow, when the sun is as high in the sky as the moon is right now, let's take a walk and see if these feelings will still be there. Until then, I shall cling to your words, hoping you'll repeat them in the sunshine of a bright new day, and everything you said, Joe, I want to hear it again." And with that I started to weep. "Annelie, what is it?" he asked.

"Nothing, Joe. I always do this when I'm happy."

He brushed away my tears, and we kissed again. Inside Mommi had made some tea. "I wasn't spying on you," she said. "I just thought you might be cold."

When I went to bed, Florian, my cat, purred contentedly on the pillow beside me, and I could hear the hens through the bedroom walls, softly muttering as they rearranged themselves in their boxes.

As I lay there, I thought about everything that had happened that night and the unfamiliar feeling of bliss I was experiencing inside. Was I falling in love with Joe? I had never felt this way before. By the end of the evening I had come to trust Joe, but I was afraid to trust my own feelings. I had already had too many bad experiences in my life. How could I separate what might be true love from mere infatuation or a moment of rapture? I fell asleep looking at the wondrous dark blue sky, wishing on a star, and thinking about the walk Joe and I would be taking the next afternoon.

I didn't wake up until late morning. I could smell my mother's cooking. She was already fixing Sunday dinner. I heard Joe chatting with her, telling her all about his mom, his pop, and his six older sisters and their families back home in Indiana farm country. It was all so relaxed and easy. Joe had a kitchen towel hanging from his hip pocket, and every time Mommi washed and rinsed a kitchen utensil, he would pick it up and dry it. He had already dried all of the breakfast dishes. I had slept through the first meal of the day. I felt neither guilty nor embarrassed, thinking this had given my parents the opportunity to get to know Joe better without my being present. We all learned about each other, and he instantly became a part of our family. He had already enchanted my mother.

That afternoon we took our walk. Across the road was a beautiful pine forest. I had walked the path along the shady side many times, sometimes alone, sometimes with Prinzi. That day it was with Joe. After going some distance, we stopped on the path and Joe took my hands in his.

"Annelie," he said, "if anything has changed since last night, it is that I'm more convinced than ever that I want to spend the rest of my life with you!"

He stopped me in my own tracks. All of my plans, KLM, a business career, traveling around the world—what was going to happen to all of these? Instead, he was making a believer out of me. He was making me believe in love at first sight.

He waited for a response. I did so by kissing him as passionately as I knew how and told him how happy he had made me. But neither one of us uttered those three little words. Deep in our hearts, though, we knew we had found each other.

Later that afternoon Joe had to catch the *Holledauer Bockerl* to get to Freising, then Munich and on to Frankfurt. We walked to the station together, and it was a very emotional good-bye. We didn't want to let go of each other. Joe promised to put in for his next three-day pass as soon as he got back to Rhein/Main Air Force Base the next morning. Then he was gone. I went home and wrote my first love letter.

Everything left unspoken the day before was now written in my letter to Joe. When it was finished, I didn't have the courage to send it. My heart was filled with love, but in trying to express it, my sentiments came out sounding like something from *Modern Romance* magazine. I didn't want him to perceive me as a love-struck teeny-bopper, even though by definition I was a teenager, having turned seventeen just one month before. I wanted him to know I was a mature young woman who was in love with him and that I considered our romance anything but trifling. I decided to wait a few days and tucked the letter away in my desk drawer. I was hoping to hear from him first.

He did not disappoint me. Several days later, as I walked home from the station, my mother met me in the garden waving something. It was a letter from Joe. I took it from her and went straight to my bedroom. It was beautifully written, his penmanship strong and consistent. (A typically German observation.) It was also very romantic. Our relationship had its beginnings in that wonderful time, long ago, when people got to know each other before being intimate, when friendship developed over days and weeks with laughter and leisurely discovery, confidences shared and sometimes shy revelation. Passion was a cherished product of courtship and marriage, growing out of love.

It is a sentimental journey revisiting those days. Part of Joe's letter said:

I have so many things to tell you and one can never say them in a letter, but I will try. Maybe you will understand, at least I hope so. A few days before I came down I was lying in my bunk, reading a book about a girl and a GI and how they fell in love the first time they saw each other. I said to myself that what I was reading was only in a book and probably would never happen to me. But I still had hopes. What I am trying to say is that you really knocked the props out from under me and I'm very glad you did.

Being with you for even the short time I was—I think I know how you feel and I'm praying it's the same as I do ... I don't know why I didn't say it last night but I guess my heart was in my throat, and I couldn't speak. I love you, Annelie ...

I got the letter I had been saving and sent it to him the next day. Excerpts from my letter read as follows:

Dearest Joe, my only one:

I felt like a lost sheep trotting home from the station alone and just kept staring holes in the back of the train. I felt like running after it and being at your side again. I felt like screaming out loud for someone to make it stop!

... I cannot wait until I again feel the nearness of your heart, the tenderness of your sweet caresses, the burning touch of your lips.

... you've opened up a whole new world full of tenderness, kindness and happiness where there are flowers, birds and heavenly melodies to take the place of all the scars and blemishes of this earth. I'll be counting the hours until you return ...

Those were very romantic times.

Joe came down once more in March of that year, and his second visit was as significant as his first, if not more so. I had gotten off the train in Freising on my way home from work, to await the arrival of his train from Frankfurt. We had planned to spend the evening in Freising before taking a taxi to Attenkirchen. When we spotted each other on the platform, we leaped into each other's arms. He swung me around. Everything had been said in those beautiful love letters we had written. Now we knew how we felt about each other and said those three words out loud, over and over and over. We were deliriously in love.

"Let's find a little café where we can have some wine and a quiet dinner. I have something I want to ask you," he said.

I knew of a place on lower main street in Freising, called "Die Weinstube." The Wine Bar was candle-lit, with soft music, and intimate tables for two—it was the perfect place for lovers.

The waiter brought two glasses of wine. We toasted, we sipped, and we made small talk. I could already read Joe like a book and knew what was coming. He asked me to marry him. Without any hesitation, I said I would. Joe kissed my hands. It was a beautiful moment as I watched him, a moment I shall never forget. As the evening wore on, we talked about our future. I dreamed of the life we would have together; and as I did, Joe planned it.

I discovered very early on that this man never did anything without a great deal of forethought. It became obvious that he had carefully thought through all of the responsibilities his marriage proposal involved. While I was still out in dreamland, he was explaining some of the practical considerations. Before we could set a date, he needed to be a staff sergeant, one rank higher than his current airman first class ranking. As a non-commissioned officer, i.e., staff sergeant, he would qualify for the benefits married soldiers could obtain: housing, commissary and PX privileges, medical benefits for dependents, and so on. I preferred remaining on cloud nine and not having to deal with the realities of life. Not just yet, anyway.

When the taxi we had called for arrived, I was delighted to snuggle with my fiancé all the way home in the back seat of another tiny Volkswagen. We decided not to say anything to my parents.

Mommi had made up Joe's bed on the couch, and I was heading for my chicken coop bedroom. We had just had another wondrous evening, promising each other a life together. Now there were unspoken words on another subject as desire came into the picture.

We kissed, lovingly repeating our promises, and said goodnight. As I lay in my bed, thoughts of getting married, whenever that day would come, were beginning to sink in. I never felt as right about anything in my life as I felt about telling him "yes."

Joe was able to get two three-day passes in April. When he returned to Rhein/Main Airbase after his second visit, everybody in the offices of Group Headquarters welcomed him with beaming smiles and congratulatory handshakes.

"What's this all about?" he asked.

"You've been promoted!" they said. "Congratulations, Staff Sergeant Krauter!"

That evening, shortly after I got home from Munich, Frau Bauer, our bakery neighbor, came over and told me to come to the phone quickly. Someone was calling me long-distance, a man's voice. She was sure it was my soldier boyfriend. I was worried, for this was an unusual time for Joe to call. We usually only telephoned on the weekends when he couldn't come to Attenkirchen.

I picked up the phone, "Is this you, Joe? Are you okay?" I asked.

"I'm great!" he answered. "My promotion came through, and you may now call me Sergeant Krauter, and you might also start thinking about changing your name!" He was going to put in for a three-day pass immediately. "Expect me the first weekend in May. We have lots of planning to do, and as soon as I hang up, I'll get busy filing my 'Intent to Marry' application with Group Headquarters."

We were overjoyed that we could actually initiate our plans. Our immediate plans were soon dashed, however, by the announcement that all military personnel were confined to base, resulting in the declining of Joe's request for a three-day pass for the first weekend in May. His request just happened to fall on the weekend that coincided with the annual May Day celebrations taking place in the Communist bloc countries. Moscow in particular celebrated by parading Russia's awesome array of military might and threatening weapons. Tanks, airplanes, helicopters, and a variety of short, medium- and long-range missiles with mobile launching pads, proudly paraded past Red Square.

There was no doubt that the Cold War was heating up in 1952. We had become accustomed to Stalin's saber-rattling, yet felt reasonably secure in the knowledge that the Allies were ready to defend the West on a moment's notice, despite Stalin's threat that he could overrun us overnight. Most of the German population had experienced the hot war. The terror of it all was still in our not-too-distant memories, and this evil warmongering gave us the jitters. No one wanted to dive back into the bunkers. With Joe and Freddy directly affected, the political scene came back into our home. What affected Joe affected me, and what affected me trickled into the atmosphere of our home and family.

Joe finally made it back down to Attenkirchen after things settled down and the May Day alert was lifted. He came the following weekend, coincidentally the weekend of Mommi and Freddy's birthdays, May 10 and May 11. We met in the train station in Freising on Friday evening and headed for the *Weinstube*.

Joe began with an apology: "I'm sorry I don't have a diamond ring for you in my pocket as I had planned, but I came to get engaged to you tonight!" he said. "I will have a ring for you when I return the end of May for your parents' twenty-fifth anniversary. That is when I will formally ask Pappi for your hand in marriage. That is when we will announce our engagement, and we will all celebrate together." He was working with a jeweler in Frankfurt, designing an American-style engagement ring. His dad was selling Joe's car back home and would send him the money.

We were very honest with each other regarding our finances because money was always tight, and we agreed not to burden our parents. I worried that he was spending so much on a ring for me, having to sell his car. I told him an engagement ring was not that important, and besides, it wasn't traditional in Germany anyway. A simple gold band on our wedding day would do just fine. Our commitment to each other was all that mattered.

The owners of the Weinstube had come to recognize us as regulars and greeted us accordingly. Sometimes they came over for a brief chat. This particular evening they observed something special going on at our table. We told them we had just become engaged and were about to set our wedding date. Within minutes a split of champagne arrived at our table, and the owners and most of the customers lifted glasses in a congratulatory toast. It was a cheers moment for everyone.

On the way home, we kidded around with our taxi driver, with whom we were now on a first-name basis, suggesting that as regular passengers on this special occasion, he should really consider giving us a free ride. He said no, but promised a larger than Volkswagen taxi the next time, inasmuch as we were engaged and could use a larger back seat to give us more cuddling room, cuddling that did not go beyond hugging, kissing, whispering sweet nothings, and holding hands. This was the man I was going to marry, and I felt the greatest gift a woman can give is to give herself to her husband on their wedding night. That was what I was going to do.

We set the date, Sunday, July 6, 1952, exactly four months after we first saw each other. Our parents would find out when we made the announcement, as we had planned, sometime during their twenty-fifth wedding celebration.

Joe returned to Rhein/Main Air Force Base after our engagement weekend and immediately applied for another three-day pass. I don't know how or why he was always lucky enough to have his requests honored, but I suspect those in charge of the passes knew what was going on in his romantic life. They aided and abetted his cause. Joe's fellow airmen, sergeants, and officers thought highly of him.

The best-laid plans of mice and lovers often go astray. So it went with the plans for our important family weekend the end of May. Joe couldn't make it. All of the military in West Germany was again put on high alert. Personnel was restricted to base, and all leaves and three-day passes were cancelled until further notice.

There was too much going on in Europe, both politically and militarily. The border between the two Germanys had already become one of the most fortified in the world, with barbed wire fences, mine fields, and sniper towers spanning its length.

Neither East nor West Germany ever gave up on eventual reunification. Their marked separation affected their respective economies also. West Germany was doing remarkably better than its counterpart, partially because of the Marshall Plan (which helped in the rebuilding process) the currency reform of June 1948 (which introduced the Deutsche Mark) and the infusion of millions of D-Marks that were randomly spent on German goods and services by members of the occupation and their families.

While the Allies were aiding the West German economy with monies from many sources, helping the Germans create their famous *Wirtschaftswunder,* the Soviets, rather than rebuilding East Germany, were depleting their resources and rebuilding Russia. Conditions there worsened as thousands of skilled workers and intellectuals risked their lives to escape to the West. The stories of whatever happened to the many scientists, researchers, weapons developers, and mathematicians spirited off to Russia after the war were smothered in silence. East Germany was depleted, and those who remained were poor and demoralized.

To put a halt to drain of human resources, the Russians announced in 1952 that the border between the two Germanys, the death strip that had already seen so much carnage, was going to be officially closed and reinforced with Russian troops as were the borders inside Berlin. Still, people continued to put their lives in jeopardy to reach freedom. Hardly a day went by that the newspapers weren't headlining the stories of ingenious escapes, but more often they were about lives lost in the attempt. Whenever there was such a tragic incident, it reminded us that the homestead in Bettenhausen, our entire family, was situated a mere five kilometers inside the border. We might just as well have lived on another planet, so profound were our feelings of separation. But for a stroke of luck, we could have been subjected to the same fate.

Such was the big picture of what was going on during Joe's tour of duty, but nothing hot ever happened while he and Freddy were stationed in Germany. Still, the state of readiness was ever present and the troops vigilant.

And so it was in late May that Joe had to call me, confirming that he was not able to come. All military was again on high alert. Our plans were dashed, and we were disappointed.

In Bonn on May 26 the signing of the Bonn Agreements was to take place. Germany would be guaranteed sovereignty, becoming an independent, self-governing nation. The Allied occupation was to officially end; however, troops would remain in West Germany to defend against the growing Russian threat. The next day, May 27, the signing of the treaty establishing the EDC (European Defense Community) was scheduled to take place in Paris. This treaty excluded Russia, resulting in an even deeper divide between East and West and lowering the freezing temperatures in the Cold War. It was a tumultuous, confusing time for Germans. There had already been riots in Essen. Some 30,000 people demonstrated against parts of the Bonn Agreements. Several lost their lives. Authorities expected civil unrest, unauthorized marches, and more demonstrations, escalating into riots.

The party for my parents went on without Joe or Freddy, who was also on alert. I missed Joe terribly, especially since we couldn't spring our surprise on everyone attending. But I didn't say a word. Still and all, we had a fun day. Mommi was quite surprised with the combined, and somewhat belated, birthday/anniversary gift we gave her: another oil painting I knew she had her eye on. Pappi's wallet was stinging, and my little nest egg had taken a good-sized hit. I'm sure I also asked Freddy to chip in what he could. She had so few wishes for herself and deserved so much. This beautiful painting of her beloved sunflowers would brighten her every day.

One had to learn of the arduous process the artist went through to really appreciate his work. Herr Tyrna, the artist, was a World War II refugee from the Sudetenland, a region west of Czechoslovakia, from which he had fled. He was an eccentric fellow, who claimed he was going through his sunflower period. He planted masses of them behind his modest house in a neighboring village.

Every morning he would pick three or four at the peak of their bloom, still moist with dew, arrange them in a clump of water-soaked earth, and then he'd paint. By the time they were wilted towards the end of the day, he would discard them, only to repeat the process day after day, working on the same painting until he was satisfied that it was finished. He used up dozens of blooms for each of his works. As a result, his sunflowers looked so alive you wanted to reach out and touch their prickly leaves. Today my mother's sunflower painting graces a wall in my living room. It is precious to me.

Joe came down the weekend of June 7. This would be his last visit before we'd be married. He finally had the opportunity to ask my father for consent. Pappi gladly gave my hand, knowing that I had truly given my heart. Now everybody knew what they had been surmising, and we celebrated.

We had a lot of paperwork ahead of us, red tape, as Joe referred to it. He had already filed his application to get married with Group Headquarters, the prescribed procedure for all GI's intending to marry German nationals. In our case, citizenship was not an issue. I was American-born and had a valid United States passport. The glitch we had to deal with was the fact that I was under age. There were documents, written in German that had to be translated and notarized. The most important of these was the parental consent. We had to get our blood tests, schedule an interview with the base chaplain, and, most important, secure the required consent form issued by the Armed Forces and signed by Lieutenant Colonel Chima, Joe's Group Commander. And I needed to travel to Rhein/Main Air Force Base.

I worked until June 16 after giving my two weeks notice to surly Herr Haacke. He was surprised when I told him about the new life I was about to begin. He wished me luck, saying I would need it, considering how young I was. My fellow workers were more sincere as I said my good-byes to them. My hope that Herr Haacke just might have come through with a small bonus in lieu of vacation days was a pipe dream. All he wanted to know was what day would be my last.

I was thinking about a modest wedding. My parents couldn't afford anything fancy, and we would need funds for our honeymoon and starting housekeeping. Of greatest importance to me was whether the savings in my bank account would pay for the white suit I wanted to be married in. I had a white hat, wrist-length white gloves in the style of Grace Kelly, and white platform shoes with ankle straps, all very chic for 1952. My mother performed another one of her miracles by coming up with four yards of white sharkskin fabric from her stash of 14th Street bargains she had salted away in one of our overseas trunks, among the last of the Lady Pepperell sheets.

I had to fit in a visit to Frau Zirzow before I left for Frankfurt, and she came to the rescue in a big way. Delighted to see me so happy, yet somewhat surprised that I was tossing out all of the plans I had had and discussed with her so often, she encouraged me to follow my heart. She looked at the sharkskin fabric I had brought along, and we talked about a white suit. She had all of my measurements in her book and told me to come back after I returned from Frankfurt. She would design something for me in the meantime. "You did have a straight cut skirt in mind, didn't you?" she asked.

"Yes," I said, "with a slit up the back."

On June 18 I boarded the train for Frankfurt, where Joe met me on the station platform. I spotted him long before the train came to a halt. He was so tall, standing head and shoulders above the crowd, and so handsome dressed in his Air Force blues. He had arranged for me to stay with Technical Sergeant Marvin Singleton and his wife, Mary Beth. They lived in a cute house in an area of occupation-requisitioned housing in the small town of Neu Isenburg, just three miles outside the main gate of the base. This couple from Missouri was so welcoming to me that I never felt like a stranger. Their two children, who were gamboling around, were admonished to settle down and greet their houseguest. I would stay with them for the next five days.

We got our most important appointments out of the way first: the blood tests at the dispensary and our appointment with the military chaplain. The latter one was interesting. "You are German," he said to me. "This man comes from a farm in Indiana. I am glad to see you so happy to start married life together, but I must make you aware of your different cultural backgrounds and the challenges you might be facing in the future."

I think he overemphasized the differences. I had many cultural experiences by now and had profited from them all. He didn't go any deeper into my background other than to comment on my command of accent-free English and ask how it was that I came to live in Germany. I told him I was a student of languages and happened to be born in New York, the daughter of German immigrants who had decided to return to Germany. That seemed to satisfy him, and I was glad he didn't ask when our family returned to Germany or under what circumstances, or I would have had to recite my mother's canned speech.

As children she had coached Freddy and me, when asked, to simply tell people that our family was stranded in the United States when the war broke out and eventually exchanged with Americans who had the same thing happen to them on the other side. The exchange was effected by the State Department. End of story. The chaplain signed off on the necessary documents. Lieutenant Colonel Chima did likewise, signing the Armed Forces consent form on the recommendation of the chaplain. We had accomplished our mission.

Joe's friends in Group Headquarters, those that were married and living in base housing, filled our evenings with dinner invitations. I met wives and children and was delighted with their friendliness. Joe's other buddies, the single men, took us dining and dancing at the NCO Club. It was a whirlwind five days.

I didn't want to leave Joe, the air base, or the many friends I had made, even though he promised we'd soon be living there. On that day I had no choice. I had to return. Once I boarded the train to Munich, all I thought about was getting home quickly, so I could attend to the many details that had to be finalized.

I had copies of the documents issued by the Air Force in my possession. All were in English, and now I would have to translate them into German and have them notarized, then filed with the Attenkirchen *Buergermeister*, Herr Schreck, who had the powers of a Justice of the Peace and would marry us. His aide, Kathi Schmidhuber, recorded the date we had chosen to be married in the mayor's appointment book and guided me through the process of the civil ceremony. She said it would be very short and legally binding. We had no church wedding planned.

I sent out the announcements stacked on the desk in my bedroom. There was no need to send invitations. Joe's family was back in Indiana and could not attend, and most of my relatives were stuck in the Russian Zone. My godmother in Hamburg, Tante Karla, was not able to come. Therefore, the announcements. My mother had planned a garden party reception for friends and neighbors in Attenkirchen, and either she issued verbal invitations, or I penned a note on the announcements.

Meanwhile Joe was putting in for his leave and making arrangements for our honeymoon. He contacted Special Services to check on whether accommodations would be available at the time we needed them and at which R&R facility. There were two sites provided for members of the Armed Services in Europe. One was Berchtesgaden, close to Salzburg; the other was Garmisch, south of Munich. Both were beautiful towns in the Bavarian Alps, and I'm glad we didn't have a choice in the matter. Special Services would advise us when the reservations came through.

Joe had become the personal aide to Colonel Lucion N. Powell, the superior in Group Headquarters who had replaced Lieutenant Colonel Chima, following the latter's rotation to the United States. Colonel Powell called Joe into his office one morning and asked him if he was aware of how inconvenient the timing of his leave was. The annual officers' Efficiency Reports were due, and Joe was crucial to getting them out. These were highly confidential papers and understandably more important to Colonel Powell than the timing of our wedding. He would be willing to approve a three-day pass, but ten days' leave at this time might not be possible.

For several days everything was touch-and-go, making both of us quite nervous. Colonel Powell was not insensitive to our predicament and pressured others to submit their findings as soon as possible so he could dictate his summations. Joe worked deep into the night getting them all typed. In the end, everything fell into place: the ER's were done, Joe's leave was approved, and the reservations for our honeymoon in Berchtesgaden were confirmed.

Joe arrived in Attenkirchen on Thursday evening, July 3. The next day, we took the train to Munich to pick up our rings. Saturday was planned to be an at-home day when we would all be together. Mommi and several of her lady friends were going to cook and set up for the Sunday afternoon reception following our civil ceremony. It would be a busy day, but very relaxed.

Instead, the aide from the mayor's office, Kathi Schmidhuber, contacted us early in the morning. She told us that *Buergermeister* Schreck had been called out of town for the weekend, but the second *Buergermeister*, Herr Bauer, a local farmer and Justice of the Peace, could marry us if we got there by noon. It was Saturday, July 5. Our announcements said we'd be married on July 6!

We rushed around like mad, getting ready. Frau Zirzow had fashioned a beautiful suit for me, the jacket cut in the popular Chanel style. She had accented the revers with white-on-white trapunto embroidery, all done by hand. My suit rivaled Paris and Milan *haute couture*. Joe looked dashing in his dress uniform.

We gathered in the tiny office of the municipality. Standing in front of Schmidhuber's desk, on top of which documents awaiting signatures were spread, as well as the municipality's journal into which our marriage would be registered, were: Mommi, Pappi, Freddy, Joe and I. Herr Bauer was off to one side. The ceremony would be in German. Freddy was our *Trauzeuge*, our witness. He had maneuvered himself next to Joe, standing in such a way that nobody could see him poke Joe in the ribs with his elbow when the *Buegermeister* posed that all important question: "Do you take this woman to be your lawful wedded wife?" And the time had come for Joe to respond, "Ja!"

That's all it took, just one little "Ja," and Joe had married me without understanding a word of what had been said, nor was he able to read any of the documents he had just signed. Today, some fifty plus years and four sons later, it is more than okay.

I don't know how my mother managed it, but the reception planned for Sunday happened on Saturday instead. In the early evening, friends and neighbors started to come, and my parents presented a beautiful buffet. Our baker neighbors came with their gift of a luscious wedding cake, Freddy showed up with a bunch of his buddies and cases of champagne, beer, and wine, and we celebrated deep into the night. It was a perfect summer evening. Pappi had hung lights in the plum trees.

Frau Zirzow had insisted I have a special gown for the honeymoon. She had designed a delicate, light-green nightgown for me. The hemline, hand embroidered and scallop-edged, was tulip cut in front, which made it fall open thigh-high as I moved about. To this she added a demure, sheer negligee. I'm sure she imagined me coming down a sweeping staircase into marriage looking like a Greek goddess. Zirzow knew how to create drama. Little did she know because of a shift in plans, we were to spend our wedding night at home with the chickens clucking away on the other side of the wall.

Mommi helped me slip into my gown. We hugged. She told me to let everything that happened before wash away. Her eyes glistened with tears. She asked me if I was all right. I told her I was fine, a little nervous.

Joe was over by the window as I came into my bedroom. He turned and reached out for me. We stood there like two little kids, just holding hands and looking out the window. The moment we had been anticipating had finally arrived. We fell into each other's arms, hugging, kissing, touching; there was no more holding back. We walked across the room and sat down on the edge of the bed. We talked, and then we kissed, and then we talked some more. For the first time Joe uttered the words I was to hear from him so many more times throughout our years together.

"From now on, its just you and me, Babe." He asked me if I was happy. I told him I'd let him know in twenty-five years.

Joe nestled me into the pillows. There was passion, there was desire, and there was a resounding R-R-R—I—P ! My gown! Joe had been sitting on part of it, and as I leaned back, it wouldn't give. My beautiful gown! Frau

Zirzow's beautiful gown. It was torn from tulip hemline to bust line. I was totally exposed. We fell back and both of us burst out laughing. Joe was all over me. "You're taking advantage, Joe," I giggled.

"My intentions exactly," he said.

It wasn't until the wee hours of the morning that we finally drifted off to sleep in each other's arms. And then the rooster crowed. It worked with his hens, but it didn't work with us. We were awake, but we didn't get up, not for quite a while. Loving and the dawning of a new day. I never dreamed such happiness would be mine.

My mother and Frau Wiese, a lady friend, had planned a going away brunch for us the next morning. Freddy made it just in time. We had a wonderful time reminiscing about how lovely our garden reception had been and how smoothly our entire event had gone, despite its tumultuous beginning, starting a day earlier than scheduled. Now we could all laugh about it.

It was not so funny to my Uncle Willi. For years he reminded me how angry he was when he arrived in Attenkirchen on the early afternoon train all the way from Munich expecting to attend our July 6 wedding, but found us gone and the event over. All that was left for him was a cup of coffee and a piece of leftover wedding cake. I loved teasing him about it. I told him Joe and I just couldn't wait any longer, and he of all people could surely identified with that.

I dressed in my fashionable going-away outfit, picked up my packed suitcase, and off we went in Freddy's borrowed car, heading for the Munich-to-Salzburg Autobahn and our honeymoon destination, Berchtesgaden.

Freddy dropped us off in front of our hotel and plunked our suitcases on the sidewalk. He had no time to come inside and have a beer.

"Got to get back to Freising and return Lieutenant Kibbick's car," he said. "Besides, I've got a date tonight!"

We knew it wasn't with beautiful blonde Vlosta. She was long gone back in the USA. It had to be with some hot *Schatzi*.

I hugged and kissed my brother, thanking him for bringing Joe to me. Freddy turned around, slapped Joe on the back, and said: "Take good care of my Sis, *Schwager* (brother-in-law). I'll pick you guys up on Friday." I didn't cry when I left my parents, but when I stood there with Joe, watching Freddy chasing his own life again, I lost it. Joe understood completely.

We checked into the Hotel zur Post, the R&R facility maintained by the Armed Forces in Berchtesgaden. We were shown to our room in the annex, a building adjoining the main hotel overlooking the town square. It was a lovely view if you cared about people-watching, which was not our pastime when we were in our room.

We had no transportation, but the hotel provided busses to take us to the various tourist attractions. The most interesting tour we took was to the *Kehlsteinhaus*, also known as Hitler's Eagles Nest, atop the Obersalzberg. From its heights, Hitler could overlook the country he was born in, Austria, and the country he had ruled, Germany. It was commissioned by Martin Borman, Hitler's personal secretary and the National Socialist German Worker's Party, and presented to Hitler as a gift on his fiftieth birthday in April of 1939. The engineering feats and architecture of the building left us speechless. Even the car park on the man-made flat halfway up the mountain was imposing. We walked into a tunnel bored deep into the mountain, over 100 meters in length, until we reached a grandiosely designed brass-plated lift that ascended into the interior of the Teahaus, or Eagles Nest, in less than a minute. From there the panoramic view was one of indescribable beauty.

On another day we took a boat ride on Koenigsee, said to be the most beautiful of all the lakes in Bavaria, as well as the deepest at more than 190 meters. There is a famous chapel on an island in the lake, accessible by boat only, called St. Bartholomae. Most of its building blocks date back to the 12th century. The faithful from all over the world are known to make pilgrimages to it. The most remarkable part of the tour was the boat ride itself, as it ran in total silence because the boats run on electric engines, and there are no houses or roads around the lake.

We visited the underground world of the salt mines, as well. Dressed in traditional miners' garb, we slid down the same wooden rails as the miners before us, hundreds of meters deep into the grottos, some of which were full of water forming underground lakes that we rafted across.

Our days were filled with adventure; our evenings were out on the town, dining and dancing. We ate most of our meals in the hotel. Breakfast in the morning room was sixty cents. Dinner in the elegantly appointed dining room was two dollars. I recall the heavy white linen tablecloths with swastikas woven into their repeat pattern. It made us think of the German officers of Hitler's elite, who must have dined at the same tables, draped with the same cloths we were now using. Such were the spoils of war. All of this was now ours to enjoy at $1.50 per day, military scrip.

At night we fell into bed and into each other's arms. Passionate, lusty, and playful, we got very comfortable with each other. How was it possible to be so deeply in love? I made a promise to myself that I would always put Joe's happiness ahead of my own. He filled my heart so completely.

Our honeymoon was sheer magic. *Traumhaft schoen—maerchenhaft*

(A beautiful dream—like a fairytale). Only later in life did we realize how fortunate we were to have had the opportunity to spend it in one of the most beautiful places in the Bavarian and Austrian Alps.

Freddy picked us up as he said he would and drove us back to Attenkirchen. The next morning he would drive us up to Rhein /Main Air Force Base. My last night at home. I felt sentimental, but guarded against getting sad about leaving and about spending my last night in the chicken-coop bedroom.

I carted my dowry to the car: four Lady Pepperell sheets, four pillow-cases, and a vacuum cleaner I couldn't use. It needed a transformer to re-duce the German 220 voltage to our American appliance wired for 110. While I repacked my honeymoon suitcase with fresh clothes, Mommi and I had our last mother/daughter talk before leaving. We had always been extraordinarily close and confided in each other. When she asked me if Joe was good to me, I knew what she meant and didn't feel as though she had invaded my privacy. I told her we had a wonderful honeymoon. Joe was a loving husband and nothing was said about the past. I assured her it was possible for me to have a happy life and that I had put away all of my old troubles for good. She said that's all she wanted. And then she gave me this parting advice, "Keep your family together, support your husband in all of his endeavors and always go to bed hand in hand."

"How could I miss with you and Pappi as my lifelong examples?" I asked.

We said our good-byes. Pappi called me "Mutzi." He told me he'd get the overseas trunk Mommi had packed my things in on its way by rail freight Monday morning. Joe gave him our address: Schuetzenstrasse 6, Neu Isenburg. They stood by the garden pump, arms linked, smiling and waving as Freddy pulled out of the driveway. I had to swallow hard.

We were on the waiting list for government quarters and received a monthly "Class Q" allotment in the amount of $137.10, which was in-tended to defray the cost of renting from private German individuals until base housing assigned us an apartment.

Joe described the "apartment" he had found for us in Neu Isenburg, a short drive outside the gates of the air base. The description sounded too bad to be true. It was. Freddy, following Joe's directions, pulled up in front of Schuetzenstrasse 6, an old two-story house built right along the street with only a two-foot-wide sidewalk for pedestrians. We opened a gate, and our landlady, Frau Zahn, rushed towards us. She was a big, busty, German mom type. Reaching out for Joe, she seemed genuinely happy to see him and shook his hand, almost pumping his arm out of its socket. She turned to greet me, congratulating both Joe and me on our marriage. Turning to Freddy she started to apologize for not speaking a word of English, when he delighted her with a hearty German hello.

She led the way into the house and showed us to our apartment. One room. It was as wide as an Army barracks cot is long, plus maybe about two feet. This is where we stacked our suitcases that doubled as a nightstand. Covered with a cloth and a lamp on top, it was a fine arrangement. There was a wooden table with two chairs along one wall, a potbellied stove in the corner, an armoire on the other wall, and to our immediate right as we walked in was a small chest of drawers with a washbowl and water pitcher on top. The well-worn, bare floor was scrubbed and polished. To cozy the place up a bit, she had placed an area rug in the small space left in the middle. The window was above the bed, overlooking a narrow courtyard.

I asked her where the bathroom was. She took us outside across the courtyard to a shed where there was a one-holer. A roll of familiar pink German toilet paper that felt like recycled cardboard was off to one side on top of some newspapers. In the same shed was a laundry area with cold running water and a stove with large kettles to heat water. Wood was stacked neatly nearby. All of this was there for me to use on laundry day. Whenever we required hot water to wash up in our room, we were just to holler up the steps where her kitchen was, and she would bring down a kettle full. What cold water we needed, we could fetch by the pitcher from the shed. With that she went upstairs and told us to call on her anytime.

Joe's buddies from Group Headquarters had piled our table full of wedding presents. There were flowers, cards, a bottle of champagne, a small radio, a toaster, a pressure cooker, a French fryer, a baby bottle (no thanks—not yet!), and an envelope with thirty dollars in military scrip. I was taken back by such generosity.

I finally got to meet "Tutor," Joe's best friend. His name was actually Staff Sergeant William S. Tutor, but everyone knew him as Tutor or just plain Toot. He was a large man, every bit as tall as Joe, and he came from South Carolina. He was the son of a preacher and quite a character. He was the one who had collected the money from the guys to go shopping in the PX for our wedding gifts. He had a German live-in girlfriend named Ursula Hentschel, who had a cute two-year-old daughter named Ellen. They were originally from Berlin. Tutor introduced his girlfriend as Sue, and that was what we all called her. I don't know exactly how they met, but their relationship eventually ended in marriage. Sue and I became best friends.

Our love nest in Frau Zahn's house was just fine with us. We often laughed about the cultural differences the chaplain had cautioned us about as we took turns using our washbowl. He didn't have a clue when it came to our life experiences: Joe, growing up on the farm, never having had running water in all the years he was at home, except for the pump in the kitchen, and I coming out of World War II, when a bucket of fresh water was sometimes a real luxury. But we both managed to stay ahead of the game. For Joe it was very convenient to take a daily shower in his former home, the barracks on base.

I had made a wonderful new girlfriend, Grace Rose, who took me under her wing. She and her husband, Technical Sergeant David Rose, and their two little boys, Bobby and Gary, lived in Gateway Gardens, an on-base dependent housing compound. Grace would pick me up several times a week and drive me to her apartment so I could wash my hair and take a hot, soaking bath. Grace got me involved in the activities of the NCO Wives Club and the Rhein/Main Air Force Base ladies' bowling league. She had to chauffeur me everywhere, which made me feel indebted to her inasmuch as I was unable to reciprocate.

A more serious quandary was Joe's transportation to and from work. A military pick-up bus cruised through Neu Isenburg on a regular route with designated stops to pick up GI's authorized to live off base. We soon saw that we had to buy our own car, the sooner the better. Joe called his father and again told him to sell his (Joe's) car. He needed the money to buy one over here. This time it was not a luxury, but a necessity. Pop said he'd get right on it.

I was pretty good at cutting corners to save money and did so by cooking some of our one-pot-meals in our pressure cooker in the room and doing all of our laundry in Frau Zahn's *Waschkueche* (laundry kitchen). We purchased a hot plate and an iron from the PX with the extra thirty dollars that were part of our wedding gifts. Washing, starching, and ironing Joe's khaki uniforms kept me busy for two solid days every week. It saved the money we would have otherwise spent on a laundry bill and made me feel I was contributing to our savings.

On weekends we usually walked to nearby *Gasthauses*, cafés, or bars for German food. On Saturday nights we ate at the NCO club. The food was good old American style, which was a treat for me. The meals were affordable, there was always a live dance band, and all of Joe's buddies and their wives and girlfriends were there. Many of these couples had become my friends, too, and they included us in their circle.

Grace and Dave Rose and their boys had become our closest friends. Hardly a Sunday went by that we didn't pile in the car with the Roses and take long drives along the Rhein, exploring castles and stopping in picturesque villages for a stein of beer or a glass of Rhein wine. We would dine in quaint inns, ordering one of Germany's most popular dishes, *Wienerschnitzel,* costing just two Marks fifty per serving including all the trimmings. Other times we would pack our own lunches, drive up into the nearby Taunus Mountains, and picnic in the woods where we would encounter nature-loving Germans enjoying their favorite pastime of wandering through their beloved forests.

One day Joe came home with two pieces of terrific news. The first one was that we had been issued a thirty-dollar per month commissary allowance. No more did I have to impose on Grace to shop for my list of groceries. But nothing could top the second bit of news. The American Express office on base had left a message for Joe that a wire transfer of funds had arrived from his father.

Several days later Joe bought a '47 Chevy club coupe from a buddy rotating to the USA. The car was in good shape for a five-year-old model. It had a cream-colored body and a dark green top, no dents and only a few scratches in the original paint, faded from the sun.

I could hardly wait for Joe to come home with it. Even Frau Zahn was excited. She let Joe pull into the courtyard, and we spent that first weekend cleaning it up. I shampooed the upholstery, waxed the inside trim, and washed the windows inside and out. Joe simonized the outside and shined the chrome. It was the most beautiful vehicle I had ever seen. I called Mommi and Pappi and told them we'd be down the following week-end if Joe could get a pass.

The first ride we took was to Grace and Dave's house. They were so happy for us although I still had to rely on Grace to get around during the day. I began to prepare to test for an international driver's license, but had to wait until the following year before I could take it. I had to be eighteen. Nonetheless, Joe and I were inching closer and closer to the American way of life for military families in occupied Germany.

The post-war period was a glorious time to be in Germany. The German people still loved the Americans, things were inexpensive, and we had the freedom to go any place we chose within our financial limits. That became our problem more often than not, though Joe and I had decided that for the duration of his tour we would do as much and see as much as we could, enjoying life to the fullest in our beautiful surroundings. Without the responsibility of children and having acquired our own transportation, we were spending every last dime. By the end of the month, we were scraping for money to buy groceries.

That's when Sue, Tutor's German girlfriend, and I would put our heads together and make "stone soup" with whatever was left in our meager larders. We often shared our thirty-dollar commissary allowance with them, and between whatever we both had left and reaching back into our war-time experiences of making a meal out of nothing, we scraped by. One Thursday night at the NCO club, Bingo night, all four of us were spent down to our last few dollars after buying Bingo cards when I hit on the last game. It was not the usual cover-up, but an "H." I stared at my card. The game was going fast when all at once I realized I had it! Bingo! I won! The caller came over and handed me twenty dollars. Enough for pork and beans for all of us until the end of the month.

One of the favorite pastimes of American couples was to get to-gether at each other's houses for dinner and an evening of cards. I learned how to play pinochle, Joe learned how to play canasta, and both of us began learning how to play bridge. Dave and Grace invited us for just such an evening. The boys sat at the table with us for supper. Three-year-old Bobby was seated in a regular dining chair; Gary, still a toddler, was in his high chair. We had finished our meal, and Grace was serving vanilla ice cream with fresh blueberries. Gary was trying to hit his mouth with his baby spoon, missing just about every time, when out of frustration and without further ado, he picked up his bowl and upended it on his head! I was amazed at Grace's non-reaction. Remaining completely calm she said, "Now Gary, you're going to have to lick all of that ice cream off of your face, aren't you? And look there's a whole blob on the tray, too, and all those blueberries!"

A German mother would have raced for the washrag as ice cream and berries still drizzled from the top of the child's head and down his nose. Grace, instead, reached for her camera. I was amazed at her child-raising techniques. Was this the American way, or was this really Grace's way of enjoying the antics of her little boys? I do believe the latter. She was a loving and patient mother. I took mental notes for the future.

Joe and I got hooked on bridge. The couple teaching us was Master Sergeant Bill Harper and his wife Gloria. We'd go over to their apartment about once a week to learn more and more about the game and perfect our bidding. Soon we were dealing out hands.

Randy, their only child, was remarkably intelligent at five years of age and doted on by his parents. Bill followed Joe home from the base one afternoon and asked to come in; he had a favor to ask of me. He told us Gloria had to go to the Army hospital in Wiesbaden as soon as possible to have an operation. Would it be possible for us to come and take care of Randy while he stayed with Gloria for the several days and nights? Of course it would. He had only to go ahead and schedule her surgery, and we would baby-sit.

Randy was happy with us since we had become so familiar to him. I brought along some German children's books, which I translated as I read them to him at bedtime. The Harpers' apartment was spacious and beautifully furnished, and Randy had his own bedroom, half again as big as our one-room digs at Frau Zahn's. For the next few days we intended to enjoy playing house at Bill and Gloria's, complete with a young child.

We sat around in the evening after I put Randy to bed and dreamed out loud about someday having our own family. Joe knew how I felt about having children in Germany. We wouldn't. We had talked about it earlier and were doing our best practicing birth control using the only methods available to us at that time; rhythm, protection or abstention. There was no magic pill.

I had told Joe some of the war history of our family and how the issue of differing countries of birth within it was one of the stumbling blocks complicating our already complicated lives. If it were at all possible for me to be in control, our children would not only be 100% American, they would also be born on American soil, the same as Joe and I had been. Perhaps I was a bit over the edge on the subject, but I was adamant about it.

Another reason was that I was still so young and really wanted us to get to know one another, get used to each other's wants and needs and daily living habits. This would be especially important after we served out Joe's tour of duty and began our lives back in the States. We knew this extended honeymoon we were on would eventually end, and we would have to begin seriously planning for our future. Perhaps there would be an opportunity for me to get more education, with college courses and the like. It was not the right time to start thinking about children.

Joe grew quiet as he lay on the couch staring at the ceiling. "Penny for your thoughts, Joe?" I said.

"You know, Annelie," he said, "some of the pieces don't fit."

"In what way?" I asked. He proceeded to reminisce about that wonderful weekend when we first met and what had attracted him to me besides the obvious. He said it was my sense and sensibilities. At seventeen, I was the most mature girl he had ever met. He knew our family had gone through rough times; Freddy had told him about our many separations and later war experiences.

"But you seem to have come out of all of this a completely different person than your brother. Your character, your moral values were impeccable to me. In your first love letter you wrote something about our love for each other washing away all the scars that remained from earlier times. I had no idea what that really meant, just figured the scars you were referring to were the indelible memories of the war. Nonetheless, the remark stuck with me. Then on our wedding night when I discovered…"

I knew what was coming, and I finished the sentence for him. I felt that old panicky feeling returning and getting its grip on me. I started trembling and weeping, and as I often do when fright overcomes me, I started hyperventilating. It scared Joe. I headed for the balcony to get fresh air. Joe followed, and somewhat bewildered, put his arms around me.

"Not so tight, Joe. I've got to relax and breathe deep, and I'll be okay." He was afraid I was going to faint.

Somehow I had known this moment would come, but I figured I would be the one to broach the subject when the time was right, and it would be much later in life. I never thought how my not being a virgin would affect Joe. How unfeeling of me. I was just thinking of myself. After all, I thought, he was twenty-three, and I was not ignorant of the fact that he surely had had some life experiences, but didn't let it bother me. I really didn't want to know.

We went inside. "Joe," I began, "before I start spilling my guts, please tell me your uncertainties about me are not rooted in that good old double standard where boys will be boys and are expected to sow their wild oats, but marry only girls who are pure as the driven snow. That would be very disappointing to me."

He admitted, being a man, that men thought about that, but he reverted back to what had been confounding him all along and repeated his remark that the pieces just didn't fit.

So I told him about Pops, the American sergeant, the good samaritan, who orchestrated our family's escape from Russian occupation and how grateful I was to him. He meant everything to my family and to me. We owed him our lives. He had maneuvered us across the border deep into the American Zone. How we admired his courage and resourcefulness! How I had trusted him and never recognized how he began to manipulate my young and innocent mind. How he convinced me that our family would be forever safe. The death threats against Pappi, my worst nightmare, would never come true.

"Just let me make love to you," he had said. "We would have this very special bond between us and a very special secret that would be ours alone. You would always know that you, too, had a part in saving your family."

All I had to do was submit. All I had to do was … Then, how he raped and violated me on different occasions and in different ways, knowing that I would never tell.

Joe was stunned. It was not an easy story to tell. Now it was his turn to weep. He anguished over the trauma and the hurt I bore all by myself. He felt sorry and angry and guilty, all at the same time, and started to apologize.

"Please don't, Joe," I begged. "You don't have to. I have worked through this tragic event over time and been able to put it away. You brought it to the surface, and now I believe I am finally putting it to rest."

He asked if anyone else knew. I said "Yes, Mommi and Pappi." He never thought to ask how, and under what circumstances, they found out. I left it there.

We turned off the lights and walked down the hall as Mommi had said, hand in hand. It had been an emotional night. We spent what was left in each other's arms. I felt Joe's caring and protective love engulf me. He was my husband, my lover, and now he had become my best friend. I could not imagine life without him. Our devotion to each other reached depths that newlyweds do not normally experience so early in their marriage. When I awoke the next morning, I felt a huge weight had been lifted from my heart. I felt cleansed, as though I had been reborn.

The following weekend we took off for our first visit to Attenkirchen. We were like two carefree teenagers, anxious to get home and show off our car to my parents. It was a solid, eight-hour drive, even though we had Autobahn most of the way. Joe was a good driver and quickly adjusted to Autobahn driving, where there was no speed limit. There was a rest stop high in the mountains called "Java Junction." It was a facility maintained by the EES (European Exchange Service) for the exclusive use of the Armed Forces. I was amazed at all the services offered. There was a snack bar, a PX, lounges for both men and women, American Express and Western Union services, international telephone hook-ups and a filling station with at least eight pumps. At the far end of the parking lot was a mini-park with an overlook that offered views of the valleys below. There were even benches so travelers could rest a while and breathe in the mountain air. It was a lovely spot and just about midway on our trip. We made it our regular stopping point whenever we drove home, both coming and going.

Our weekend in Attenkirchen was wonderful. Mommy and Pappi looked great and were overjoyed to see us. Freddy came home from Freising too. He was very interested in what our lives were like at Rhein/Main Air Force Base—so interested in fact—that he wanted to put in for a transfer and asked Joe to help him.

There were three squadrons of C-119's—the well known aircraft nicknamed the "Flying Boxcar"—that comprised the 317th Troop Carrier Wing and Freddy was still very interested in becoming a radio operator and getting on flying status. Added to this was his desire to transfer into Joe's outfit. In preparation for this transfer, he had to be proficient in Morse code and other subjects required to meet the criteria of the "AFSC" classification of radio operator/flying status. Joe told Freddy to get transcripts of his 201 file and he would take them back to Group Headquarters and hand them over to Lieutenant Jolly, the personnel officer; however, Freddy would have to put in for the transfer himself. Joe would be on the lookout for the paperwork and pass it on to Lieutenant Jolly as soon as it arrived.

To those who didn't really know my brother, it appeared as though lady luck was always on his shoulder. The rest of us knew how driven with ambition he really was and how hard he worked to achieve and "make his own luck." He was always preparing for whatever goal he had set for himself. And so it happened that Lieutenant Jolly came into Joe's office one morning, wondering if he knew how to reach Airman 1st Class Frederick O. C. Wiegand, to tell him a slot matching his classification had opened up and if he wanted to test for the position, he had to appear in his office on such and such a date.

Lieutenant Jolly of course knew of Joe's relationship to Freddy and delighted in passing the news on to Joe, even though this was not the normal channel of communication. That was still to come—but Joe had the pleasure of tipping him off. Freddy still would have to do it on his own. There were a number of airmen testing for the same slot. The highest test scores would be the determining factor.

Freddy transferred from his former radar sight—the 604th AC & W Squadron in Haindlfing to the 317th Troop Carrier Wing, 40th Squadron, at Rhein/Main Air Force Base in late September 1952. He was not on flying status yet, but he had achieved his "own version" of flying status, because he was walking on air! There wasn't a happier guy around.

We usually drove home to Attenkirchen every two to three weeks, as long as the weather held out. Sometimes Freddy came along. It was now autumn and driving could be treacherous at times, especially through the mountains. You could suddenly be shrouded in fog so dense, only ten meters of pavement were visible ahead or find yourself hanging onto the wheel when you suddenly came upon icy road conditions. The nights started to get very cold. It was on just such a night when after a long, nerve-wracking drive, we finally made it back to Frau Zahn's. Our room was ice-cold. We tried to get a fire started in the old pot-bellied stove. Stuffing it full of kindling and more and more crunched-up newspaper, Joe would try to light it, but it just wouldn't take off. He came up with a really bright idea and said, "wait a minute, I'll be right back". He went outside, empty glass in hand and came back in with several ounces of gasoline he had fetched from the jerry can we kept in our car. He poured some onto the newspaper stuffed in the belly of the stove and quickly attempted to light it with his Zippo lighter. All the lighter would do was spark—no flame. He kept spinning the wheel against the flint, when suddenly a spark ignited the gasoline fumes that had built up and there was this huge dull "k-a-a-h-BOOM!" It knocked Joe on his rear end and Frau Zahn came flying down the stairs screaming: *"Was ist los? Was ist passiert?"* (What's going on? What happened?)

We scared the heck out of her—and ourselves. It really could have been tragic. After that, Frau Zahn had a fire going for us every evening and our room was warm and cozy when we got home.

Finally, on Friday, December 5th, after waiting almost five months, the long awaited call came from base housing: S/Sgt Joseph Krauter, Jr. and his dependent had been assigned a third floor, one bedroom apartment on Bahnhofstrasse 48, Neu Isenburg. We were ecstatic! It was in one of those typical old German apartment houses with a center staircase that went round and round and had generous landings on each floor. There were two apartments per landing—one to the left and one to the right. If you leaned over the banister at any point, you could see the skylight at the top of the building, or the tiled floor of the main entry hall at street level. Each apartment had a buzzer that released the house door downstairs. A quick peek over the banister from your own landing and you could see who was on the way up.

We were told there would be a slight delay, however, because the apartment was not in move-in condition. Although it was empty of all furniture and furnishings that base housing equipped Government quarters with, it still had to be cleaned and painted. The German clean-up crews were running at least two weeks behind. With the up-coming Christmas holidays, even that schedule could be iffy. Christmas was on my mind too and I hoped we could be in by then. We asked if we could clean it up ourselves—please! "Go right ahead, was the response, call when you're ready for base housing to deliver all your furnishings."

I didn't know what a "GI Party" was, but I soon found out! Joe called Tutor and Freddy, Susie came along, of course, and among the five of us, we made the dust fly! By late Sunday afternoon, we had that place whipped into shape! Everything sparkled. Joe called base housing first thing Monday morning and told them we were ready for delivery. As soon as they could load up our furnishings, we were ready and waiting.

It was a jewel of a little apartment. We had an entryway, a kitchen with balcony, spacious bathroom, living room with dining area at one end and a lovely bay window overlooking Bahnhofstrasse at the other end. The bedroom was large enough for two twin beds (which we promptly pushed together), nightstands, dressers and the like. The entire apartment was furnished with brand new mahogany furniture, oriental rugs, table and floor lamps, bed and table linens and several dozen towels of all sizes. The kitchen was completely equipped with pots and pans, cooking gadgets and silver flatware. The breakfront in the dining room was loaded with the finest hand-cut crystal goblets in varying sizes, all in sets of twelve. The crowning glory was a complete set of beautiful Rosenthal china. "Rosenthal!" Twelve place settings complete with every serving piece imaginable. There is a Grimm's fairytale which tells the tale of a *Tischlein Deck Dich*—a magical little table that sets itself with the finest china and laden with the tastiest delicacies you could wish for—suddenly appears. That is how I felt. The only thing missing—because Christmas was in the air—was our first *Tannenbaum*. We bought our first live Christmas tree for our first Christmas together, along with our first "real" load of groceries at the base commissary. No more thirty-dollar limits. Merry Christmas everybody!

All of this was ours now and I could tell it to the world on our very own telephone. For the first time ever I had a telephone—WE had a telephone! I called my parents, Joe called his, and together we told them of our good fortune.

I started making a list of all the couples we owed for dinner. It was a long one. I was not well versed on the art of throwing a cocktail party and the mere thought of inviting everyone at once unnerved both of us. So, we stuck to small intimate dinners for four or six at a time and I cooked German cuisine, of course. Our very first guests were Herr and Frau Zahn for *Kaffeeklatsch* on a Sunday afternoon. Frau Zahn was totally speechless when she entered our apartment and I felt she was sincerely happy for us. We had become very close friends—even though we almost demolished her place when we caused an explosion and blew out every last bit of soot from her pot-bellied stove! We were so thankful nothing happened that night and often chuckled over a remark Joe made after we lay in bed: "Bet ya Frau Zahn won't need a chimneysweep for the next two years!"

I had been corresponding with Joe's Mom and all of his six sisters from the very beginning of our marriage. We exchanged lots of photographs and Joe helped me set up a poster, family tree fashion, complete with pictures of each family group. It didn't take me long to memorize the names of all of his sisters, their husbands, their children and who belonged to whom. I learned about their lifestyles through these photos. The activities of the children—Joe's nieces and nephews—were especially charming: high school girls cheerleading in their adorable flippy skirts and lettered sweaters, boys posing with their basketball team wearing their numbered jerseys, basketballs tucked underarm. A younger nephew, Max, standing proud in his brand new band uniform holding his flute. Pop Krauter coming up the lane carrying two empty buckets, having just "slopped the hogs." Mom Krauter standing next to her lily bed by the kitchen window, holding the day's freshly gathered eggs in her crumpled up apron. Another photo of Pop having just returned from fishing with a son-in-law standing next to a bucket filled with his catch of the day—the limit—proudly holding a large-mouthed lake bass. This was traditional Americana in the truest sense of the word, not the America—the New York City America—that I knew.

I had now taken my rightful spot on the Krauter family tree. And certainly our children would grow their own branches. As far as lifestyle was concerned, Joe confided in me that he had no desire to ever return to farm life after completing his tour of duty. He either wanted a career in sales or if that were not possible, perhaps we would remain in the military. Whatever he decided would be fine with me.

Christmas of 1952 was wonderful. Freddy, Joe and I drove down to Attenkirchen to be with Mommy and Pappi. We brought along everything we could think of in the way of American food stuffs from the commissary: coffee, tea, cocoa, cigarettes, tobacco, spices, ketchup and other products familiar to them, but either unavailable or unaffordable on the German market.

We talked about our apartment and what a paradise of a place it was. I told Mommy I wished she could see it. She said she would surprise us with a visit very soon. Jolting me back into the reality of her world, she went on to tell us that she was going back to New York early in the New Year; possibly as soon as February. She had to, if she wanted to retain her American citizenship. The last time she entered the United States was in 1948. Five years had passed and 1953 was the year she would have to return for the required six months' residency. She showed me the letter she had received from the American Consulate in Munich. "What about Pappi?" I asked. He would have to stay in Germany. Immigration quotas had loosened up considerably, but still did not include his category. He could, however, ask for another review of his case.

As we drove back to Rhein/Main, I thought of nothing else than my mother returning to New York. I understood why she had to go, but I had very mixed emotions about her leaving. I suddenly viewed her from a totally different perspective. I was still her daughter, of course, but I now identified with the woman and the wife, and I felt for my father. In a way, I was her equal now—married to a husband I loved with all my heart—just as she did Pappi. How was it possible for her to always find the inner strength to move resolutely forward? Pappi got us to Germany as a result of the many choices he made. She was going to spend the rest of her days doing what she could to get us back to America, and if that meant another separation, so be it! It had to begin with her retaining her citizenship at all costs. Freddy and I were a given. We knew, and she knew, we were destined to return and live in the United States.

There was a message for Joe when he got back to the office after our Christmas holiday. It was from his best buddy, Lavern "Squeak" Myers. Joe was surprised and delighted to hear from him and told me how they had gone all through elementary school together, and were later the "star players" on the Sidney High School basketball team. After graduation they enlisted in the Air Force together. Routine background checks for Government clearance were performed on all inductees and Squeak's revealed that he still had an outstanding traffic ticket. He was held back until the fine was paid, and as a result, it put him three days behind Joe in processing and they never caught up with each other.

Squeak was a very gifted athlete and after going through basic and receiving his stateside assignments, he played basketball for his various units. He was eventually transferred overseas and earned a spot on an Air Force traveling team. He played intramural basketball against other Air Force and Army teams all over the European Command.

Squeak was stationed in Lyons, France, when he called Joe to let him know that his team was playing in a tournament at an Army base in Wiesbaden, Germany—a stone's throw from Rhein/Main. He wanted Joe to come and watch some of his games. He had also heard that he had gotten married to a "German gal" and he wanted to be introduced to his bride. I was looking forward to meeting him too. Joe had told me so many wonderful stories about their growing-up years; it was obvious, Squeak was the brother Joe never had, and to me he would be the first person I would meet, who was even remotely connected to Joe's background.

As I had expected, Squeak was a terrific guy, warm and outgoing, with the personality of a man "who never met a stranger." We attended several basketball games and invited Squeak and his buddy, S/Sgt. Joe Sturgess, to visit us in Neu Isenburg, staying as our houseguests if their schedules allowed. They told us they didn't have to report back to their home base until January 2.

Perfect! We could celebrate New Year's Eve together at the NCO club. There was just one hitch in the plan. Actually, two. We had invited Freddy to come with us too, and neither he nor Squeak were sergeants. Freddy was an airman 2nd class, Squeak was an airman 1st class. According to regulations, neither one of them were of high enough rank to access the NCO club. What to do?

Several weeks earlier, a regulation had been passed that authorized military personnel to wear civilian clothes to off-base non-military functions. Joe called home and had his Mom send him a box full of his best clothes. We outfitted Freddy in Joe's blazer and a pair of dress trousers, which I shortened to make them fit. He added his own white shirt and tie and he was ready to go. With Squeak we had to be a little more creative. He had airman 1st class chevrons on his jacket and needed to have those of the next higher rank. I just happened to have an extra set of staff sergeant chevrons in my sewing basket. I promptly removed his and sewed on the staff sergeant chevrons—three stripes and a rocker. Voila! Annelie had just promoted airman 1st class Lavern Myers to staff sergeant Myers!

That party was probably the most memorable New Years Eve celebration we ever had! To this day we still attend Sidney High School reunions and never fail to run into Squeak and his delightful wife Marty. Our conversation, of course, always goes back to recalling the outlandish coup we pulled off. Admittedly, we had more guts than brains. What in the world were we thinking of?

❊ ❊ ❊

The year 1953 began with our family's facing another separation. Mommi would soon be leaving for her six-month residency requirement in the States. It seemed important for all of us to be together before she left. Towards the end of January, Joe, Freddy, and I drove down for a long weekend.

Pappi and I had always celebrated our birthdays together. We made a big deal out of the fact that the dates were so close, his on January 29, mine on February 3. We viewed ourselves as soulmates, which we truly were. Besides, we had to hold our ground, in that we were the counterbalance to Mommi and Freddy, whose birthdays fell on May 10 and May 11. We had a friendly rivalry on this issue. They claimed their birthdays as being closer together than ours. We claimed the days in between our birthdays were party days. So, if you really wanted to have a blast, you would come to our party, guaranteed to last for days.

This occasion, however, turned out to be more of a going-away celebration than a birthday party. Everyone was quite upbeat. Mommi would be back in six months, and with all of our lives being so busy, time would pass quickly. I had reservations. I was not thinking about the passage of time as much as about the outcome of her six-month stay. I knew how much she loved America and wanted to be back there for good. I also knew she would not only initiate a review of my father's case by the powers that be on the other side, but gather all the assistance she could to help his case. We had privately discussed this, and I knew how determined she was. If everything went her way and she accomplished her goal, the downside would be that Pappi would have to sacrifice all of his hard work and everything he had built up in Attenkirchen and go back to America, only to start over again at age fifty-something.

Both parents knew that neither Freddy nor I would stay in Germany. Freddy was a Yank through and through and would never adjust to the German lifestyle. I could have, but they knew my intentions were to follow Joe home to Indiana. Whether Indiana would become our permanent home was a decision we would make when circumstances presented themselves. One thing I was certain of: Joe would never consider living in Germany unless we stayed in the military and were ordered to serve another tour there.

I felt sad and guilty for having been party to thrusting these life-altering changes on my parents, especially on Pappi. I'm sure deep down he had to be disappointed that his long term plans for Mommi, Freddy, and me might not come to fruition, but, as Joe once said to me in private, Pappi did not have to saddle himself with the responsibilities of his children's futures anymore. We were adults and ready to make our own way in the world, and he had to take care of himself and Mommi and do what was best for them.

Several weeks later Mommi was on her way. She had planned a couple of stopovers before she finally left. Joe and I met her at the station in Frankfurt and brought her home to Neu Isenburg for a visit, two days. She loved our apartment as I knew she would, and enjoyed meeting some of our friends—the military families I had told her about, who had extended their hands of friendship to us early on. And Frau Zahn, of course, came for afternoon *Kaffeeklatsch*.

I voiced my concerns about Pappi and asked how he was coping with this latest turn of events, with her leaving, and she assured me he was fine. I promised her that Joe, Freddy, and I would look after Pappi and visit more often than before. Joe and Freddy would alternate, putting in for three-day passes and if need be, I would stay with Pappi for longer periods to help him get caught up on household chores, which I knew would take a downhill slide with Mommi gone.

We said our good-byes at the train station, tearful, of course. She knew I had very mixed emotions, but told me to have faith and always look up, emphasizing her remark by pointing skywards. Things would work out, just keep praying.

Continuing on her journey, she had planned a last stop in Hamburg to visit her sister, my Tante Karla, before she flew to New York, where Elsie and Werner would greet her at the airport. Her stay with them was brief, just long enough to share the family news and have a good rest before she moved on. She was on a mission.

Friends of ours, Edith and Rudi Meyer, were a flamboyant German couple of means and talent. Between the two, they spoke six languages. Because they were childless, they had carved out careers for themselves in service to the wealthy of New York. They would work seasonally, functioning as butler and maid, traveling companions and translators or housekeepers in the oceanfront mansions of their employers. They spent winter months in Florida or on some island in the Caribbean, or even as part of the crew on an ocean-going private yacht.

When they found out about my mother's coming and her temporary situation, they invited her to stay in their apartment in the Bronx and apartment-sit while they worked the season in Florida. Perfectly wonderful digs for Mommi! Before the week was out, she had found a job as a cook at Ilsa's Restaurant in Chelsea, an area on the West side of lower Manhattan.

In the meantime, Pappi was buying new trees and hiring people to help care for the chickens and tend the strawberry farm. Most of his day laborers came from in and around Attenkirchen, the same people we had known for years, while he was selling textiles to a developing customer base in Munich and surrounding areas. In the end, he worked for his textile manufacturer full time, inasmuch as the US Occupation as we knew it was being phased out. Although Allied Forces remained in Germany, restructuring was taking place. As a result, the Quartermaster Corps in Munich, where Pappi had been employed for many years, was scaling back, and he did not see a future there.

Pappi was doing all right under the circumstances, staying busy and focused on the future. His plan had been one of providing a comfortable German rural living on the plot of ground he had bought, with children and grandchildren nearby. The prospect of that was becoming more and more remote. Even after Mommi returned, things might not be the same.

Occasionally I would catch him in a reflective, somewhat melancholy mood. He was a lonely man. He never said so, but I knew it. I could feel it. I promised myself to give him reasons to be happy and optimistically look forward to a future that would include all of us.

The Air Force was also busy reshuffling duty stations. What had been the 433rd Troop Carrier Wing, a reserve unit from Ohio called back to active duty and assigned to Rhein/Main Air Force Base, was due for rotation to its home base in Dayton. As the 433rd was phased out, it was replaced by the 317th Troop Carrier Wing. All personnel not due for rotation automatically became part of the 317th. Ultimately, the entire 317th Troop Carrier Wing, comprised of Group Headquarters, the 39th, 40th and 41st squadrons, was transferred to Neubiberg Air Force Base, just outside of Munich.

Joe received his orders to transfer on March 12, 1953. Freddy was already on site. Assigned to the 41st squadron, my brother was among the first bunch to transfer to Neubiberg. I shook my head in disbelief. How could we be so lucky to be transferred so close to home and Pappi at a time when he needed family around him the most? We would be less than an hour's drive from Attenkirchen. This was more than mere coincidence. This was a small miracle. I searched around to find someone to thank. It occurred to me that thanking God would be a good start.

It was at this time my spiritual life began manifesting itself. I began believing more and questioning less. Although I wasn't even close to where my mother was in her deep faith and her total trust and acceptance in the ways of the Lord, I began to recognize and believe in a higher power. As I would reflect on the course of our family's history and the many things that happened, both individually and collectively, I realized there was no other logical explanation, but that the hand of God was directing our lives. Oftentimes complete strangers would emerge and save us from near tragedy. On other occasions, circumstances would dramatically change, allowing us to find our way out of the darkness. Then out of the blue, unbelievable moments of joy and happiness would shower upon us. Our transfer to Neubiberg was proof that it had happened again.

This spiritual presence in my life did not come to me as a sudden revelation, but rather bit by bit as I began to sort things out. It seemed more as though I had entered a period of spiritual growth, and ever so slowly, I became a believer. The child who had always known the Ten Commandments, the little prayers, the hymns, and the many Bible stories was still there, but she was a woman now and began to see God's big picture and how she fit into His plan. I became convinced there are angels walking among us.

Military personnel receiving orders to transfer to Neubiberg Air Force Base left early, Joe included. While the men were installing the newly organized 317th Troop Carrier Wing in their duty station, their dependents stayed behind at Rhein/Main. A month would pass before all families were relocated. Those with children had priority.

Five weeks later Joe called with news that we had been assigned off-base housing. We were the last of a group of childless couples to be relocated. They moved us to a section on the southeast edge of Munich called Ramersdorf. It was high-end residential with a main shopping street, Rosenheimer Strasse, and close to good public transportation. Joe went on to describe the apartment.

His first word was "Huge." "Hold on a minute Joe," I responded. "The last time you described an apartment to me it turned out to be Frau Zahn's little bolt hole."

He assured me this would be different and went on to say we were located on the fourth floor and had a beautiful view of the boulevard below, flanked by city parks with bike paths. In the distance you could see the Munich skyline with its towering steeples, and looking southward, the Alps were visible on the horizon.

"Huge" was an understatement. Our living room was unbelievable. It ran all the way through from the main boulevard in front of the apartment building on Claudius Keller Strasse, to the access road behind, where there were courtyards and parking areas. Our little apartment in Neu Isenburg could have fit into our new Ramersdorf living room alone. There was a sunny, eat-in kitchen, separate dining room, and a sweeping master bed-and-bathroom suite, large enough for Joe and me to chase each other around in. A spacious entry hall welcomed visitors and featured a powder room and guest bedroom off to one side.

I telephoned all my relatives, as well as all of my friends in Attenkirchen and Freising to let them know that we were now in Munich. Additionally, I got in touch with as many of my former schoolmates from Private Handelschule Sabel as I could, informing them that the red carpet was out. Our apartment was located off-base in an ungated community, and we were integrated among the *Muenchner Buergers* (citizens of Munich), so all they had to do was find our house number, ring the doorbell, and come upstairs.

If there was such a thing as Bavarian heaven, this was it. Joe and I had the best of all worlds. We were living the free and easy American lifestyle, headquartered in the most picturesque part of Germany and enjoying the good fortune of being close to home.

Pappi spent at least one night a week with us. Freddy had a key to the apartment and laid claim to the guest bedroom, and Uncle Willi came, too.

His first visit left him speechless. He thought he had walked into a movie set. Was this some kind of a practical joke we were playing on him? It normally took a lot to rock Willi back on his heels, but our place bowled him over. He drank wine from a crystal goblet and I served him cake on Rosenthal china. He had removed his shoes, and his stocking feet were luxuriously digging into the Persian rugs that covered our gleaming hardwood floors. Jokingly, he invited himself to spend the night in our guest bedroom, taking a hot bath in our giant tub first.

"Joe will soon be home. Plan on staying over, Willi. We'll find a *Gasthaus* down the street and go for dinner together—*Wienerschnitzel*—and then we'll come back here, and you can enjoy! Please stay. We'd love to have you!"

He thanked me, but took a rain check. He had to get back to Emmi, whose apartment was also in Munich. He hadn't moved in with her, but regularly spent several nights a week at her place. But he promised to drop in as often as he could. Willi and I continued to enjoy each other's company, especially when we had those knee-slapping chats, reminiscing. He got the biggest kick out of drawing comparisons between my chicken coop bedroom of yesteryear and my sumptuous quarters of today, at my ripe old age of eighteen, compliments of Uncle Sam.

Having reached the age of eighteen, I was old enough to test for my driver's license. I couldn't keep asking my friends for rides. We had our own car; therefore, learning to drive became my top priority. I called the issuing office inside the McGraw Kaserne in Munich, US Army Headquarters for a good portion of Bavaria, and made an appointment to take the written test. I knew it would be tough, but I wasn't worried. I had been preparing for months. There were over a hundred road signs one had to commit to memory. They displayed symbols only, inasmuch as they were the standard employed by Western European countries, where each country had its own language. I passed and was given an appointment the following day for my road test.

Our '47 Chevy was sporting a brand new paint job, navy blue over robin's egg blue.

It was beautiful and shiny, and Joe loved it. Most evenings after work, we drove out into the rural areas around Munich so I could practice driving. Sometimes we drove back to the base so I could practice parking in the lots that were empty after work. Pete Mulligan had taught me well in his little Fiat, and everything came back. I only had to learn to manipulate the gearshift more smoothly; it was on the steering wheel in the Chevy and not four on the floor as in Pete's car. I thought I did well and felt confident. I knew Joe felt trepidation, but he had sense enough to hold his tongue.

Joe drove me to the building on the Kaserne grounds where I was to pick up my tester. Freddy followed us. After wishing me luck, Freddy and Joe headed back to the base. I thought I saw Joe swallowing hard as he not only waved good-bye to me, but also his precious car. He was more worried about his precious car than he was about me.

An Army sergeant, clipboard in hand, got up from behind his desk and said, "Okay, young lady, let's get this show on the road." We got in the car. There were no seatbelts back then.

"Put the car in reverse and back around this building," he said. "Then put it in drive and head forward, merging into the right lane of traffic."

"What do you mean, put it in reverse and back around this building?" I said. "I would never back around a building where I had no visibility going around the corner, besides having a bunch of temporary posts with chains indicating one lane traffic only. Isn't that against the law, or at the very least an indication of very poor judgment?"

"Do as I say, young lady, and let's go!"

And with that, concentrating on swinging wide enough not to clip the outside corner of the building with my car, I not surprisingly got tangled up with the temporary barrier and knocked down every post and about 150 feet of chain, that had been painted safety yellow. I left nothing standing, and all he could say was: "What did you do that for?"

I got out to look at my left front fender. "My husband is going to kill me!"

"Let's keep going," he said, pointing to a wide-open parking lot. He wanted me to show him how to angle-park and parallel-park.

"Okay," he said, "now let's proceed around the block and just follow existing traffic as it moves along the thoroughfares. I'll tell you when to turn to head back to my office, and you'll be finished."

That was it! He signed off on the road test. He scrawled "PASSED" on the form clipped to his board, went inside, and issued my driver's license.

I couldn't get back to Ramersdorf fast enough. It had started to rain when I left the McGraw Kaserne. I was glad to have my license, but very upset. I had taken another look at Joe's fender before I got in the car, and it looked awful. I headed straight for Grace Rose's apartment, which was around the corner from us.

She had hardly opened her apartment door when I blurted out what had happened to me and to our car. Grace, in her usual unperturbed manner said, "C'mon, let's have a look." Dave, her husband, restored old cars as a hobby, so everything we needed was at hand. She gathered up some rags, a bottle of rubbing compound, and a can of Simonize car wax.

"Grab an umbrella," she said, as we walked out the door.

The rain poured down as the two of us huddled under the golf umbrella. Grace rubbed and buffed and polished and shined until she had miraculously removed all of the yellow paint and softened the surface scratches to where they were hardly visible. Only one or two scratches had gone through to the bare metal.

"Dave'll take care of those. We'll just have to figure out when," she said. "When you get home, park up against some bushes, so Joe won't see that fender right away."

I drove home thinking more about what a great friend I had in Grace than worrying about Joe's finding the damage. Her sense of humor wiped out what guilty conscience I might have had. Joe discovered the damage the next day, but didn't make a big deal out of it. I was relieved.

We were adjusting to married life, and both of us liked the military, realizing that we were living it under the best circumstances. Had it not been for the routine maneuvers Joe had to go on, and C-119 fly-overs the base personnel had to perform, there would have been little else to serve as reminders of why we were stationed at Neubiberg. Our base, along with all the others in the EUCOM (European Command) had to diligently maintain its around-the-clock state of readiness.

Every day was a learning experience for me. I became active in the NCO Wives Club, more so than I was at Rhein/Main, and participated in their service projects. We would visit orphanages and bring American party treats: cake, ice cream, candy, popcorn and such, and clothing gifts to the children; then stay and play with them. They loved pin the tail on the donkey. The children were well cared for and not needy as far as their daily subsistence was concerned, but they did have social and emotional needs. I enjoyed helping out and facilitating communication inasmuch as few young children could understand English, much less speak it back then. So I acted as the interpreter. I enjoyed it a lot even though I occasionally came home saddened.

Joe and I were a popular couple. I'm sure much of that popularity was due to the fact that we had in-depth knowledge of the area, and I was always quick to respond to friends' inquiries regarding where to go on a day trip, what out-of-the-way inns to stop in for a fine German meal, and what cities and towns to visit while auto-touring through the Alps and taking in the scenery along the way. Invariably, we were invited to come along. Because I didn't have the responsibility of children, I was sometimes quick to accept such invitations without always checking with Joe. This would occasionally get me into a bind with Joe, as he didn't always want to go. I found out early in our marriage what a homebody he was. We compromised.

We enjoyed many on-base activities: parades, celebratory dinners, dances, movies and a variety of active and spectator sports. The facilities were extensive with a chapel, schoolrooms, and club facilities for all levels of the military, officers, non-commissioned officers, and airmen. The base was like having our own village. To the military and their families it was the norm and an accepted lifestyle. To me it was a new experience. It was a much smaller facility than Rhein/Main and was, therefore, more intimate.

Joe loved the sports, especially football games. Coming from the soccer world, I didn't understand the first thing about American football. I thought it was a terribly rough and tumble game and wondered how you could catch a ball shaped like an ostrich egg, whose crazy bounces could not possibly be anticipated, then throw yourself on the ball after it finally stopped bouncing only to have everybody else pile on top. Just looking at that heap of humanity, I hurt for the guy on the bottom and hoped he'd make it out alive. The spectators went crazy yelling, but they seemed to understand every play. I sure didn't. But I must admit how much I enjoyed the camaraderie of the fans, and the food and socializing before and after the games.

One evening after a game, Master Seargent Bill Trimble and his wife Peg invited a bunch of us over for chili supper. What in the world was chili, I wondered? Joe couldn't believe I had never eaten it. It was not a staple on German-American tables, which is why my German-cuisine-cooking-parents never served it, nor did it show up on the menus of restaurants we patronized. There the usual fare was pigs knuckles and sauerkraut, *Hasenpfeffer, Sauerbraten*, and *Wienerschnitzel*—dishes equally unfamiliar to Joe. But when I tasted it, I knew I liked chili and wanted to learn how to cook it. I thumbed through the pages of my *Good Housekeeping Cookbook.*

"Joe, tell Freddy to come over for chili supper," I said excitedly a few days later.

There it was, gently simmering away on the stove with that marvelous tomato and Mexican seasoning aroma wafting through the apartment. The table was set, Freddy arrived, and we sat down. Proudly I ladled out my concoction. Extra chili powder and hot pepper flakes were on the table if anyone wished to increase the flavor. Smilingly I watched as my husband and brother began to enjoy. Not even a spoonful had been swallowed when they began to crunch down on something and immediately commenced spitting out kidney bean after kidney bean. What was going on here? The beans were still so rock-hard they clattered as they hit the table. I watched in disbelief, shocked and embarrassed. How was I to know you were supposed to soak the beans overnight?

We participated in the black market, openly and shamelessly. The Americans had coffee, tea, cigarettes, nylons, Revlon cosmetics, and perfumes. The Germans had beer steins, cuckoo clocks, Meerschaum pipes, Hummel figurines, and fine woodcarvings. There were opportunities galore to trade. Shop owners were more than willing to barter for anything they had, and ambitious solicitors would ring our doorbells in the early evening. And so we were all busy trading. It became somewhat of a sport, although self-limiting.

Every household was authorized to purchase two pounds of coffee per week. Adults were issued one-and-a-half cartons of cigarettes per week. That meant Joe and I could accumulate up to eight pounds of coffee and twelve cartons of cigarettes every month. That pile of stuff represented a small fortune on the black market. I was crazy about crystal goblets called *Roemer*. Every German bride dreams about having them. One carton of cigarettes would trade for one goblet. I collected eight, one in every jewel tone available. Joe wanted to bring back gifts from Germany for his parents and his six sisters. I suggested we get them anniversary clocks, also known as 400-day clocks, manufactured by the renowned Schatz clock makers.

One evening a solicitor came to our door. When we told him we were in the market for seven Schatz clocks, he almost turned that many cartwheels. We arranged to have them delivered in two-week intervals, and he crated them for us, ready for overseas shipment. All Joe had to do was take them to our APO and send them to the farm. Joe's Mom stored the boxes for us until we got home.

Joe and I both smoked at the time, not heavily, but enough to hold back a carton a week for ourselves. There were times, however, when I was trading so heavily we ran out. We could buy German cigarettes. The most popular brand was "Zuban," but they tasted so awful, we had to resort to buying a can of Prince Albert tobacco and cigarette papers and roll our own. There was no restriction on how much tobacco you could buy at the PX. The only problem was it was fine-cut pipe tobacco and kept falling out of the ends of our hand-rolled cigarettes even though we twisted them shut. And then you had to be careful lighting your cigarette. Sometimes the twisted ends would flare up and singe your eyebrow.

Somewhere I had read about President Jackson's wife Rachel smoking a pipe in the privacy of their presidential quarters. I admired her self-assured, if somewhat naughty, behavior. I figured if she smoked a pipe, I would give it a try. There was a tobacco shop nearby on Rosenheimer Strasse that sold beautiful Meerschaum pipes. I bought one for Joe and a delicate cherry-wood ladies pipe for myself. At first we enjoyed puffing away, but soon discovered that pipe smoking was not that much fun. We were constantly repacking and relighting the tobacco, and the pipes got juicy, making the smoke taste bitter. The only solution was to stop trading away our cigarettes or quit smoking, which we were not willing to do.

The summer of 1953 was full of activities. Freddy was living his dream of flying all over the world with his crew from the 41st Squadron. Joe and I grabbed every opportunity we could to tour and explore Bavaria. We had a lovely mini-vacation at the Eibsee Hotel, another one of those R & R facilities offered to the military outside of Garmish at the foot of the Zugspitze, Germany's highest Alp. Garmish had a high-class nightclub called Casa Carioca for the occupation forces to enjoy. It had a huge retractable dance floor, which exposed an ice rink. The dining booths, set in tiers, began at dance floor level and continued upwards with the uppermost tier under a domed roof simulating a starlit evening sky. We had the good fortune to get ringside seats to a performance of a Holiday On Ice troupe on a world tour. It was a memorable evening, like a second honeymoon.

I had introduced Freddy to my girlfriend and former schoolmate, Marlou Schneppenhorst. She was a couple of years older than I, still living at home with her parents and working in her father's optical firm in Munich. She and Freddy really hit it off. I wasn't sure whether they were in love; all I knew was that they had a nice relationship. The four of us often planned Sunday outings together and usually wound up visiting Pappi.

On one such visit Pappi surprised us with astounding news. Mommi's spadework in New York was bringing results. She had been working with the Swiss Consul and US Immigration. Pappi showed us a letter from the American Consulate in Munich asking him to come in for a conference. He was to bring his current *Reisepass* (German passport) with him. "Please contact us as soon as you can after your conference, okay, Pappi?" I begged.

A week had gone by, and we hadn't heard from him. Then one afternoon the doorbell rang. There stood Pappi. He was so out of breath he could hardly speak.

"*Guck mal her!*" he said. "*Du glaubst nicht was ich in der Hand habe!*" (Look here! You won't believe what I have in my hand!)

With that he slapped his passport on the kitchen table, the same way he used to slap a trump on the table while playing Skat with his buddies. He had opened his passport and was pointing at it: Immigrant Visa #258 issued to Otto Wiegand, signed and sealed by the Vice Consul of the American Consulate in Munich, 10 August 1953. I leaped, I laughed, I cried, I danced with Pappi. This was unbelievable after all these years. I couldn't wait for Joe to come home from Group Headquarters, but Pappi couldn't stick around until he did. I promised him we'd come to Attenkirchen on the weekend with Freddy.

It was the end of July, 1953, and after much negotiation between the United States and North Korea, a truce had been signed. The Korean War was over. There were rumors that the servicemen who had served might be offered early discharge. Joe's service time was the Korean War period. Nothing had happened yet, but it gave us something to think about.

At the same time, Joe's friend Tutor who had enlisted a year earlier than Joe, was due for rotation. He and Susie had lived together for quite a while, first in Neu Isenburg near Rhein/Main and more recently outside Neubiberg. Tutor was not going to leave his family behind. They made plans to get married.

I was helping Susie with some of the details of the wedding, and although we had little lead-time, we managed to get the event quickly and beautifully in place. When the day arrived, August 31, 1953, Staff Sergeant William S. Tutor, Fuqway Springs, North Carolina, USA, and Ursula "Susie" Hentschel, Berlin, Germany, were united in holy matrimony in the chapel at Neubiberg Air Force Base. Joe and I were witnesses.

Susie's mother Erika and her younger sister Karin were in attendance. They came all the way from Berlin. The chapel was packed with wedding guests, military personnel from Group Headquarters and all three squadrons, their wives and German girlfriends. Afterwards everyone was invited to a reception at the NCO Club, which also turned into a going away party. Tutor, Susie, and little Ellen, Susie's daughter, seemed very happy, but there was also a sad side to this occasion. Susie had to say good-bye to her German family.

In early September the announcement came down from the Pentagon. For those who qualified, an early discharge was being offered. Joe and I talked it over. Tutor was on his way home. Mommi was already in the States. Pappi had his visa and was getting ready to join her. Freddy would rotate as soon as he could, and Joe qualified for early discharge. What were we waiting for? Joe put in his request for an early out.

In late September Freddy had an opportunity to be part of a crew that ferried C-119's back to Dover, Delaware. The airplanes were destined to be either mothballed or overhauled and placed back into service. Freddy had seven days to get back to his home base on a space-available basis, which gave him enough time to visit friends and/or relatives in the United States before he had to make his way back to Neubiberg. On one occasion, he flew on to Baer Field, Fort Wayne, Indiana, and made his way about thirty miles west to rural North Manchester, where Joe's parents lived on a farm. His intention was to introduce himself to Mom and Pop Krauter and meet the family I had married into.

In his pocket he had a picture of Sharon, Joe's niece. She was the daughter of Frances, one of Joe's older sisters, and she was a beautiful girl, just a year younger than I, and still in high school. Freddy had an ulterior motive: he intended to meet her. Much as Joe and I fell in love at first sight, Freddy and Sharon must have followed the same pattern because he came back a changed man.

Pappi had many details to attend to, insuring the farm would be left in good hands. It was a foregone conclusion it would not be sold. No more closing the door and walking away from his life as circumstances had forced him to do many times before.

The perfect solution presented itself. Willi stepped forward and voiced his desire to lease the farm. A simple lease agreement between Pappi and Willi was drawn up and notarized. The agreement stated it would be renewable every three years and Willi had first option to buy if Pappi ever decided to sell.

Now that the most important details were finalized, Pappi was ready to book passage. His target date was late October. I drove home from Munich several times to help him pack the things I knew Mommi would want. Out came our faithful overseas trunks that were still in good enough condition to make one more Atlantic crossing. Packed to capacity, we sent them on their way by ocean freight.

Willi made plans to move out of his quarters in Munich and return to Attenkirchen. Soon he would become the commuting farmer who still had a day job in Munich, living the same lifestyle my father had for so many years, with its unending hours of work and demands on personal energy. He eventually married Emmi, the love of his life.

On October 19 in the midst of all of the changes taking place in Pappi's life, we received our orders. Joe's request for an early discharge had been approved, and we were to report to Bremerhaven on November 8, 1953, for separation from USAFE (United States Armed Forces in Europe). We were scheduled to sail November 10.

We had three weeks to get ready. Because we wanted to take our car back home and drive it from New York to Indiana, Joe had to take it to the ocean freight yards in Bremerhaven two weeks prior to our departure. He had to get it serviced and safety checked, documenting that it was in perfect running order. After driving it to the vehicle transport docks in Bremerhaven, most of the gas had to be siphoned out of the tank, leaving just enough to drive the car on and off the boat.

Joe arrived home in Munich by train. In the meantime, I had arranged to have our dog Chippie, a snow-white German Spitz, vet-checked, crated up, and air freighted directly to Mom and Pop on the farm. When he arrived in Fort Wayne, he had to be quarantined for ten days before they could pick him up.

Packing up our household goods and personal effects was not a problem. The military set the schedule and informed us when a crew would come in and pack everything we owned. Several days before we had to leave for Bremerhaven, two huge crates filled with our earthly belongings were hauled out of our apartment. Inside were all of our wedding gifts, a cuckoo clock, a 400-day clock, my precious, deviously acquired, black-market crystal goblets, to which I had added twelve place settings of Hutschenreuther china. It wasn't Rosenthal, which was a bit out of reach, but certainly the best and most affordable second choice. Besides, I fell in love with the Autumn Leaves pattern and envisioned the festive Thanksgiving dinners I would someday be serving to my family.

We spent the last several days in our Ramersdorf apartment living out of suitcases that were packed and ready to go. I had had no problem leaving Rhein/Main Air Force Base, but leaving Neubiberg Air Base, my city of Munich, our life style—all of that was difficult. There were last-minute dinner invitations to say good-bye to our wonderful friends. All were laced with promises to keep in touch. But saying good-bye to Grace Rose was the worst. And Gary, the funny little kid who dumped the bowl of ice cream and blueberries over his head, made me cry. Grace and I promised to write to each other, a promise that turned into a vow we have kept over the years.

Taking *Abschied* (bidding farewell) to Attenkirchen, Willi, our neighbors, especially those who were privy to the courtship of Joe and Anneliese, all of my childhood friends, the Kettner Family, and Herr Rusch, my mentor, was almost more than I could bear. And there was this other thing: Pappi had instilled in me such deep devotion for his fatherland; I don't remember a time when I didn't carry this inexplicable love within my heart. It had nothing to do with politics; it was wrapped up in culture, music, tradition, and a passion for the beauty of the land. In my case, there was the added magnetism of having grown up in Bavaria, the place where I spent my *Jugendzeit* (years of my youth). And then there was Attenkirchen, this little village that became our haven after the war and whose people wrapped their arms around us. They helped me become the person I am today. It was there that I experienced normalcy again. There were bad times, but there were also good—sometimes the best—times. And I met Joe in Attenkirchen.

Our car was already in Bremerhaven, and we had to take my little train, the *Holledauer Bockerl*, to Freising to make our connection back to Munich. I was awash in tears as I spotted the *Bockerl* chugging towards our train station in Attenkirchen, which had been witness to so many of our family's tears of joy and sadness. Had I known that this would be our last ride on my beloved *Bockerl*, my emotions would have gotten the best of me. The last commemorative train ride was in the fall of 1969, after which stretches of track were systematically removed. Today a green walking path winds its way through Attenkirchen where the tracks used to be.

In Pappi's passport there is a triangular stamp that documents his departure from the "Bundesrepublik Deutschland" as *Ausreise 782* (Departure #782). It is dated 23.10.53. On the previous page, directly underneath his Immigrant Visa, there is another stamp that reads: "US Department of Justice, Immigration and Naturalization Service, admitted Nov. 4, 1953, New York, N.Y." Pappi beat us back to New York.

The morning of November 8, 1953, Joe and I checked into the processing center in Bremerhaven. We were one of the first ones in line. In his attaché case he had everything we needed: passports, medical certificates, his orders, and his entire 201 file. Processing went quickly. We were finished by mid-morning and given our boarding passes. Boarding would begin at noon on the day we were scheduled to sail, November 10, 1953, on the military troop transport ship, the MSTS *Eldon H. Johnson*.

We had two days to hang out. There was not much to do in Bremerhaven, at least nothing we were aware of or interested in, and the temporary billet provided by the military was far from a luxury hotel.

"Let's go visit Mommi's sister in Hamburg, my Tante Karla. She would be so surprised and happy to meet you," I said to Joe. I showed him where Hamburg was on the map and what close proximity it was to Bremerhaven, an easy train ride.

We took the shuttle from Bremerhaven to the next station where we could pick up a connection to Hamburg. Having just missed the express train, we made a run for the local, which was already boarding. As we flopped down in our seats, happy that we had just made it, I took stock. Yes, there was my large handbag sitting on the bench next to me. Joe had his shaving kit on his lap, but where was his attaché case?

"Joe! Where is your attaché case?" I shouted.

We had left it in the net above our seats in the shuttle we had left, and the train we were on was already speeding through the countryside on its way to Hamburg. Joe's orders, our passports, ship boarding passes—our entire lives—were contained in that case. Joe's face turned white. I thought he was going to pass out. In panic he shouted: "Let's go pull the emergency cord and stop this train!"

Luckily, the conductor had just entered our rail car to check tickets. In near hysterics I ran towards him and explained what had just happened to us. "*Nein, nein*," he cautioned. "Don't pull the cord! Our first stop is coming up in a few minutes and you'll be able to catch the next local back to the shuttle station where you came from."

We got off and boarded the return train. Because the conductor had radioed ahead, the stationmaster was waiting for us. "This is totally against the rules," he said, as he pointed to the shuttle we had come down on from Bremerhaven, "but come, walk with me."

There it was, out in the train yard, about 150 meters from the end of the platform in readiness to pull back into the station and board passengers on their way back to Bremerhaven. He helped me onto the first car and proceeded to accompany us as we searched the nets tucked up against the dark ceilings, going through car by car, praying we would find Joe's case. Finally, in the next to the last car, there it was. Even the stationmaster was happy for us as we sighed in relief.

"*Da habt Ihr aber Glueck gehabt!*" he said, shaking his head. ("You really had some luck!")

We sailed for New York the next day. Thank goodness our crossing was a lot smoother than our spontaneous, almost unlucky, train ride to Hamburg. We docked in Staten Island on November 20. As the ferry took us across New York harbor to Fort Hamilton and the New York Port of Embarkation, we could see the Statue of Liberty and Ellis Island in the distance. Those haunting memories! I could feel how happy Joe was as we stood side by side, his hand covering mine holding onto the railing. We turned to each other, "Welcome home, Annelie" he said. I couldn't speak.

There was a rush of activity following our arrival. Our car was in storage at the Brooklyn Army Base and ready for pickup. Joe was advised to get it as soon as possible or incur additional storage charges. On November 24 he drove himself to Camp Kilmer, New Jersey, where he was honorably discharged from the United States Air Force.

It was Thanksgiving. Time to celebrate and give thanks. Seated around the table were Mommi, Tante Elsie, and Onkel Werner, my cousin Marianne, Joe and I. Pappi had cooked a beautiful meal.

School outing to Lindau am Bodensee after graduation from Private Handelsschube Sabel in Munich.

Freddy with a plane after achieving flying status.

Freddy about the time he brought Joe to Attenkirken to meet me.

Mommi and Pappi in the strawberry field during the period they first met Joe.

Just before Joe left to go back to Rhein Main AFB. The weekend we met, Freddy took this picture. (Now our favorite.)

Our only wedding picture.

The chickens outside the little square window of my bedroom where we spent our wedding night.

Freddy's 1950 Buick broke down, so we had to borrow a station wagon to go on our honeymoon, Freddy driving us.

```
                    S t a t e m e n t
            -----------------------------


We, the undersigned, herewith give our consent to
the marriage of our daughter, Anneliese C. Wiegand,
to S/Sgt. Joseph Krauter Jr., AF 16335933.



Attenkirchen, . 16. . . June 1952


(Bürgermeister)                    (Mr. & Mrs. O. Wiegand)



                    Translation
                    Übersetzung :


Wir, die Unterzeichneten, geben hiermit unsere Ein-
willigung zu der Heirat zwischen unserer Tochter,
Anneliese C. Wiegand, und S/Sgt. Joseph Krauter Jr.,
AF 16335933.
```

Parental Statement.

Our honeymoon hotel in Berchtesgarden.

Atop Hitler's famed Eagle's Nest.

Horses and happiness on this honeymoon.

Down into the saltmines we go.

Together.

Hospital visit with Joe's best friend Bill Tutor and future wife Ursula Hentschel during his recovery from an appendicitis operation.

Grace and Dave Rose, their sons Bobby and Gary.

New Year's Eve, 1952. (l to r) Bill Harper, Joe Sturgis, Joe's childhood buddy "Squeak," Freddy, Joe, me, Gloria Harper.

hen we said our good-byes to Mommi and Pappi the next day, we told them we would be spending Christmas on the farm with Mom and Pop Krauter. They understood completely and were happy for us. Joe was anxious to get going.

"Be careful, my two, and call us after you arrive in Indiana," Mommi called, as she and Pappi stood by the curb and waved until we were swallowed up by the city traffic and couldn't see them anymore.

We crossed over the George Washington Bridge into New Jersey. Joe said something about heading in the direction of Philadelphia, where we would pick up the Pennsylvania Turnpike. It sounded as though driving home to the farm wasn't going to take as long as I thought it would. But then we drove, and we drove, and we drove. The vastness of the country was amazing. Heretofore, New York was the only America I knew. The farthest west I had ever been was to Riverdale, New Jersey, where the *Bergwald* was, the summer camp the German American Vocational League (DAB) owned, where our family often spent summer vacations in the early forties. It was only an hour's train ride from Penn Station.

Joe seemed to know exactly where he was going, so I just sat back and tried to relax as my thoughts turned to what lay ahead. I had primed myself as much as possible in Germany by putting a big chart on the wall with all of Joe sisters' children listed in chronological order. I asked Joe to randomly quiz me while we were driving: Okay, Gladys was married to Kenny, Jean was married to Neil, Jenny to Charlie, Frances to Cappie, and so on. I had corresponded with each sister and requested recent photographs of the children. All of them would be coming to life, and I wanted to be able to immediately recognize each family group.

All the trees were bare through western Pennsylvania and Ohio. It seemed strange. In Germany, especially in Bavaria, the forests are predominantly firs that stay green all year round. When we started out the next morning, there was no snow on the ground; still all the frost-covered tree branches and shrubs were glistening white. Autumn colors earlier in the season must have been spectacular I thought, with all the hardwoods displaying beautiful golden, fiery orange, and deep red leaves.

As we crossed into Indiana and neared the Fort Wayne area, I could sense Joe's excitement. He started giving me a narrative of the familiar landmarks we were passing. Road signs indicating how many miles it would be to North Manchester began showing up at crossroads. I reached into my purse and took out several letters I had received from his mom. The return address, Rural Route #2, North Manchester, Indiana, was what I started looking for, a street sign that would indicate this "Rural Route #2 Road."

We were back out in the country after we passed North Manchester. Joe said we still had to go beyond Sidney, the closest town to the farm. "Town" was stretching it a little. Sidney was more of a hamlet, but I compared it to the German villages I was familiar with although the architecture did not compare in the least. It didn't take but a blink of an eye to drive through Sidney, and we were in the country again.

"Joe," I said, "when is the Rural Route #2 street sign ever going to show up?"

"Just be patient," he answered, as we turned off State Road #13 and onto a road that was hardly improved gravel nor wide enough to accommodate two-lane traffic. I felt we must be getting close. "OK, Joe," I said, "now where is the sign?"

"Just keep looking ahead," he said. "We'll soon be turning into a lane and crossing over a bridge."

I saw solitary farmhouses and barns here and there. Some had silos. I noticed all of the mailboxes were on the same side of the road. All were different, and not one of them was standing straight, each seeming to pick its own degree of leaning. Joe knew all the farm families and mentioned their names as we passed their mailboxes. He turned into a winding lane, no wider than a set of wagon tracks. Weeds that had been mowed were growing between the two tracks. "Where's the bridge?" I asked.

"We just crossed it," he answered.

The bridge consisted of two boards, each a little over a foot wide, spanning a creek that wound its way from somewhere behind the barn across the meadow in front of the farm. It rippled through Pop's hog lot, creating a muddy watering hole for the pigs, before it disappeared into a culvert near the road.

I could see a two-story farmhouse on top of the hill, partly concealed by huge trees. Joe said they were sugar maples. And there they were: the two crates containing our household goods, which had arrived and were waiting for us. They were standing next to Pop's garage, a somewhat dilapidated farm building. Our dog Chippie came out of the garage as he heard our car driving up. He didn't recognize us, just sat there looking quizzical. He never even barked.

We had arrived at the farm, Joe's home. All at once, I felt overwhelmed. How would they receive me? He was the much loved baby brother and only son of a family that included six older sisters. How would Joe's parents react when he presented this unknown wife from Germany? I sighed, not looking at my husband. After we parked, I reached for Joe's hand, and we walked towards the door. Trying to control a case of the jitters, I hesitated a moment. "Joe," I said, my voice shaking, "I hope I don't disappoint them."

"Annelie" he said, wrapping his arm around my shoulder, "you don't have a thing to worry about. Now come, I want you to meet my mom."

Joe's mom opened her arms to me. "Come here, Honey," she said.

She was a tall woman, five nine, large-boned, and rather heavy set, the epitome of a mom, smothering me in her chest. It's something Joe never forgot about as a little boy. He had often reminisced about his mom, telling stories about her. I liked that about him because in Germany one says if a son loves his mother, he would always love his wife. My Pappi certainly felt that way about his mother.

Pop stood off to the side, smiling, but holding back a bit, not knowing whether he should just smile or hug me. His offering to my welcoming was a hearty handshake and a couple of sentences in the broken German he had rehearsed, recalling the days of his childhood when only German was spoken in the farm home of his immigrant parents. I smiled, put my arms around his neck, and hugged and kissed him. It was my way, and he did not object.

I looked around. I had come to a wooden farmhouse, built in the 1860's or 70's. The first floor had a kitchen with a panty, large enough to hold a work station where Mom could roll out her pie dough, with compartments full of flour, a sifter, sugar, and tubs of lard up above. There was a fine dusting of flour all over that room, reminding me of my Oma's kitchen on bread-baking day except Mom Krauter's baking area never shut down. She prepared fresh pies for every meal.

Her dining room and parlor, both large rooms, had individual doors leading out to a porch that spanned the front of the house. There were flower boxes wired to the porch railing all the way around. Though they were empty now, I could well imagine the nasturtiums and petunias that tumbled out of them in the summertime. I had seen pictures. And there was that all-important porch swing, providing the setting for traditional courtship.

Mom had furnished the farmhouse with what little she had in a homey and loving way. There were areas in the parlor that had a designer look. She had a carpenter come in and open up the staircase that led to the upstairs bedrooms, adding shelves for knick-knacks and plants. It gave the room a beautiful, airy look. At the far end of the parlor were French doors that elegantly closed off a guest bedroom. Flowered wallpaper adorned the walls and coordinated with Axminster rugs on the floor. Her hand-crocheted doilies were displayed on tables, and a beautiful heavy afghan was draped over the back of the couch. A pot-bellied stove kept the downstairs warm and took the chill off the upstairs bedrooms.

I had lived in many places, most recently in our elegant apartment in Ramersdorf. But what came to mind was the farm house in Bettenhausen, the home of my grandparents that had sheltered generation after generation of the same family. But it didn't come close to the cozy, warm, and welcoming atmosphere Mom Krauter had created in her home.

These were wonderful farm people, hard working, not wealthy. Pop still farmed with horses. I had no problem using a hand pump to get water to wash nor going outside to the privy. I didn't like it, but it wasn't a new experience for me. I had used an outhouse many times before; as well as enjoying the luxury of a chamber pot. I had dug in the dirt many a day to transplant strawberries and forked steamy, fresh-from-the-chicken-coop fertilizer. I had come from a similar background.

That evening Mom served her typical farm supper: pan-fried potatoes, homemade sausage, cole slaw, cottage cheese, her own lumpy applesauce, and freshly baked pie. All of it was delicious. We would always eat in the dining room. Supper on the farm was early, around five o'clock, which meant by eight, Mom and Pop were ready to go to bed. Eight o'clock was not our usual bedtime, but that night, our first night on the farm following a long drive home, we were ready for bed, too. The next day would be Sunday and all of Joe's sisters and their families would be coming for dinner. Dinner on the farm was at noon. It would be a pitch-in (new word for me) a welcoming home feast.

Mom said goodnight and went upstairs, while Pop turned off the lights. When he came back into the parlor, he was carrying a bottle of blackberry brandy in one hand and two glasses in the other. As he thimbled out a small amount of brandy into each glass, handing one to Joe, he mumbled something about being thankful to have his only son back, safe and sound, and also meeting me. Pop was not given to showing his feelings, much less expressing them, but on this occasion it was hard for him to hide his emotion. His lips quivered as he spoke, and his eyes began tearing up. I took a sip from Joe's glass and hugged Pop as we said goodnight. I really liked him.

Joe's bedroom was in the northwest corner of the house with a panoramic view of the farm. To the north were Pop's fields and the woods. To the west you could see the creek winding along a hedgerow, and past Pop's huge barn and the barnyard. There farm life played itself out among the animals and the farm machinery, all according to the seasons. Earlier that evening, we had watched the sunset. Now we were standing at the same window looking at the shadowy landscape, still visible in the faint glow of a golden horizon. A pastoral scene of Indiana, painted by the Hoosier artist, T.C. Steele, couldn't have been more beautiful.

"Happy to be home, Joe?" I asked.

"Very. Thanks for coming with me."

Joe had a double bed. It was twice the size as our first bed at Frau Zahn's and quite old-fashioned with an iron headboard, footboard, and railings. The mattress was a three-inch thick pad on top of bare springs. They squeaked as we got into bed, making us both giggle as Joe turned off the lights.

Breakfast was early: oatmeal and cream, and delicious fruit, pears, peaches, cherries, all canned by Mom. Her personal touches were all over the house. I complimented her on the hand-embroidered pillowcases we had slept on. She had even crocheted lace edgings. I couldn't imagine how she found the time and energy to do that along with all of the farm work and raising seven children. She was an amazing woman, not at all the simple hardworking farmwife I had perceived at my first impression.

She was easy to talk to. I told her how in Germany, discounting wartime, beds were especially fussed over. They were presentations with fine linens, fluffy pillows, and down comforters. I told her the story about my mother and her stash of Lady Pepperell sheets. Both she and Pop got a kick out of that. But we didn't have the luxury of sitting around the breakfast table and chatting very long. Not that morning. All the girls were coming for dinner. Mom still had several pies to bake, and time would pass quickly.

Pop went down in the cellar to separate the cream from that morning's milking. Joe stayed behind to help his mom with the kitchen clean-up so I could go upstairs, make our bed, and get more settled into our room. I hugged Mom before I went, to thank her for making me feel so welcome.

I was still fussing with my hair and touching up my make-up, when I could hear happy voices mixed with squeals of delight floating up from the parlor as Joe's sisters were beginning to arrive, and he was reuniting with them. I was very nervous. What would they think of me? Normally, I was a rather self-assured person, but on this occasion my stomach was full of butterflies.

I took a couple of deep breaths and went downstairs. I spotted Joe's oldest sister immediately. "You must be Gladys," I said, "I'm so happy to meet you."

She seemed surprised, not only that I recognized her, but that I had picked her out of the crowd and greeted her first. Joe had a special place in his heart for his oldest sister, and I knew that. Mom had contracted scarlet fever during her first pregnancy, and Gladys was born a cripple. She also had a speech impediment and walked with a limp. But other than that, she was as bright as a penny. She was born with an iron will, which served her well as she made her way through life independently.

Someone grabbed me by the shoulders from behind and spun me around. It was Jenny. She and I had become pen pals. We were already friends; all we had to do was meet each other in person. Jenny had made it possible for Joe to attend Logansport Business College by inviting him to live with her and Charlie in Adamsboro, a small town near Logansport. Charlie drove a school bus, gathering up all the farm children in the area and taking them to Logansport schools, Kindergarten through 12th grade. Joe rode the same bus back and forth into town with all those little kids, as Charlie conveniently added Joe's stop in front of the Logansport Business College to his route.

Jenny was eight years older than Joe, intelligent and always reaching for more knowledge. She chided all of the other sisters in a good-natured way that she and Joe were the only educated ones. They were the only two out of seven siblings that had graduated from high school. The rest dropped out to go to work or get married, or both. In any event, they all left home early. Most of them were still in their teens.

Jean, Joe's youngest sister, stood off to the side with her husband Neil and their four little blond girls. Jean was pretty and so "with it." Perhaps I got this impression because of the first picture I saw of her, clutching Neil's arm, sporting an upswept hairdo, ruby red lips, nylons with seams, and high heeled shoes. Neil was a handsome young soldier in uniform. Jean reminded me of a typical World War II babe. And could she play the piano! Her hands flew across the keys as she played ragtime and pounded out songs to the boogie-woogie beat. Most remarkable of all was the fact that she was self-taught.

Helen stood poised and elegant, regal. Beautiful and serene, she greeted me the way a Sunday School teacher might greet a newcomer, sort of a blessed welcome. She was married to Clifford and had two daughters, Sereta and Glenna. Glenna's nickname, which everyone used, was Punky, reminding me of Mutzi, Pappi's nickname for me.

Frances lived in Sidney, two-and-a-half miles from the farm. I felt as though I already knew her. She was one of Joe's older sisters and the mother of Sharon, the niece my brother was so hotly romancing. Freddy had visited them several times before Joe and I got home; a connection had already been established. Meeting Sharon for the first time left no doubt in my mind as to why Freddy had fallen for her. She was movie-star beautiful with thick chestnut brown hair, full lips, a delightful personality, and the smallest waist I had ever seen.

And then there was Bernice, Joe's second oldest sister. Her reputation had preceded her. Since childhood, she was the rebel. As an adult, she was outspoken to a fault. Joe and I both smoked, and I had heard through the grapevine that she disapproved of that, for me, anyway. The fact that Joe smoked was okay. I had made up my mind that I would be very considerate with my occasional smoking and always go outside, but I was not going to let Bernice intimidate me. She and I would have to approach our relationship carefully and let our friendship grow slowly. Her husband Vern was a game warden, a neat fellow, tall and handsome. They had two sons. Max, the younger, was a delightful twelve-year-old who had practiced German phrases to greet me. I was impressed. The other son Jack, several years older than I, was already married and serving in the Air Force, just like his Uncle Joe. Rumor had it that Bernice was not the greatest mother-in-law in the world. I was glad she wasn't mine because I was happy with Mom Krauter. In fact, I had no problem calling Joe's parents "Mom" and "Pop" from the moment I met them. It came very naturally. As for Joe's sisters, with lives so intertwined, I would make no attempt to penetrate this circle of sisterhood. If I were invited in, I would come, but I was content in the knowledge that Joe and I were committed to each other and we would make our own lives alongside the rest of the family, most likely not in the same environment.

I was relieved after we met each other, and ready for a smoke. I asked Joe to come out on the porch and join me. There they were, all six of them, my brothers-in-law. They had had the same idea. The "outlaws," as they referred to themselves, were already puffing away. They invited me into their midst, assuring me that from that day forward I would always be one of them, an outlaw.

Helen gathered everyone to give thanks before dinner. Most of the younger children had been playing outside or in the barn and came running in like a thundering herd. Standing in a circle, as everyone held hands, Helen said a moving prayer, which seemed to be spilling out of her heart. Among other things, she thanked the Lord for Joe's safe return, for bringing "Lee" into the family, and in closing, she asked that our marriage be specially blessed. I was so touched I could not hold back my tears.

The children filled their plates first and sought a place to sit—on the floor, on the staircase, at Mom's tiny kitchen table, or the older ones at a card table in the parlor. Then all the adults gathered around the dining room table.

I had never tasted better food in my life. This was a feast straight out of the heartland. My parents were excellent cooks, gourmet cooks, trained in their professions. But these ladies were of the earthy variety. They cooked stick-to-your-ribs chow and it was scrumptious.

Chicken, pan-fried in lard and butter, roast pork, scalloped potatoes, mashed potatoes with chicken gravy, creamed corn, green beans with ham, baked beans tasting of brown sugar and honey, cole slaw, ambrosia salad, waldorf salad, and on and on. The sideboard was laden with sticky buns, cakes, berry and custard pies of every kind imaginable, and from Mom, baked especially for Joe that morning, a still-warm Dutch apple pie. My taste buds had never experienced anything like it. I was going to pay close attention when Mom cooked and ask lots of questions. She cooked without recipes.

In December I busied myself with Christmas preparations, helping Mom put up the tree and other decorations, while Joe strung lights around the front porch. Pop didn't do much after completing his daily farm chores, except sit, rock, chew tobacco, and listen to basketball games on the radio. The folks had no television set and were not interested in buying one. Considering the short evenings they kept, going to bed soon after the sun went down, they really didn't need one. It made for boring evenings for Joe and me. Sometimes I brought Chippie inside for an hour or so, even though I knew Mom didn't like animals in the house. She tolerated him, and I didn't take advantage. Occasionally I'd take him for walks the way I used to, but even he had changed. He was just as happy to stay in the garage or the barn and true to his breed, hunt and kill rodents. He and Pop had become buddies, which made up for my loss.

I had sent Christmas cards and letters out to our friends and was looking forward to the holidays when we would uncrate the 400-day clocks we had sent home and give them to Mom and Pop and each of Joe's sisters. Freddy had purchased a lovely diamond ring for Sharon and sent it back with us. Joe was to pull off the big surprise and slip it on her finger Christmas Eve.

I missed Mommi and Pappi a lot. I told myself it was the season. Beginning with the first Sunday in Advent, the days leading up to Christmas were always filled with festive anticipation and nostalgia in our family. Perhaps the knowledge that they were in New York and on the same soil as I contributed to my missing them. At least their letters were uplifting, as they wrote about what they were doing to restart their lives. They were still so goal-oriented and energetic compared to Joe's folks. But then they were almost a generation younger, too. The age difference made a big difference in how I related to Mom and Pop, who seemed almost like grandparents rather than in-laws. Joe's oldest sisters were closer in age to my parents, and it probably would have been more natural for me to relate to them as the next older generation.

It was at this time that I learned about the Hoosier phenomenon called Indiana High School Basketball. As sparsely populated as Kosciusko County seemed to be during the week, on Friday nights everyone came out of the woodwork and converged on their respective high schools. Crowding into small, at times less-than-regulation-size gymnasiums, they enjoyed the spectacle known as Hoosier Hysteria.

Sidney High School, Joe's alma mater, had the smallest gym in the county. It was referred to as the Cigar Box. There was one set of bleachers, three rows high on each side. One side was for spectators; the other served home team players, the visiting team, the scorers table, a few VIP's and coaches and teachers. At the far end was a stage where cheerleaders could boost themselves up, find a place to sit, and stay out of the way. On the stage was a lectern from which introductions were made. Folding chairs were off to the side.

It all seemed very organized until tip-off time when the madness began. I thought my eardrums would burst. I had never heard such yelling, screaming and carrying-on. There was no way Joe could hear me asking questions about the game, nor would he attempt to answer them if he did, so involved was he in the action on the floor. We were sitting in the first row. All I could do was protect my toes, my feet, my entire person from being run over by ten hot and sweaty, panting young boys running past with reckless abandon,

Everybody knew Joe. For four years he had been one of the stars of the Sidney High School basketball team, and everyone crowded around him at half time. Sometimes he was able to introduce me. Other times I got so lost in the crowd, he couldn't, so people started introducing themselves. That's when I heard names such as Stub Frantz, Turkey Heater, Shorty Rector, Doity Riggs, and two sisters named Pansy Plant and Leafy Plant. This was like living among the characters of a book by Mark Twain. Then, off to the side I noticed young women whispering among themselves and pointing at me: probably Joe's old girlfriends.

This was Joe's heritage. This is where he grew up, among these people. He loved them as much as I loved my people in Attenkirchen. They were wonderful and I knew we would often come home to Sidney to visit and spend weekends with the folks on the farm. But I also knew this was not where Joe wanted to build our future. We needed to move on. I had never intended to stay in Attenkirchen for the rest of my life, even if I hadn't met Joe, so it wasn't unnatural that we'd both want to look down the road.

Time passed slowly. Joe had put out feelers for a job, but he had not received any responses. Perhaps things would open up after Christmas, surely after the New Year.

I learned how to play euchre, and occasionally Mom and Pop would stay up a little later and play with us. Pop and I would always take on Mom and Joe. Pop delighted when I, as a beginner, played the right card assisting in winning the game. He could be quite humorous. Other evenings, we split our visits between Gladys and Kenny, who lived close by in South Whitley, and Frances and her family in Sidney. Both of them had television sets. Gladys and Kenny were TV junkies, spending hours in front of the TV, munching popcorn. Just to make sure we wouldn't go home hungry, Gladys would serve pie and coffee. Frances and Cappie, on the other hand, had a lively household. In Frances's words, she had two families. Of their six children, three were born early on in their marriage and were around my age and Freddy's. Thirteen years later, a set of twin girls were born, and just for good measure, one more baby girl after that. All of these little girls, cute as they were toddling and crawling around, did not make for relaxed TV watching.

The Sunday before Christmas the family gathered at the farm to celebrate with Mom and Pop. The family had grown so large that they drew names for their gift exchange. I was not familiar with the practice, but thought it a clever idea. No one went home without a present. Joe and I gave away the 400-day clocks we had brought home from Germany as gifts for his sisters. We had kept it secret, and they were all surprised.

Christmas Eve arrived, and the four of us—Mom, Pop, Joe, and I—

spent it with Frances and her family. At a pre-arranged time late in the evening, Joe sat on the floor in front of Sharon and said that Freddy had sent along a little something for her. He slipped the diamond ring on her finger, and she was overwhelmed. Within minutes the telephone rang. It was Freddy asking to talk to Sharon. She picked up the extension in another room, and an hour later she came back. With mascara and tears streaking down her cheeks, she announced her engagement to Freddy.

Joe's sister Jenny had invited us to celebrate New Year's Eve at their house in Adamsboro with their friends. We accepted the invitation, which included spending the night. Our New Year's resolution was to get our lives on track for the future. We would begin immediately.

Joe had always said he did not wish to follow in his father's footsteps and become a farmer. He knew he wasn't cut out for that lifestyle. He was destined for a career in sales. But good jobs, any jobs, were scarce. Employers required either a college degree or years of experience in a given field. Joe brought neither to the table. Before he enlisted, he had worked for Ted Harp, owner of Sidney Feed and Implement Company, bookkeeping and overseeing inventory control, as well as selling feed and farm implements. That was the extent of Joe's experience in the business world.

It was time to go back to see Ted Harp, not to seek employment, but to ask for his assistance in finding a sales job with a large company. Ted had major suppliers and many contacts in high positions within these corporations. Delighted to see Joe again, he promised to do what he could to help. In the meantime, he offered Joe the opportunity to go out and sell fertilizer to the farmers in the area. He couldn't put him on a salary, but he would pay him commission on his sales. Ted had heard that Joe brought home a young wife from Germany and figured he could use all the money he could get. Joe and I couldn't have agreed more.

Soon thereafter a letter arrived from the A.E. Staley Company, Decatur, Illinois, requesting an interview with Joseph Krauter, Jr. This was an important, well known company in the agricultural industry, manufacturing farm feed supplements, with sales representatives covering the entire Midwest. All of their salesmen were known to be making a fine living. I urged Joe to get dressed up and look the part of a super salesman. We went clothes shopping in North Manchester's finest (and only) men's store, Patterson's, and Wible's shoe store, for a pair of the most up-to-date shoes.

We were on our way to Decatur. For his interview, Joe appeared in a gray flannel suit, white shirt, tie, blue suede shoes, camel-colored overcoat, and Homburg hat. With his black wavy hair and Clark Gable mustache, he was gorgeous. They would fall over themselves to hire him.

A.E. Staley Company was situated in downtown Decatur in a stately old building. We walked into a spacious, marble-floored lobby. I blew Joe a kiss as he entered the elevator and found a bench from which I could watch the elevator doors. I sat there all morning, not able to concentrate on the book I had brought along to read. After he came back down, he looked crestfallen. I could tell right away he had not gotten the job. On the way back to the farm we tried to figure out what went wrong.

In later years Joe and I would amuse ourselves, not only over our own naiveté, but over what the Staley people must have thought when this young, good-lookin' guy showed up looking more like an applicant for a job as a Las Vegas croupier than an average, good old boy, ready to call on grain elevators and mingle with farmers. He was just so doggoned handsome. I was convinced these high-powered executives were also practicing job protection of their own.

I was very disappointed. When we arrived home, Mom comforted her baby son. "Give it time," she said. "Something will turn up." The more I heard this purring "Mom-talk," the more restless and irritable I became, and the family began to notice it. Sometimes I would walk into the kitchen, and Joe and Mom would be talking. As soon as I appeared, they would stop. It bothered me, and at night in bed I would give Joe an earful.

Our life, the way we had known it, had changed drastically. We used to lie in bed upon awakening and snuggle for a little while. These mornings Joe felt obligated to get up and help out. I missed the moments of intimacy terribly, now that I needed them more than ever. I used to be able to loll in bed, just long enough to stretch, do some deep breathing exercises, and think about what I had to do that day. Now I felt like a floozy if I didn't pop right out of bed with the rest of the family and get busy. Doing what?

Mom's hobbies were crocheting and talking on the party line, another one of those rural systems I had to get used to. All those different rings: two longs and a short, three longs, two shorts and a long. I kidded Joe about it, calling it the Hoosier Morse Code. Mom got me started on doilies, and I completed two or three, but I was doilied out. I could only sit and crochet for so long and then in silent frustration I had to get up and go for a walk. Joe and I were spinning our wheels.

Sometimes I felt selfish, and other times I felt for Joe, realizing he was stuck between a rock and a hard place, being kind and responsive to his mother in the daytime and placating me at night. Joe had a loving relation with his mom, and I recognized her need to talk to him and tried to give him time to be with his parents without me. But a farmhouse in winter in

Indiana can be confining if you don't have much to do. Something had to change.

I told Joe I was going to go to work until something turned up for him, but I needed safer transportation than our '47 Chevy. Even Pop said that we would have been better off had we sold it in Germany before coming home. In his words, it was a piece of junk. Several days later, a 1952 Chevy club coup was sitting in front of Pop's garage. Along with our trade-in, Joe had to spend the better part of his mustering-out-pay to pay for the car, inasmuch as no one would extend credit without a steady job.

Meanwhile everyone had put out the word that Lee was job-hunting. Joe's sister Bernice came to my rescue. She called soon after she heard to let me know that the Jomac Glove Factory in Warsaw was hiring piece-workers. There was money to be earned, not much, but definitely employment. I had to be able use a sewing machine, and I told her I could.

Pop and Joe drew a map to show me how to get to Warsaw, winding through the back country, which would take me through a burg called Packerton. It was about a ten-mile drive one way. I had no trouble finding the Jomac complex on the outskirts of Warsaw and walked into a small office building, asking to fill out an application for employment.

"Piece-work or office help?" a lady inquired.

"Where could I earn more?" I asked.

"Piece-work of course," if I were a good seamstress and fast. I filled out the application and handed it to her. She told me to have a seat.

After a short wait, a gentleman called me into his office and asked why I would not consider a position in the office. They had an opening, and my application indicated a wide range of office skills, including taking dictation, which would be an asset. Tongue in cheek, I told him I could only take dictation if he spoke German. And besides, I was really keen on earning money. It was my only motivation. I would welcome the opportunity to see how well I could do out in the factory. He told me I could start the next day or the first day of the following week, whichever I chose, and gave me the name of the forelady I was to report to in the sewing room. Working hours were from 7 AM to 4 PM, half-hour for lunch, two fifteen-minute breaks. As I walked out the door, thanking him with a German handshake, he told me to come and see him if I changed my mind and would rather work in the office.

Euphoria is what I felt all the way home. I ran into the farmhouse and threw my arms around Joe and the folks, celebrating my successful job hunt. I was so happy and I called Bernice right away to thank her for her tip.

At 6:30 AM the next morning, I was out the door. It was an easy drive to Warsaw, sometimes a bit slick, sometimes snowy. But the plows were out before dawn and made the wintry roads passable. I was told to come to work dressed casually. Blue jeans and a sweatshirt would do. No elegant working clothes like the ones we had purchased for Joe.

Every morning three or four stacks of cutout patterns in the shape of a hand were placed on my worktable to the right of my sewing machine. To the left on the floor were two bushel baskets. For each glove, I had to sew two cutouts together, flannel side out, canvas side in. The forelady demonstrated the first one for me, and it looked easy enough, except she was an absolute whiz-bang on the machine. How skillfully she could maneuver the inner and outer twists and turns of all five fingers, sewing them together with the identical selvedge width from pinky to thumb! And I don't think it took her over thirty seconds. Then she showed me how to turn the gloves so the flannel would wind up on the inside and the canvas on the outside. These were work gloves, sold in hardware stores, farm elevators, and garden shops.

I was off to the races. I could already see the dough rolling in. By midmorning my basket load was looking good when a whistle blew, indicating our first fifteen-minute break. The ladies headed for the lounge out in the warehouse, a corner, that is, somewhat privatized by stacks of cardboard boxes. Everybody smoked. Me too. I thought of Bernice who told me she had many friends working at Jomacs and wondered how she dealt with their smoking habits.

As I looked around and chatted with my new co-workers, getting acquainted with several at a time, I realized we were full of lint from the flannel side of the material we worked with. Every exposed hair on our bodies was covered. Eyebrows, eyelids, nose hairs, hair on our arms—and everyone's hair-do had a dusting of white fuzz. I looked at my reflection in the mirror and saw the same fuzzy snowbird. I decided I would drive home from work that afternoon looking just like that. I thought it was comical.

What was not so comical was what the forelady, who was in charge of quality control, had done to my basket full of gloves during the break. She was coming towards me with her poking device to demonstrate how she had checked my gloves for tight seaming. She had stuck that thing into every finger and gave them all a good poke. There wasn't a single glove in that mess she had created that passed her red-hot-poker-test. Everything I had sewn so far had to be re-sewn and the holes closed up.

"Wouldn't it be possible to tag my first load as seconds and sell them as is?" I suggested. It was common practice in the textile industry and somebody had to do it.

"No, Honey," she said. "We only manufacture first-line goods around here."

Joe was happy to see me that evening and anxious to hear about my first day in the textile industry. He thought my experience hilarious and got a real kick out of my dusting of white fuzz, which had built up so thick by the end of the day it was now making me sneeze. When I pulled out the two chits I had tucked away in my bra, my earnings for the day, we both had another good laugh. Nevertheless, I was dedicated to my new career and promised myself I would get better. Determined to stick it out, I knew I could earn at least enough money to pay for my gas and then some. My job got me out of the house. Joe could help out at home and have quiet visits with his Mom. It was a good arrangement for now.

Privately, Joe and I were still considering re-enlisting in the Air Force. We talked about it in bed every night, weighing the pros and cons. According to government regulations, Joe could not re-enlist until ninety-one days had passed following his honorable discharge. He would lose one stripe and go from staff sergeant status back to airman first class. This would mean there would be no government quarters, and we'd be back on our own, seeking inexpensive off-base housing. I was willing to do whatever Joe chose. The only thing I would never stop would be urging him to apply to Officers Candidate School. He was officer material, not only in my opinion, but also in the opinions of his former commanding officers at group headquarters. He had a beautiful letter of recommendation written by Captain Billy Reaver, meant to attach to his application to OCS if Joe chose to re-enlist some time in the future. We would have to wait until the end of February before we could make a decision.

Mommi and I had been corresponding ever since we arrived on the farm. Perceptive as she always was, she read between the lines of my letters. Although I never complained, she picked up on my frustration and disappointments, that things were not going as well for Joe as we had expected. She announced she was coming for a short visit, alone, "just to meet Mom and Pop Krauter," she said. Perceptive as I was, I knew she wanted to have a good talk with me to make sure I was okay; that I wouldn't get too restless—explaining that these were the hurdles one had to overcome in marriage.

I was glad about her timing. I had been working at Jomacs for several weeks, which made my outlook more positive. When I told her about my initial work experiences including the red-hot-poker-lady story, she too had to laugh. Pop Krauter and my mother were on the same frequency right away. Out came Pop's rusty German, which reflected the Swabian dialect of his parents' roots, and he and Mommi had a jolly time talking about the old country.

Just as important was her intention to meet Frances and family, especially Sharon, the young lady Freddy had become engaged to. Mommi's reaction was very similar to mine. She was happy with her and pleased that Freddy and Sharon had found each other.

Mommi's visit was a breath of fresh air. Pappi was doing well, working in his profession for Schaller & Weber, the well-known German butcher store on Second Avenue and 86th Street in Yorkville. As soon as she got back to New York, they would have to go apartment hunting. Edith and Rudi Meyer were due to come back from their seasonal work in Florida, and their apartment, which my parents had been sub-leasing, would be needed by the Meyers.

Shortly after Mommi's visit, Ted Harp of Sidney Feed & Implement Company came through with another job lead for Joe. A representative of a farm fertilizer company by the name of F.S. Royster Guano Company told him he was being transferred, and both he and his company were looking for a replacement.

Ted called his friend, Morgan V. Ray, general manager of the Indianapolis district office, and told him about Joe, describing him as a clean-cut young man who grew up on a farm, recently discharged from the Air Force, brief sales experience with Ted's company, married, and eager. Mr. Ray told him to send Joe down for an interview.

Joe hitched a ride with one of Harp's truckers, who was picking up a load of fertilizer from the plant. Joe interviewed with Ray and came home with a job! We had to move to either Connersville, Shelbyville, or Rushville. We chose Rushville.

We were not even in Rushville a day when a tall, red-headed pastor came to our door and invited us for Sunday services at his church and dinner at the parsonage that evening. The next morning, the milkman came to our door wanting to sign us up for his route and asked us if we enjoyed dinner at the parsonage the previous evening. I asked Joe, "What's going on here? We've moved from one small town USA to another. We're still in Mark Twain country."

The biggest employer in Rushville was the International Furniture Company, and this time I applied for an office job and got it. I was assigned to the scheduling department, where my responsibility was to respond to a daily stack of postcard inquiries that came in from Sears Roebuck stores all over the Midwest and tell them when to expect delivery of their orders. I was coached on how to track an order in a manufacturing schedule and how to estimate an out-the-door delivery date, providing everything went smoothly, which meant no running out of fabric, upholstery frames, or employees not showing up for work. I enjoyed the job. I had my own desk, but spent most of my time walking up and down the production lines in the factory, where I met the most interesting people. There were women upholsterers in the sample room who would have a mouthful of tacks in one cheek and a wad of gum in the other. They spat tacks onto magnetic hammers to fasten dust covers to the bottoms of wood-framed furniture and, without missing a chew, responded to my inquiries between taking drags off their cigarettes. I was amazed and amused.

As spring wound into summer and planting time eased off, Joe's coverage of his territory with its constant travel slowed down. It was also the time of year when the company held its annual sales conference. Mr. and Mrs. Ray gathered the sales force, wives included, and invited us to the Elk Lake Lodge in northern Michigan for a week's stay, during which time business meetings were conducted, group outings for the wives planned, and rest and pleasure combined to make all of us feel part of the corporate family.

Shortly after the convention, Mr. & Mrs. Ray invited Joe and me for a Sunday afternoon barbecue. They had a beautiful home near Pleasant Run Golf Course on the east side of Indianapolis, a lovely residential area. We were the only guests.

Joe and I felt something important, something good, was about to happen. Surely he wasn't going to be fired in this elegant setting. As we gathered around the dining room table and the wine glasses were filled, Ray announced Joe's promotion to assistant district manager of the Indianapolis office. This was more than Joe and I could have ever dreamed of. Then he turned to me and asked how I felt about leaving Rushville and moving to the big city. What could I say, other than I was overjoyed? All further details would be discussed at the office on Monday morning. Ray indicated he would like our move to be completed by August.

Unterschrift des Paßinhabers

Otto Wiegand

Es wird hiermit bescheinigt, daß der Inhaber die durch
das obenstehende Lichtbild dargestellte Person ist und die
darunter befindliche Unterschrift eigenhändig vollzogen hat.

Freising   14. Okt. 1952
den

Landratsamt Freising (36)

Im Auftrag

Nr. 3985254

Pappi finally made it back to
the States.

PERSONENBESCHREIBUNG

Name _____ *Wiegand*
(bei Frauen auch Geburtsname)

Vornamen _____ *Otto*
(Rufname unterstreichen) *Karl*

Geburtstag _____ *29. Januar 1903*

Geburtsort _____ *Gottlashausen*
(Kreis, Land) _____ *Tennessee*

Größe in cm und Gestalt _____

Gesichtsform _____

Farbe der Augen _____

Unveränderliche Kennzeichen _____

Beruf _____

Wohnort _____

Nr. 3985254

Pop Krauter slopped the hogs.

Joe's parents said good-bye when their youngest child left for Germany.

Joe's sisters (l to r) Jean, Jenny, Helen, Frances, Bernice, Gladys.

Mom Krauter with family members and dog Buddy. Sister Jean is on the stoop.

My first view of the farm from the road.

Elderly farmwife and Mom's neighbor Irene Slater painted the farm this way.

My German dog Chippie adjusted well to farm dog Buddy.

All in the family: Freddy proposed to Frances' daughter Sharon. We carried the ring from Germany.

Freddy and Sharon's marriage was August, 1954.

I couldn't wait to share the news with Mommi and Pappi.
They were happy for both of us and especially proud of Joe. They
wanted to be sure we'd let them know all about Indianapolis. It was an
option they would consider in the future if Freddy and Sharon also stayed
in Indiana.

They were not living in the Bronx anymore. Mommi had found a
partly furnished apartment on East 83rd Street in Yorkville, close enough
for Pappi to walk to work. They were settled in and ready to welcome Freddy
home. He had received his orders to rotate in late April and was in the
midst of preparations to separate from USAFE when Pappi asked him to
be sure to squeeze in one last visit to Attenkirchen to see how Willi was
doing, check out the farm, and say good-bye.

Freddy did not have to return to the States by sea like the rest of us.
He flew directly to Dover Air Force Base on a space-available basis, and
like a homing pigeon, he made his way to his old stomping grounds,
Yorkville. This time he didn't have to look up a buddy to bunk with or some
old girlfriend. He could go straight to his parents' apartment. Freddy was
honorably discharged from the Air Force at Camp Kilmer, New Jersey, on
May 7, 1954. A few days with Mommi and Pappi, a visit with Tante Elsie,
Onkel Werner and Marianne, as well as checking in with old friends was
all he had time for. He had to get to Sidney, Indiana. Sharon was waiting.

I had heard that the employees of the International Furniture Company were extended the privilege of purchasing furniture at factory cost. As
a recent employee, I asked my office manager whether length of employment was a prerequisite for taking advantage of the opportunity. He said

the courtesy was extended to all employees in good standing, as long as they had the cash. I told him about Joe's promotion and our transferring to Indianapolis. In effect, I was giving him my notice, but at the same time, I wanted to be able to work as long as possible.

I did not want any pay. If it were possible, I wanted to build up an in-house credit account, against which my furniture purchases could be charged. He said he would work something out. Little did he know there were times when I couldn't locate an order in a schedule and just made up a shipping date. Customers deserved some kind of response.

Joe was busy, too. He traveled every day, breaking in a newly hired trainee, taking him around and introducing him to the accounts in his territory. Our weekends were spent apartment-hunting in Indianapolis, and we found a townhouse development in the 1200 block of North Arlington Avenue on the east side. Units were still being built, but models were open for viewing. One requirement was that we needed to be near public transportation so I could get a job downtown. The location was perfect, just two blocks from the Tenth Street bus line. We rented and moved in on schedule: August 1, 1954.

As children in Germany, we had thought of the Midwest as the wild West. We really didn't make a distinction between the Midwest, the Far West, or the Southwest. Anything that indicated "West" in America was automatically "wild." I'm sure these perceptions were based in the cowboy Westerns and gangster movies we saw when young and living in Brooklyn before repatriation. Chicago spelled gangster territory, as in Al Capone's time, and Indianapolis brought John Dillinger to mind. So my preconceived notion of Indianapolis was a bit squirrelly. Just a week or so before we moved in, the Dresser Drawer murder occurred. A young woman's body had been found stuffed into a drawer in a room on the fourth floor of the Claypool Hotel in downtown Indianapolis. So I had apprehensions about the city to which we were relocating.

The first Monday morning after our move, I got spiffed up in my best dressed-for-success outfit and went downtown to seek a job. I had studied the want-ad section of the Sunday edition of the *Indianapolis Star* the day before and circled several interesting ads. Goodman Jewelers had an opening in the office. With paper in hand I boarded the Tenth Street bus and headed for the Circle in downtown Indianapolis. I walked around the block to Washington Street where Goodman Jewelers was located.

"I'm here about the job you have advertised in the paper," I said and was ushered to the back of the store to an open-scape office behind a counter, where I was introduced to the credit manager named Johnny Combs.

The job involved interviewing customers who wished to buy merchandise on credit and taking their applications. I told Mr. Combs it sounded like something I could handle, and he hired me. "How soon can you start?" he asked.

"I can start tomorrow," I answered.

He walked me out through the store and introduced me to Raymond Goodman, a gracious businessman. It seemed a wonderful opportunity to be hired by an old respected firm in downtown Indianapolis, where '50s department stores, fine restaurants, and specialty shops of all kinds flourished.

I caught the bus the next day and began my job. The store opened at 9:30 AM; I had planned to be there ten minutes early. As I walked in, sales people were already behind their jewelry counters and office girls at their desks. Everyone smiled broadly at me, one salesman greeting me with an exaggerated "Good M-o-o-r-ning!" I went to the ladies lounge, checked my hair and make-up, returned to my desk, and tucked my purse away. It was 9:30, and I was ready to go.

I had two co-workers, an older lady named Kay and a younger one around my age, Kathy. Kay taught me the ropes. I observed as she took an application from a customer and cleared credit. I had to call the Merchants Association, then the customer's bank, verify employment, and contact two or three more references submitted by the applicant where he or she had been extended credit. Once I had gathered all this information and noted it in the margin, I gave the application to Combs, who had the authority to either extend or decline credit. This entire process usually took no longer than a half hour, sometimes a little longer if the applicant had some kind of negative history or conflicting information.

The next two days I took my bus and appeared ten minutes before opening, just as before, and the smiles kept getting broader. Some of the salesmen even bowed from the waist. "Joe," I said that evening, "these are the nicest people I've ever met in life. As soon as I appear, they almost usher me through the store!"

By Friday morning the most demonstrative of the salesmen came out from behind his counter and gave me one of those sweeping low bows in the manner of a courtier bowing to his lady fair. Kay, who had been standing at the credit counter watching the spectacle said to me, "Do you think you could come in a little earlier next week?" I was astounded.

"But Kay," I said, "I've been arriving ten minutes early every day! The store opens at 9:30, doesn't it?"

"Yes, for the public," she said, "but the credit office opens at 8:15."

We are in Indianapolis, dressed for success and a life full of promise: Joe at the F.S. Royster Guano Company, Lee at Goodman Jewelers.

I apologized to Combs for the misunderstanding, as well as to Mr. Goodman and his sister Sara, the firm-jawed spinster who helped her brother run the store.

"I told Johnny Combs there was something wrong here," she said. "This young lady's work seemed to be so correct, and yet she hasn't been to work on time one single morning this week!"

They all forgave me for the misunderstanding and I went on, making a special effort to regain the respect of the Goodman family and be a valued employee.

Joe's and my life shifted into a period of stashing cash and living frugally. My check, $29.55 per week after taxes, is what we lived on. It paid for food, transportation, drugstore items, and a $5.00 weekly payment on some limed oak end tables I had purchased on credit from the Fairway Furniture store downtown. Joe's monthly income covered rent, utilities, telephone, a small monthly premium on an insurance policy, and unforeseen expenses. What was left over, we banked. Thank goodness Joe's job included a company car and a limited expense account.

Joe began traveling on the road, staying out in the field two, sometimes three nights per week: a pattern, which was to last many years. One night I was alone and in typical German *Hausfrau* fashion, I started cleaning the apartment after I came home, so it would be done before Joe got home and we would be able to relax over the weekend. It was a hot August night and quite late. I had waxed myself into the corner of the living room and curled up on our two-piece sectional with the intent of staying there and watching the eleven o'clock news until the floor was dry. I had latched the screen door, but the front door was open, allowing a shaft of light to fall out across the sidewalk and onto the street.

Suddenly I heard footsteps that stopped and were followed by a soft whistle. The footsteps started up again, and the shadow of a man appeared, stopping in the shaft of light outside our door, whistling again. My heart leapt, and I was frozen in fear. What to do? The phone was out in the kitchen, the extension upstairs. I can't even remember making the decision, but I got out of the chair, marched to the front door and slammed it shut as hard and as loud as I could and attached the safety chain, all in one motion.

Scared to death, I raced upstairs to get to the telephone in our bedroom. Before I dialed the police, I peeked out the window from behind the curtain. My scary imposter turned out to be a neighbor who was harmlessly walking his unleashed dog and whistling for him. I was still imagining dresser drawer murderers behind every bush. I spent an uneasy night, wishing Joe were home.

Freddy and Sharon planned to marry the end of August. Both had jobs with the Heckman Bindery in North Manchester. They had been working all month long, redecorating the apartment they rented on Main Street. It was a nothing place above a hardware store, but they turned it into a honeymoon nest by the time the date came to tie the knot. We saw each other frequently, and we stopped in every time we drove up from Indianapolis to visit the folks on the farm.

Things were going well with the four of us, but I yearned to see my parents. I needed to see Pappi. Wouldn't it be wonderful for us to spend Christmas in New York, to be together at that time of year, which had always been our family's special time? Freddy and I began hatching a plan.

The Goodman Jewelry Company was gearing up for the holidays. On the schedule were the Post-Thanksgiving-Day Sale, pre-season sales the entire month of December, Christmas week, and after-New Year sales. It was without a doubt the most important time of the year for them. I didn't ask, I told Johnny Combs I needed to go to New York to be with my parents for Christmas. He knew nothing of the former accusations against Pappi, the incarceration of our family, repatriation, bombing, fleeing and all the troubles of the war. Nor did Raymond Goodman.

"Lee, you've just started working," he said. "You haven't been with us long enough to even qualify for a vacation, and the upcoming Christmas season is our biggest retail period. I can't spare you, it is out of the question."

"I must go, Mr. Combs. I simply must. And if you don't let me go, then I'll just have to leave."

"You do that, and you'll not have a job when you get back," he said. It was still early in the pre-Christmas season. We had several weeks to go until Christmas Eve, but business was rapidly picking up. I got good at clearing credit quickly. Customers appreciated that, as did Combs.

One evening as I was leaving the office, he stopped me and asked, "If you really decide to go, when would you be back?"

"Mr. Combs," I said, "Joe has to be back on January third, and I plan to return with him." I guessed that meant I would still have a job with Goodman's when I got back.

Joe got permission from Mr. Ray to drive the company car. It was our only transportation and more roadworthy than Freddy's clunker. We got in the car and headed east.

New York is magic at Christmas, streets sparkling with lights, people bustling about with smiles on their faces, carols wafting out of the stores. We drove into the city on Christmas Eve, just as it was beginning to get dark. "Take Park Avenue uptown," Freddy had told Joe. Park Avenue is the most beautiful, festive avenue in the world at Christmas with its lighted trees in the median of every block from midtown Manhattan all the way uptown past Central Park.

We were fortunate to find a parking space close to the brownstone apartment house on 83ʳᵈ Street where Mommi and Pappi lived. We rang the doorbell in the vestibule. A buzzer answered and unlocked the door. We could see both of them outlined at the top of the stairs, three flights up, Mommi in a cook's apron covering her good dress, Pappi in his usual white shirt, tie, and knitted vest. The closer I got, the more difficult it was for me to breathe. I fell into his arms as he said, *"Hallo, mein Mutzilein"* ("Hello, my little Mutzi"). Mommi already had her arms around Freddy and Sharon. Pappi's hand reached out for Joe.

From inside the apartment Christmas lights were shining brightly, and the smell of roasting meat and anise cookies was in the air. It was hard to believe. After so many years, we were finally home, together in the land we always knew was meant to be ours.

※ ※ ※

June 21, 2005

This book is for you, Mommi and Pappi. I wrote it to honor you and to share my memories of our lives together with my own children and with Freddy's, so they can keep these memories alive for their children and those children can do the same for generations to come.

You instilled in us the values of strength, loyalty, and love.

Mommi, your work ethic and correctness were inbred in us, as you lived your life by example.

Pappi, you taught me the value of knowledge and a deep reverence for nature—from the smallest blade of grass to your beloved seas, to every living creature on earth.

In spite of everything that happened to us, you both raised us in an atmosphere of forgiveness, with no regrets, no bitterness, never any feelings of revenge or animosity. You taught us to believe in the goodness of man and strive to bring out the best in ourselves.

I thank the Lord for blessing Freddy and me with such remarkable and loving parents.

Mutzi

EPILOGUE

My parents left New York City in 1955 and settled in Indiana. They purchased a small neighborhood restaurant in Indianapolis and once again became self-sufficient, respected business people in the community of Irvington on the eastside of the city. Pappi died of a heart attack on August 2, 1962, at age 59. Mommi lived until she was 96. She joined Pappi on April 17, 1999.

Freddy and Sharon had three children and divorced after 23 years of marriage. Freddy lives in Greenwood, Indiana, with his second wife of 25 years, Darlene. He has two stepchildren. Darlene is Freddy's caregiver as he sadly struggles with Parkinson's Disease.

Sharon remarried and lives in Indianapolis with her second husband, Gene.

Onkel Werner died in 1984 in his late seventies. Tante Elsie was 84 when she died in 1991. Tragically, my cousin Marianne was killed in an automobile accident in 1978 at age 44. She left a husband and four children.

Tante Lene died in Bettenhausen in 1989. She was 70 and though in poor health, most say she died of a broken heart, having never recovered from the death of her beloved Willi Buechner who fell in the Second World War.

Onkel Willi died in 1996 at age 75. Emmi, at 84, suffers from arthritis, but still lives independently in Attenkirchen under the watchful eyes of their two daughters, my cousins Monika and Anna, and their families.

Onkel Karl, the last of my father's siblings to die, passed away in Berlin in 2002 at age 88.

His wife, my Tante Lisbeth is still alive. Their daughters, my cousins Marlene and Ulla live nearby.

The elder Wohlparts, Kaspar and Rosa, came to visit their married children often, but never returned to live in the States themselves. They passed away in Freising, Germany. Their daughter Inge and her husband live on Long Island. Son Alfred, my playmate from Crystal City, whom I thought such a nerd, went on to become a teaching professor with a degree in Forestry and a doctorate in Botany. He is also master hiker and a published author. He lives in Oak Ridge, Tennessee, with his large family.

The Mulligans also settled in Indiana to be near our family. Naomi preceded Pete in death in the 1980's. Pete lived to be 102 and passed away in the Veterans Home in Lafayette, Indiana, in 2001.

Sergeant Lavern "Squeak" Myers, Joe's childhood friend, had a career as an English teacher and coached Indiana high school basketball after his discharge from the Air Force. Retired, he and his wife, Marty, live in Elkhart, Indiana. We see each other several times a year.

Technical Sergeant David and Grace Rose retired from the Air Force and settled in the Napa Valley. Grace remarried following Dave's premature death, and still lives in the Napa Valley with her second husband Al. They are avid square dancers and participate in National Square Dancing Competitions. We remain in touch.

Staff Sergeant William S. Tutor and his German wife Ursula (Hentschel) divorced a few years after his discharge from the Air Force and return to North Carolina. Ursula and her daughter, Ellen, never returned to Berlin to live. Re-married in the States, she lives in Miami Beach with her second husband Murray. Our two families are friends through the second generation.

Joe's parents, Joseph and Jenettie Krauter, and all of his sisters with the exception of the youngest, Jean, are gone. Jean lives in Florida with her second husband, Don.

And as for us, Joe and I settled in Indiana. In 1964 we founded a family business in the basement of our first home in Indianapolis. With our four married sons, their wives, and sixteen grandchildren, we just celebrated our 53rd wedding anniversary.

APPENDIX

Federal Bureau of Investigation

Freedom of Information / Privacy Acts

Release

Subject: *Otto Wiegand*

FEDERAL BUREAU OF INVESTIGATION

Form No. 1
THIS CASE ORIGINATED AT: NEW YORK, NEW YORK

NY FILE NO. 100-17239   JK

REPORT MADE AT	DATE WHEN MADE	PERIOD FOR WHICH MADE	REPORT MADE BY	
NEW YORK CITY	7/17/42	7/10,15/42		b7C

TITLE	CHARACTER OF CASE
OTTO KARL WIEGAND	INTERNAL SECURITY - G ALIEN ENEMY CONTROL FOREIGN FUNDS

SYNOPSIS OF FACTS:

Subject born 1/29/03 in Bettenhausen, Germany.
Entered U.S. illegally 5/24/26 at NYC. Visited
Germany 4/22/37 and returned to U.S. making legal
entry on 9/24/37. Filed Declaration of Intention
#273051 in Brooklyn, N.Y. 8/29/38. WIEGAND, a butcher,
has lived and worked in N.Y.C. since first arrival in
U.S. Has purchased no war or defense bonds to date.
On 4/24/39 purchased $1,000 worth of Rueckwanderer
Marks and in 1938 paid $400. for a mortgage on father's
home in Germany. Admitted membership in DAB and RDV
since 10/1/36. Denies affiliation with any other clubs
or official status in any although he assisted in the
actual building of DAB Camp Bergwald at Riverdale, N.J.
Admitted giving free room and board to [   ] a
German who escaped from Canada from September 1939 through
February 1940 but denied any knowledge that [   ] was an
escapist from Canada. Subject has Alien Registration
#3427342. WIEGAND was arrested pursuant to Presidential
Warrant on 7/10/42. Premises searched, no contraband
found. Photographed and fingerprinted at NY office and
following interview was delivered to Immigration and
Naturalization Service authorities at Ellis Island
pending hearing before Alien Enemy Hearing Board.

b7C

- P -

NEW

DETAILS: AT NEW YORK, NEW YORK.

This investigation is predicated upon the fact that the

APPROVED AND FORWARDED:	SPECIAL AGENT IN CHARGE	DO NOT WRITE IN THESE SPACES

100 - 123329

RECORDED & INDEXED

COPIES OF THIS REPORT
5 - Bureau
2 - USA
1 -
1 -   ONI   b7C
1 -   G
1 - Immigration and Naturalization
2 - New York

301

subject was ascertained to have been a member of the Deutsch-Amerikanische
Berufsgemeinschaft [   ] seized   b3
under a subpoena of the Federal Grand Jury and on the basis of which facts
a: Presidential warrant was caused to be issued by the Attorney General.

        Pursuant to the Presidential Warrant Special Agent [   ]   b7C
accompanied by [   ] Special Squad #1, New York Police Department,
at 10:00 a.m. on July 10, 1942 took the subject into custody at his place of
business at 60-54 69th Avenue, Ridgewood, Brooklyn and upon obtaining a consent
by the subject to a search of his premises by the arresting officers, the subject
was taken by Bureau automobile to his home located at 68-58 60th Lane, Ridgewood,
where a search of his premises resulted in finding no contraband but which produced a photograph album containing numerous snapshots of the subject and other
persons in the process of building Camp Bergwald at Riverdale, New Jersey. Also
was found a receipt for $1,000.00 which the subject had on April 24, 1939 paid
for Rueckwanderer Marks together with two papers written in German concerning a
mortgage in the amount of 1500 marks which the subject purchased by a loan of
$400.00 to his father. Another paper written in German and taken at the time
of this search was ascertained to be a humorous explanation by several friends
of the subject for his being out late on the evening of March 19, 1942 and was
intended to mollify the feeling of subject's wife on his return home.

        Following a search of the subject's premises he was brought
to the New York office by the arresting officers in a Bureau automobile where
he was photographed, fingerprinted and his arrest is referred to by number
G-CD-665 on July 10, 1942.

        Thereupon the subject was referred to the reporting agent
for questioning, during which interview he furnished the following information
about himself:

        Full Name. —OTTO KARL WIEGAND.

        Date and Place of Birth. January 29, 1903 at Bettenhausen,
Turingen, Germany.

        Date and place of entry into the United States. Subject made
an illegal entry on May 24, 1926 as a deserter of the S. S. Resolute at New York
City, on which ship he had sailed from Hamburg, Germany as ship's butcher.
He entered legally September 24, 1937 at New York City on the S. S. Deutschland
from Hamburg, Germany.

        Subject exhibited German passport #2821 issued to him April
22, 1937 for the purpose of making a visit to Germany with his family. The

American vice-consul in Berlin, Germany on September 9, 1937 issued to the subject immigration quota visa #3642, identification card #942272, permitting the subject to make lawful entry into the United States under the immigration quota. The subject stated that his visit to Germany in 1937 was made for the purpose of visiting his parents and relatives and so that he might introduce them to his wife and two children whom they had never seen.

Marital status. Subject was married May 31, 1927 at New York, New York.

Family. His wife ALMA WIEDRICH WIEGAND was born May 10, 1903 in Germany and naturalized in Brooklyn, New York in 1938, the exact date being unknown. Her present occupation is a housewife.

His son FRIEDRICH OTTO KARL WIEGAND was born May 11, 1931 at New York City. He attends P.S. 88, Brooklyn, New York.

His daughter ANNA LIESE CARLA WIEGAND was born February 3, 1935 in New York City. She attends P. S. 88, Brooklyn, New York.

Relatives in the United States. His sister, ELSIE WIEGAND KNOCH, 1704 First Avenue, New York City is 35 years old and an alien. She is a chamber maid and has been employed at the Essex House, the St. Regis Hotel, the New Yorker Hotel and others. Subject could not verify her present employment.

The subject denied that he had any other relatives in the United States.

Relatives in Germany. His father FRIEDRICH WIEGAND, age 60, lives at Bettenhausen, Germany is a farmer and was in the German Army during the last World War but is stated by the subject not to be a member of the Nazi Party.

His mother, EMILY AUGUSTA LOESSER WIEGAND, age 61, a housewife, lives at Bettenhausen, Germany.

His brother ERICH WILHELM WIEGAND, age 31, is a factory worker and when last heard from resided at Bettenhausen, Germany. Subject stated he was unable to say whether or not his brother ERICH is a member of the Nazi Party.

His brother ERWIN KARL WIEGAND, age 30, was, according to the subject, killed in Russia last year having been in the German Army on that front.

Subject's brother KARL OTTO WIEGAND, age 28, formerly a butcher in Berlin is understood to be in the German Army at the present time.

- 3 -

Subject's sister LYDIA AUGUSTA WIEGAND KIRSCHNER, age 41, is a housewife residing in Muehlbach, Germany. Her husband is said to be a government office worker and member of the Nazi Party.

His sister BERTHA KELLNER WIEGAND DREISSEGACKER, age 37, is a housewife residing in Bettenhausen, Germany. Her husband is stated to be a farmer but not a member of the Nazi Party.

His sister HELEN LYDIA WIEGAND, age 22 is still residing at home with her parents in Bettenhausen, Germany.

His brother WILLY WILLY WIEGAND, age 21, when last heard from was employed as a butcher at Bettenhausen, Germany.

Continuing he explained that he had other uncles and aunts and cousins in and around Bettenhausen, Germany but that he could not recall the names of all of them. He added that he last received correspondence from relatives in Germany in September 1941.

Education. Subject stated that he had eight years in public school and three years of continuation school during which latter years he learned his trade as a butcher.

Occupation. Subject advised that he is a butcher and has never had any other trade. He stated that he formerly was a member of the Amalgamated Meat Cutters Union, Local #372 and that his social security number is 099-03-9162.

Employment. Subject stated that when he was 14 years of age he became an apprentice butcher in Westphalia under one HERMAN BREIBENBROOK and that he was thereafter employed in Altoona and Hamburg, Germany under ALBERT HUEGNER and CARL TIMPPER.

He stated that he obtained a job in the George Kerns Packing House on West 38th Street and 10th Avenue the second day following his first arrival in the United States and that after being employed there for approximately six months he obtained a job in the Derby Division Company on First Avenue and 40th Street, New York City where after a period of about six months he obtained a job as a packer in the meat packing plant of the H. C. Bohack Co., Inc. in its plant on Metropolitan and Flushing Avenues and after remaining in that position for approximately one and one-half years he changed his employment to Oppenheimer & Co. in its retail store at 711 Columbus Avenue. After being employed there for nine months he returned in 1929 to H.C. Bohack Co., Inc. and was there from 1929 until August 1940, being employed at various retail meat markets of that concern.

Subject advised that in August of 1940 he opened his own

- 4 -

meat market operated under the style of "Wiegands Quality Meats" at 60-54 69th Avenue, Ridgewood, Brooklyn and that he has operated this business as his own since that date.

Since his arrival in the United States subject has resided at numerous addresses in New York City, Bronx and in Brooklyn and that since September 1938 he has resided at 68-58 60th Lane, Ridgewood, Brooklyn.

The subject admitted that he is a citizen of Germany and has never become a naturalized citizen of the United States although on August 29, 1938 he appeared before the clerk of the United States District Court, Brooklyn, New York and filed Declaration of Intention #273051 based upon his Certificate of Lawful Entry, number 2-592035 indicating his lawful entry into the United States on September 24, 1937, which lawful entry removed the defect of his previous illegal entry into this county. The subject produced his Alien Registration card number 3427342 and his Alien Enemy Certificate of Identification, number A-42148.

The subject denied that he has had any actual military training or service with the Army or the Navy in either Germany or since coming to the United States. In that connection he produced his Certificate of Registration indicating that on February 16, 1942 subject had duly registered with Local Board #283 located at 6903 Fresh Pond Road, Ridgewood, and had been assigned order number 11160, serial number T-1833.

When questioned concerning his financial status, the subject advised that he has a savings account with the Ridgewood Savings Bank located on Myrtle Avenue, Ridgewood, which account has a balance of approximately $50.00. In addition WIEGAND stated that he owns the meat market business which he has conducted at 60-54 69th Avenue, Ridgewood. He stated that he does not own any other property in the United States.

As to property owned by the subject in Germany, he stated that he purchased on April 24, 1939 $1,000.00 worth of Rueckwanderer Marks which he obtained from the Forman Agency at Myrtle Avenue, Ridgewood and which was transferred to his account in the Deutsche Bank and which was verified by receipt of a letter dated April 24, 1939 directed to the subject from the above mentioned bank indicating that the sum of 4100 marks was held in his account in Berlin and that he would receive 3% interest on this amount. The subject advised that when he purchased the Rueckwanderer Marks he had over $1,000. saved and that he liked the investment feature of the exchange rate offered at that time obtaining as he did 4.10 marks for every dollar he invested. He further stated that he thought that at some time in the future he might want to return to Germany although he was not sure. However, he stated that he thought it would be good to have this amount available to his account in Germany as his children might want to take a trip or go to school in Germany.

- 5 -

Continuing the subject advised that he loaned his father
$400.00 in 1938 and had received in return a mortgage on his father's farmhouse
in Bettenhausen, Germany. This transaction is borne out by a printed letter of
the Deutsche Bank dated May 9, 1939 acknowledging the receipt of a power of
attorney which the subject advised he had to forward in connection with this
transaction. The above mentioned papers taken during the search of subject's
premises are being retained in the files of the New York Field Division. Subject
denied that he had any other property in Germany or in the United States.

When questioned as to whether he had purchased any war or
defense bonds as his part in helping the war effort of the United States, the
subject advised that he had purchased none to date but that on June 22, 1942
he had signed pledge number d-161567 simultaneously exhibited to the agent,
which pledge card indicated that he would on September 1, 1942 through the
Ridgewood Savings Bank at Myrtle and Forest Avenues, Brooklyn, purchase $1.00
per week of Defense Bonds and stamps.

Subject advised that he originally came to the United States
because times were bad in Germany and it had become increasingly difficult to
earn a living in Germany. He stated that he originally wanted to become a
farmer in the United States but that once he obtained a job upon his arrival,
he never made any further efforts to become a farmer. He indicated that he
has been treated fairly and professed a great love for this country saying that
living conditions and standards of conduct were much better in the United States
than in Germany.

When questioned as to his attitude on the present war he
stated that he hoped the war "would soon be over", adding that he wanted the
United States to win soon. He stated that he would be willing to fight for the
United States against the Axis but would prefer not to fight against the
German Army in view of the fact that he has brothers in it. He claimed that if
his brothers were not in the German Army he would not hesitate to fight with
the United States against Germany at all. Continuing he claimed that he would
not help Germany in anyway nor would he aid even his brothers if they were to
contact him in the United States as spies. He claimed that he would report
them or anyone else immediately.

Concerning his membership in the DAB, WIEGAND stated that
he joined the Brooklyn unit October 1, 1936 and paid his dues regularly until
October 1941. He stated that one [   ] had introduced him into membership. Subject advised that he attended meetings at irregular intervals at a
rented store used for these meetings which store was located at Woodbine and
Woodward Streets, Ridgewood, Brooklyn. He stated that the leaders of the
Brooklyn unit during his membership were, in chronological order, [   ]
and [   ] and that the monthly dues were paid by him at the rate of

b7C

- 6 -

$1.00 a month.

He claimed that he was at no time an officer of the DAB
but admitted that he had volunteered occasionally to write postcards inviting
the members to a proposed meeting, social function or some other similar event
and claimed that the main reason for his joining the DAB was the social feature,
indicating that he looked forward to associating with German people and to
attend social functions which would be sponsored by the DAB. Subject stated
that around October 1938 the alien members of the DAB were "excluded" from full
membership in the DAB and that he had at that time and on the suggestion of
FRITZ ZEGLIN, joined the Richsdeutsche Vereinigung and had paid $1.00 a month
dues to this latter organization from that time until around October of 1941.
He stated that he had attended one meeting only of the RDV and that this meeting
was held in a saloon on Madison Avenue, near Onderdonk Avenue, Ridgewood.

Despite the fact that theoretically aliens were excluded
from membership in the DAB, WIEGAND advised that he continued payment of his
dues to that organization and to attend all meetings. He stated that the
only difference in his status was in that he was no longer allowed the vote
on questions at the meeting. He declared that his actual membership was considered to be that of an "unconstitutional" member after the aliens were
excluded.

He stated that he continued as a member of the DAB and RDV
until he heard that these organizations were dissolved immediately after the
United States entered the war, and that he had "on orders" which he believed
came from FRITZ SCHROEDER, destroyed his membership book, dues cards for these
organizations having been told that if they kept the books there might be some
trouble over it.

The subject advised that the DAB purchased Camp Bergwald
at Riverdale, New Jersey in 1938 and that he contributed $10.00 towards the
purchase of this camp and had aided in the building of the main building and
during the summer months had regularly gone to the camp on weekends, taking
with him his wife and two children. He stated that he owned no bungalow or
cabin at the camp but had rented a bungalow belonging to one of the members
of the DAB for approximately $1.25 a night. He stated that he took no leading
part in the camp activities and denied that he was a supervisor or assistant
supervisor or that he was a youth sponsor or held any other official or semi-
official capacity in the camp activities.

As to the activities customarily carried on at the camp,
he stated that there were occasionally lectures together with films of a
"cultural nature" showing scenes in Germany and new developments in the
building of Germany along architectural lines and also films showing the

- 7 -

progress made by the members in building Camp Bergwald.

      The subject denied that at any time he took part in rifle practice although he stated that some of the members did participate in this until their rifles were broken. Subject further denied that there was any celebration at the camp on Hitler's birthday or on the founding of the Third Reich and he denied that his children, previously mentioned in this report, were members of any youth group at the camp.

      Subject admitted that he had received "Der Amerika Deutsche" and also that he had received this publication for approximately one year.

      Subject claimed that the DAB was first founded in 1903 when it was known as the German National Merchant Clerks Association and that it did not become known as the German-American Vocational League or the DAB until 1935 at which time it was opened to all trades and vocations. He stated that his idea of the purpose for which the DAB was founded and functioned was to foster "old German culture and to sing and foster German songs and for the social functions".

      Although questioned vigorously, the subject denied any knowledge of any connection between the DAB and the German Labor Front. Subject denied that he was a member of or affiliated in any way with any other German clubs or organizations. He denied that he had seen the German Labor Front symbol at Camp Bergwald although he admitted that the swastika banner was flown occasionally at Camp Bergwald when the German Consul was invited to visit the camp. He further denied that he had heard any discussions at meetings of the DAB of any members indicating un-American conduct or attitudes.

      The subject was thereupon questioned concerning one Comrade [   ] whom the subject was alleged to have give free board and room for several months at the outbreak of the war. [   ] was alleged to have been a German who escaped from Canada at the outbreak of the war. Although [   ] name was not furnished to WIEGAND, the subject admitted that one [   ] lived at his home from September 1939 until the latter part of February 1940. Subject stated that he had offered the use of his home to "stranded Germans" to FRITZ ZEGLIN then the German Consulate and that one day upon returning home from work he had found [   ] at his home and he claimed that he merely assumed that [   ] had been referred to him by ZEGLIN and that he had made no specific inquiry into [   ] background other than to ascertain that [   ] was from Westphalia, Germany and that [   ] had claimed to have been here on vacation at the outbreak of the war having come to the United States to visit a friend named [   ] first name unknown, who also came from Westphalia and who reportedly was anxious to return to Germany. [   ] indicated that [   ] was to pay for the return passage of both [   ] and [   ] to Germany but due to some mix-up [   ] advised subject

b7C

- 8 -

that _____ was not going to return to Germany, having gotten a job as a butcher
in New Jersey. The exact address and place of employment was unknown. WIEGAND
stated that _____ lived at his home and went to the German Consulate nearly every
day although he did not know just what activities _____ engaged in there. During
the latter part of February 1940 _____ according to the subject, went to San
Francisco or Los Angeles and sailed from there to Japan. Subject stated that he
was sure that _____ had ultimately gotten back to Germany inasmuch as he, WIEGAND,
had received a letter from his parents indicating that _____ had written them a
nice letter in which he expressed his thanks for the kind treatment he had received
from the subject while he was here.   b7C

    Subject stated that he talked over the war with _____ and was
fully aware that _____ sympathies were entirely with Germany and that further
he, WIEGAND, agreed with _____ on that score up until the attack on Pearl Harbor,   b7C
since which time subject claims he is 100% for America although he has a soft spot
in his heart for Germany. He expressed his feelings by saying, "I look upon Germany
as my mother and feel about the United States as I do my wife." WIEGAND denied
that he had any knowledge that _____ had escaped from Canada.

    The officers and important leaders of the DAB during subject's
membership were said to be:

    FRITZ SCHROEDER, President.

    JOSEPH LIEBLIEN, Vice-President, and Schroeder's representative.

    ALFRED SCHUCHMAN, Community House Camp Leader or Manager at
Camp Bergwald.

    HERMANN WIRTH, Leader of the Hudson County, New Jersey DAB Unit.

    Subject was also questioned as to his knowledge of other DAB
members who took in "stranded Germans" as he called them, and in that connection
he stated that to his own personal knowledge he knew that _____ had taken
in two German fellows for about four weeks "and most likely longer" and also
that _____ took in a German described by the subject as an "exchange
student". Although WIEGAND was unable to furnish the names of any of the   b7C
Germans boarded by the above mentioned persons, he stated that they boarded
with these persons at about the same time that he took in and kept _____ namely
around the outbreak of hostilities in 1939. Subject denied that he saw any
connection whatever between the outbreak of hostilities and the coming of these
"stranded Germans" to the homes of various persons in the vicinity.

    The subject identified a slip of paper captioned "Anmeldeschein"
dated August 29, 1938 and indicated that in his own handwriting he had made

application for membership in the DAB. This slip was on the stationery of the
German American Vocational League, Inc., 21 East 75th Street, New York City.
He was also shown a slip of paper captioned "Aufnahmeantrag" dated October 25,
1938. It is to be noted that these slips of paper, both on the official forms
of the DAB were used by the subject in applying for membership in the Reichsdeutsche
Vereinigung although this organization was not specifically mentioned by any
notation thereon. It will also be noted that the date of the membership
application coincides with the date on which subject admitted obtaining membership in the RDV. Subject denied that he took any oath whatever in connection with
the joining of the DAB or the RDV.

The following description of the subject was obtained by
interrogation and observation of the reporting agent:

Age	39
Height	5'6"
Weight	180 pounds
Build	Stocky
Hair	Dark brown
Eyes	Grey
Complexion	Light
Scars	None
Glasses	None
Mustache	Small, dark brown
Nationality	German
Color	White
Sex	Male
Accent	German
Teeth	Good
Marital status	Married.

Following the interrogation of the subject he was delivered
by Bureau agents into the custody of the Immigration and Naturalization Service
authorities at Ellis Island pending a hearing before the Alien Enemy Hearing Board.

The photograph album containing pictures showing the building
of and members connected with the DAB Camp Bergwald, Riverdale, New Jersey together
with miscellaneous loose pictures and the other papers previously mentioned in this
report are being retained in the New York file of this case.

- PENDING -

FEDERAL BUREAU OF INVESTIGATION

Form No. 1
THIS CASE ORIGINATED AT **NEW YORK, NEW YORK**   **NY** FILE NO. 100-17239 **ESS**

REPORT MADE AT	DATE WHEN MADE	PERIOD FOR WHICH MADE	REPORT MADE BY
NEW YORK, NEW YORK	8/8/42	7/21/42	**W. W. COCHRANE**

TITLE	CHARACTER OF CASE
OTTO WIEGAND	**INTERNAL SECURITY - G ALIEN ENEMY CONTROL**

SYNOPSIS OF FACTS: On 7/21/42 subject given preliminary hearing before
Assistant USA M. F. FAGAN, EDNY. Subject ordered
held at Ellis Island pending hearing before Enemy
Alien Hearing Board.

- P -

REFERENCE: Report of Special Agent. [ ] dated 7/17/42   b7C
at New York, New York.

DETAILS: On July 21, 1942 subject OTTO WIEGAND was given a
preliminary hearing before Assistant United States
Attorney M. F. FAGAN, Eastern District of New York.

After considering the facts in this case and after
interviewing this alien, the United States Attorney
ordered subject to be held at Ellis Island pending a
hearing before the Enemy Alien Hearing Board.

-PENDING-

ORIGINAL DESTROYED

APPROVED AND FORWARDED:	SPECIAL AGENT IN CHARGE	DO NOT WRITE IN THESE SPACES

100-123329-2

COPIES OF THIS REPORT
5 - Bureau
2 - USA, EDNY
1 -   ONI
1 - [ ]   b7C
1 - Imm. and Nat. Service
2 - New York

311

In the Matter of

OTTO WIEGAND

Alien Enemy

D. J. File No.
146-13-2-52-453

O R D E R

WHEREAS, Otto Wiegand, of Ridgewood, Long Island, New York,
a citizen of Germany, over the age of fourteen years, is within
the United States and not a naturalized citizen thereof and has
heretofore been apprehended as being potentially dangerous to the
public peace and safety of the United States; and,

WHEREAS, the alien enemy Hearing Board has recommended that
said alien enemy be interned; NOW, THEREFORE, upon consideration
of the evidence before me,

IT IS ORDERED that said alien enemy be interned.

Francis Biddle

ATTORNEY GENERAL

September 6, 1942

ENCLOSURE

RECORDED   100 123329 - 5

2 OCT 7 194

Presidential Warrant for ALMA WIEGAND
NEW YORK FIELD DIVISION

100-123329-5X

W A R R A N T

TO THE DIRECTOR OF THE FEDERAL BUREAU OF INVESTIGATION:

In pursuance of authority delegated to the Attorney
General of the United States by Proclamation of the President
of the United States dated December 8, 1941, I hereby authorize
and direct you and your duly authorized agents to arrest or
to cause the arrest of   Alma Wiegand, 6858 60th Lane,
Ridgewood, Brooklyn, New York,

an alien enemy whom I deem dangerous to the public peace and
safety of the United States.

The said alien enemy is to be detained and confined until
further order.

By order of the President:

FRANCIS BIDDLE
Attorney General

~~December 8, 1941~~

October 12, 1942

314

Date: **October 19, 1942**

To: SAC, New York

From: J. Edgar Hoover - Director, Federal Bureau of Investigation

Subject: INTERNAL SECURITY - ALIEN ENEMY CONTROL

I am enclosing two copies of a Presidential Warrant for each
of the following subjects:

		b7C

Alma Wiegand

According to the information furnished the bureau, these warrants
were issued on the basis of a letter received by the Department, from the
Honorable Harold M. Kennedy, United States Attorney for the Eastern
District of New York, recommending that Presidential Warrants be issued
authorizing the presentation of these aliens to an alien enemy hearing
board.

Mr. Edward J. Ennis, Director, Alien Enemy Control Unit, advised
that all of these persons have indicated a desire to be interned with
their husbands and that one Alma Wiegand has indicated a desire to
surrender her certificate of naturalization as a citizen of the United
States so that she may be interned with her husband.

In accordance with the instructions received from Mr. Ennis,
these warrants should not be executed until you are instructed to do so
Mr. Kennedy. At the time these warrants are executed, one copy
of each should be furnished to the appropriate office of the Immigration
and Naturalization Service.

Mr. Tolson
Mr. E. A. Tamm
Mr. Clegg
Mr. Glavin
Mr. Ladd
Mr. Nichols — Enclosure
Mr. Rosen
Mr. Tracy
Mr. Carson
Mr. Coffey
Mr. Hendon
Mr. Kramer
Mr. McGuire
Mr. Quinn Tamm
Mr. Nease
Miss Gandy

RECORDED: 100-123329-5X

12   OCT 22 1942

315

RECORDED

100-123329-5 October 19, 1942
CWB:jeh

Special Agent in Charge
New York, New York

Re: OTTO WIEGAND
INTERNAL SECURITY-G
ALIEN ENEMY CONTROL

Dear Sir:

For your information, the Bureau has
received from the Department a copy of an order
dated September 30, 1942, in which the Attorney
General ordered that the above named individual
be   interned   .

Very truly yours,

J. E. Hoover

John Edgar Hoover
Director

Mr. Tolson_____
Mr. E. A. Tamm___
Mr. Clegg_____
Mr. Glavin_____
Mr. Ladd_____
Mr. Nichols_____
Mr. Rosen_____
Mr. Tracy_____
Mr. Carson_____
Mr. Coffey_____
Mr. Hendon_____
Mr. Kramer_____
Mr. McGuire_____
Mr. Quinn Tamm___
Mr. Nease_____
Miss Gandy_____

100-123329-6
CWN:jeh

October 26, 1942

Brigadier General Hayes A. Kroner
General Staff
Chief, Military Intelligence Service
War Department
Washington, D. C.

Dear General Kroner:

This is to advise that information has been received
that on _September 30, 1942_, the Attorney General ordered
the _internment_ of _Otto Wiegand_
who was previously apprehended by the _New York_
Field Division of this Bureau as an alien enemy of _German_
nationality.

Sincerely yours,

John Edgar Hoover
Director

Mr. Tolson_____
Mr. E. A. Tamm__
Mr. Clegg_____
Mr. Glavin_____
Mr. Ladd_____
Mr. Nichols_____
Mr. Rosen_____
Mr. Tracy_____
Mr. Carson_____
Mr. Coffey_____
Mr. Hendon_____
Mr. Kramer_____
Mr. McGuire_____
Mr. Quinn Tamm__
Mr. Nease_____
Mr. Gandy_____

COMMUNICATIONS SECTION
MAILED 11
OCT 26 1942 P.M.
FEDERAL BUREAU OF INVESTIGATION
U. S. DEPARTMENT OF JUSTICE

FEDERAL BUREAU OF INVESTIGATION

Form No. 1
THIS CASE ORIGINATED AT NEW YORK, NEW YORK   NY FILE NO. 100-17239   HAF

REPORT MADE AT	DATE WHEN MADE	PERIOD FOR WHICH MADE	REPORT MADE BY
NEW YORK, NEW YORK	7/1/43	5/12/43;6/11/43	VINCENT K. ANTLE

TITLE   CHARACTER OF CASE
     CHANGED
OTTO KARL WIEGAND;   ALIEN ENEMY CONTROL - G
  ALMA WIEGAND   (FOREIGN FUNDS)
                                            DENATURALIZATION PROCEEDINGS - G

SYNOPSIS OF FACTS:

OTTO KARL WIEGAND afforded a re-hearing before Alien
Enemy Hearing Board No. 2, EDNY, on 4-15-43. Board
recommended internment for a second time. Subject
OTTO WIEGAND stated at the re-hearing he did not
ask for a re-hearing and that his only desire was
to be interned with his family. He denied being a
member of the Nazi Party. Subject ALMA WIEGAND,
wife, U.S. citizen, indicated a desire to surrender
her certificate of naturalization as a citizen of
the U.S. so she could be interned with her husband.   b2
Informant [   ] advised ALMA WIEGAND applied for
repatriation. ALMA WIEGAND appeared as a witness   b7D
before Alien Enemy Hearing Board No. 2, on September
10, 1942 and stated she was a citizen of the U.S.
and her sympathies were with this country. ALMA
WIEGAND also appeared as a witness in behalf of
her husband OTTO KARL WIEGAND before Board No. 2,
EDNY, on 4-15-43 and stated she did not desire
to renounce her U.S. citizenship if it were not
necessary. She stated that she loves America but
she is a public charge with her two children. JAMES
W. KNAPP, Special Assistant to the Attorney General
EDNY, stated on May 12, 1943 he recommended no
further action in the case of ALMA WIEGAND as there
was no basis for a denaturalization case against
her. Complainant states he heard faint sending signals on July 28, 1942 emanating from subject's butcher
shop.

APPROVED AND FORWARDED   SPECIAL AGENT IN CHARGE   DO NOT WRITE IN THESE SPACES
                                                          100-123329-13

COPIES OF THIS REPORT
5 - Bureau
2 - USA, EDNY
2 - Baltimore
1 - Memphis (Information)
                    G-2   b7C
                    ONI

318

REFERENCE: Bureau File No. 100-123329
            Bureau letter dated December 7, 1942, re: ALMA WIEGAND,
            ALIEN ENEMY CONTROL - G. (Bureau file No. 100-151190)
            Letter to the Bureau from New York, dated March 17,
            1943, re: ALMA WIEGAND, ALIEN ENEMY CONTROL - G
            Bureau letter dated February 18, 1943, re: OTTO KARL
            WIEGAND, ALIEN ENEMY CONTROL - G. (FOREIGN FUNDS)
            Bureau File No. 100-123329
            Report of Special Agent Manuel M. Liodas, dated January
            15, 1943, at New York, New York

DETAILS:

            The title of this case is marked changed to add ALMA WIEGAND
as a subject in this investigative report.

            Under date of July 29, 1942, a ▢▢▢▢▢▢▢▢ who is affiliated
with the ▢▢▢▢▢▢▢▢▢▢▢▢ New York City, and who resides
at ▢▢▢▢▢▢▢▢▢▢▢ Leonia, New Jersey, appeared at the New York
Field Division and furnished the following information to Special   b7C
Agent ▢▢▢▢▢ pertaining to OTTO KARL WIEGAND. He stated that
▢▢▢▢▢▢ an employee of the ▢▢▢▢▢▢▢▢▢▢▢ and presently
residing at ▢▢▢▢▢▢▢ Brooklyn, New York, which is within
close proximity of the subject's butcher shop located at 60-54 69th
Avenue, Brooklyn, had told him that he had heard faint sending signals
from 1:30 a.m. to 2:00 a.m. on July 28, 1942 which seemed to come
from the subject's butcher shop. The complainant stated that ▢▢▢▢▢
also told him that at 11:30 p.m. on July 28, 1942, he had heard these
signals again. The complainant further advised that they had heard   b7C
these sending signals prior to the time when the subject disappeared.
Commenting on the subject's disappearing, the complainant stated it is
the opinion of these people residing in the vicinity that WIEGAND is
presently at Ellis Island, having been apprehended by the Federal
Bureau of Investigation.

            ▢▢▢▢▢ also told the complainant that ▢▢▢▢▢ last summer while
working for the subject, due to the fact that the subject's son was
attending some Bund Youth Camp, had noticed in the rear of the butcher   b7C
shop electrical equipment, wires and dials. The complainant stated
that he had reported to Agent ▢▢▢▢▢ of this office the fact that ▢▢▢▢▢
▢▢▢ had seen all this electrical equipment in the rear of the butcher
shop.

OTTO KARL WIEGAND

On April 15, 1943 OTTO KARL WIEGAND was afforded a re-hearing before Alien Enemy Hearing Board No. 2, Eastern District of New York. At the origin of the re-hearing the following questions were directed to OTTO KARL WIEGAND by Chairman C. WALTER RANDALL, Alien Enemy Hearing Board No. 2:

Q Mr. WIEGAND, you know the purpose of this Board; you have been here before?

A Yes.

Q So I do not have to go over that with you. You have asked for a re-hearing?

A I did not.

Q You did not?

A Nobody did.

Q A re-hearing has been requested in your behalf and we have granted it and that it why you are here. Is there anything that you wish to tell us that you think will throw further light on your case and perhaps give us a different slant on it?

A As far as I am concerned I consider my case closed. What I am interested in is to be interned with my family, to be together in a family camp.

Q Were you asked at the last hearing whether or not you were a member of the Nazi Party?

A I don't remember if I was asked that but I can answer I was not.

Q You never have been a member of it?

A No, sir.

Q Do you know of any other OTTO WIEGAND who lives in Ridgewood?
A No.

Q You would have no idea of how your name got on a list of Nazi Party members?
A It must be a mistake. I think you are talking about the RVD or the DAB.

- 3 -

Q I am talking now about the Nazi Party.
A No I was not.

Q You were a member of the DAB?
A Yes.

Q Do you remember when you joined?
A In 1935 or 1936, I cannot say exactly when it was.

Q Was there any oath you took at that time in connection with it?
A No.

Q You did not have to sign any pledge or subscribe to any oath?
A No.

Q But you are positive you never at any time belonged to the Nazi Party?
A I said no before.

Q I know you did; I just want you to search your memory in case you have
  forgotten it.
A I would know that.

QUESTIONS BY [   ]   b7C

Q Do you know what the Nazi Party is?
A It is the ruling party in Germany.

Q What are their principles?
A I don't know; I could not answer that.

Q Were you a probationary member of the Nazi Party?
A No.

Q You never had any connection at all with it?
A No.

Q How did you become a member of the DAB, who introduced you to the group?
A I don't know that, I just joined it, that's all.

Q Can you give us the names of some of the friends you made?
A [   ]   b7C

Q Where do they live?
A Tennessee, they are in camp.

        After re-presentation of all the facts in this case and after
permitting OTTO KARL WIEGAND an opportunity to be re-heard on his own behalf,
the Board recommended for a second time that he be interned for the duration.

- 4 -

A further interview with OTTO WIEGAND was requested by a letter
dated March 12, 1943, from the New York Office to the Bureau and a copy of
which was sent to Baltimore. This interview was to cover his membership
in the Nazi Party. The Immigration and Naturalization Service, Ellis Island,
New York, advised the New York Field Division prior to the re-hearing of
OTTO KARL WIEGAND that he was delivered to their station on April,5, 1943,
from Camp Forrest, Tennessee by a United States Marshal.

ALMA WIEGAND

Under date of October 19, 1942, the Bureau advised the New York
Office that informant☐had advised that one ALMA WIEGAND had indicated
a desire to surrender her certificate of naturalization as a citizen of
the United States so she might be interned with her husband, OTTO KARL
WIEGAND.

b2
b7D

By letter dated December 7, 1942, the Bureau advised the New York
Office that Confidential Informant☐had advised that ALMA WIEGAND,
68-58 60th Lane, Ridgewood, New York, had made an application to be
repatriated.

ALMA WIEGAND appeared as a witness in behalf of her husband,
OTTO KARL WIEGAND, before Alien Enemy Hearing Board No. 2, Eastern District
of New York, on September 10, 1942. Upon being questioned by the members
of the Hearing Board, ALMA WIEGAND stated she was a naturalized citizen
of the United States and that her sympathy was with this country.

ALMA WIEGAND appeared a second time as a witness in behalf of
her husband, OTTO KARL WIEGAND, before Alien Enemy Hearing Board No. 2,
Eastern District of New York, at the re-hearing of OTTO KARL WIEGAND on
April 15, 1943. At the re-hearing ALMA WIEGAND testified under oath
she was an American citizen and she directed the following remarks to
the members of the Hearing Board:

"Q You are an American citizen?
.A Yes.

Q Tell us about your circumstances; what you think we ought to know.
A Well, your Honor, I really had to go through a whole lot the last
nine months. We had a butcher business and when my husband was taken
on July 10th, I tried to get a man to run it and I kept it up three

- 5 -

" months in the hope he would come out and he did not come out, and I appealed to Mr. Kennedy, and my Pastor appealed to Mr. Biddle in Washington, but I did not get any reply, and I appealed as an American mother with two American born children and I did not have any success. So I went to the Swiss Consul and they told me that I, as an American citizen, could not go to camp with my husband. So I said if I cannot go to camp and my citizenship holds me back -- I am married to my husband from the very first day I come to this soil -- I will be willing to offer the citizenship. I went to ▢ and ▢ referred me to ▢ and ▢ and I made the statement very much the way I make it here, telling them how I felt about the whole thing. Of course, the only thing I wanted was to go to camp; that was the reason. So I did not hear anything. I went back to ▢ and he said, your husband is too dangerous to let him out, he is too loyal to Germany. So, I said, well I am still aiming for the camp, I became a public charge with my children, I broke up my home, and I went to ▢ again and he told me he would let me know the end of March or beginning of April, and then I was in the belief I would go to camp; that was my whole aim in everything.

Q Is that what you want?
A That is what I prefer.

Q You want to go to a family camp with your two children and stay with your husband?
A Yes, of course, I love my husband.

Q It is difficult, with you as a citizen.
A I know.

Q You do not want to renounce your citizenship?
A If I do not need to, no, I have no reason.

Q You love this country?
A I have every reason to love it.

Q You want to raise your children as Americans?
A They were raised as Americans and Germans.

Q You have no profession by which you could earn a living?
A No, I have not.

Q And you lost the shop?
A I lost the shop and my home is broken up.

Q You have no means of support at all?
A No, I am a public charge, I have to admit it; it is terrible after being so long here.

- 6 -

b7C

Q How old are your children?
A Freddie is 12, Anna Liese is 8.

Q Are they at school?
A Yes.

Q What is your religion?
A Well, we are true believers in God; that is about all.

Q No particular church?
A No.

Q Is there anything else you want to tell us?
A Just that I really would appreciate it very much if you would help my
   case. I am really in a nervous condition, I really cannot take it
   any longer."

        Under date of May 12, 1943, JAMES W. KNAPP, Special Assistant
to the Attorney General, Eastern District of New York, stated he would
recommend no further action in the case of ALMA WIEGAND as the facts
developed did not substantiate a basis for a denaturalization action.

                        NAZI PARTY
              MEMBERSHIP OF OTTO KARL WIEGAND

        By letter dated February 18, 1943 the Bureau advised the New
York Office that the name of OTTO WIEGAND, Ridgewood, New York, appeared
on a list of names of former members of the NAZI PARTY.

                        - PENDING -

CONFIDENTIAL INFORMANT

     The identity of the Confidential Informant appearing in the report of Special Agent Vincent K. Antle, dated Jul 1 1943 43 at New York, New York, is as follows:

b2
b7D

FEDERAL BUREAU OF INVESTIGATION

Form No. 1
THIS CASE ORIGINATED AT   NEW YORK CITY   N.Y. FILE NO. 100-17239 BC

REPORT MADE AT	DATE WHEN MADE	PERIOD FOR WHICH MADE	REPORT MADE BY
NEW YORK CITY	3/29/44	3/24/44	ROBERT E. PENLAND

TITLE	CHARACTER OF CASE
OTTO KARL WIEGAND	ALIEN ENEMY CONTROL – G (FOREIGN FUNDS)

SYNOPSIS OF FACTS: Subject repatriated aboard SS GRIPSHOLM.
Disposition Sheet submitted.

-- C --

REFERENCE: Bureau File No. 100-123329
Report of Special Agent Robert E. Penland
dated October 4, 1943.
Bureau letter to the New York Field Office dated
March 6, 1944.

DETAILS: AT NEW YORK CITY

This case is being reopened in order to report the
repatriation of OTTO KARL WIEGAND.

By letter dated March 6, 1944, the Bureau advised
the name of OTTO WIEGAND appeared on the passenger list of the SS GRIPSHOLM,
departing from the Port of Jersey City, New Jersey on February 15, 1944 as
one of a number of persons being repatriated to Lisbon.

A Disposition Sheet is being submitted for Subject.

ENCLOSURE: BUREAU (1)

1 Disposition Sheet for Subject.

- C L O S E D -

APPROVED AND FORWARDED:	SPECIAL AGENT IN CHARGE	DO NOT WRITE IN THESE SPACES

COPIES OF THIS REPORT
5 - Bureau
1 - DIO, 3 N.D.
1 - DIO, 3 N.D.   b7C
2 - USA, ED, NY
2 - New York City

100-123329-18

20 APR 1944   RECORDED
APR 13 1944

Anneliese "Lee" Krauter excelled in both American and German schools. In her adult years, she took courses in creative writing and journalism at Indiana University, Purdue University, Indianapolis.

After one of her sons was diagnosed with Juvenile Diabetes, she spent years volunteering with the American Diabetes Association, serving in both local and national officer positions. She earned many awards in the Association and was named "National Outstanding Affiliate Volunteer of the Year" in 1990. She was also appointed to the National Institutes of Health in Washington, D.C., for service on the National Diabetes Advisory Board.

Because she also earned her certificate as a German/English translator and is fluent in both tongues without an accent, Lee has been called upon to do translation in both countries. She translated Boris Becker's interview with the press when he played in the National Clay Court (later Hardcourt) Championships at the Sports Complex in Indianapolis, following his Wimbledon win in 1987.

Lee has spoken about her life as a child in America and Germany in World War II to many schools and adult audiences and has also been a volunteer educator on living with Diabetes in schools in Indiana. Lee and her husband Joe live in McCordsville, outside Indianapolis. Their four married sons and a flock of sixteen grandchildren all live in the area.

The cover graphic is an original painting by Indianapolis artist Nhat Tran. Ms. Tran graduated with highest distinction from the University of Fine Arts in Ho Chi Minh City, Vietnam, in 1992. She specializes in abstract urushi paintings and sculptures, and in addition to exhibits in her home country, her work has been shown in museums and galleries across the United States and abroad. Several of her pieces have joined the permanent collection of the Smithsonian American Art

NHAT TRAN, IN VIET NAM. PHOTOGRAPH BY: PETER STEINHAUER

Museum's Renwick Gallery in Washington, D.C., the National Museum of Women in the Arts, the Corcoran Gallery of Art and the Indiana State Museum.